PSYCHOLOGY OF MEDICINE
AND SURGERY

01209

D0544345

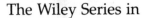

The Wiley Series in

CLINICAL PSYCHOLOGY

Titles published under the series editorship of:

J. Mark G. Williams   *School of Psychology, University of Wales,*
Bangor, UK

A list of earlier titles in the series follows the index.

PSYCHOLOGY OF MEDICINE AND SURGERY

A Guide for Psychologists, Counsellors, Nurses and Doctors

Peter Salmon

The University of Liverpool, UK

JOHN WILEY & SONS, LTD

Chichester · New York · Weinheim · Brisbane · Singapore · Toronto

Copyright © 2000   John Wiley & Sons Ltd, The Atrium, Southern Gate, Chichester,
West Sussex PO19 8SQ, England

Telephone   (+44) 1243 779777

Email (for orders and customer service enquiries): cs-books@wiley.co.uk
Visit our Home Page on www.wileyeurope.com or www.wiley.com

Reprinted December 2002

All Rights Reserved. No part of this publication may be reproduced, stored in a retrieval
system or transmitted in any form or by any means, electronic, mechanical, photocopying,
recording, scanning or otherwise, except under the terms of the Copyright, Designs and
Patents Act 1988 or under the terms of a licence issued by the Copyright Licensing Agency
Ltd, 90 Tottenham Court Road, London W1T 4LP, UK, without the permission in writing of
the Publisher. Requests to the Publisher should be addressed to the Permissions Department,
John Wiley & Sons Ltd, The Atrium, Southern Gate, Chichester, West Sussex PO19 8SQ,
England, or emailed to permreq@wiley.co.uk, or faxed to (+44) 1243 770571.

This publication is designed to provide accurate and authoritative information in regard to
the subject matter covered. It is sold on the understanding that the Publisher is not engaged in
rendering professional services. If professional advice or other expert assistance is required,
the services of a competent professional should be sought.

Other Wiley Editorial Offices

John Wiley & Sons Inc., 111 River Street, Hoboken, NJ 07030, USA

Jossey-Bass, 989 Market Street, San Francisco, CA 94103-1741, USA

Wiley-VCH Verlag GmbH, Boschstr. 12, D-69469 Weinheim, Germany

John Wiley & Sons Australia Ltd, 33 Park Road, Milton, Queensland 4064, Australia

John Wiley & Sons (Asia) Pte Ltd, 2 Clementi Loop #02-01, Jin Xing Distripark, Singapore
129809

John Wiley & Sons Canada Ltd, 22 Worcester Road, Etobicoke, Ontario, Canada M9W 1L1

British Library Cataloguing in Publication Data

A catalogue record for this book is available from the British Library

ISBN   0-471-97597-4 (cased)
ISBN   0-471-85214-7 (paper)

Typeset in 10 / 12pt Palatino bt Best-set Typesetter Ltd., Hong Kong
Printed and bound in Great Britain by TJ International Ltd, Padstow, Cornwall
This book is printed on acid-free paper responsibly manufactured from sustainable forestry
in which at least two trees are planted for each one used for paper production.

To my parents

CONTENTS

ABOUT THE AUTHOR

Peter Salmon is a Clinical Psychologist who has worked with physically ill patients in primary and hospital care for many years and has published over 100 research papers on psychological aspects of health care. He has taught medical, nursing and clinical psychology students, first at University College London, and now at the University of Liverpool, where he is Professor and Head of the Department of Clinical Psychology.

SERIES PREFACE

The Wiley Series in Clinical Psychology aims to provide a comprehensive set of texts covering the application of psychological science to clinical problems. In this book Peter Salmon shows with perceptive clarity the way in which psychology can help understand a large number of issues relating to medicine and surgery. Psychological influences can be seen to operate from the very earliest stage in which people define themselves as having problems. He shows, for example, that people seek help not necessarily when their physical symptoms are most severe, but when people find themselves unable to cope with symptoms they may have been experiencing for some time. Changes in the frequency of consultations may not signify a change in the level of symptoms but could be caused entirely by a change in social networks. Second, the book shows how illness beliefs differ between and within cultures. The same symptom that is attributed by one person to 'too much acid in the stomach' or a 'hormone imbalance' is attributed by another to 'age-related decline' or 'being over-worked'. Each of these differences may affect how a person both experiences and reports their illness. Third, the book reviews the large number of ways in which psychological treatment affects outcome, for example survival from cancer.

The text is written in accessible style with many clinical details. It is a masterpiece of clear communication. With such an enormous range of relevance, both students and practitioners in a number of fields will find this book an immensely valuable guide. It will help both in their clinical work and in their research activities. Health professionals working in fields related to medicine and surgery are seeking to take a more complete account of the psychological processes of the people they treat. This book both is a measure of how far this collaboration has come, and will greatly enhance further joint working in the field of psychological aspects of health.

J. M. G. Williams
Series Editor

PREFACE

Recent decades have seen explosive growth in psychological research into physical illness and health care. Several factors help to explain this. One has been psychologists' ingenuity in turning clinical phenomena into fertile laboratories for studying psychological theories. In parallel there has been growing recognition amongst clinicians in all professions that many of the challenges that they and their patients face are psychological. Fortunately there has also grown the appreciation that responses to these challenges are better guided by psychological theory and research than purely by intuition, prejudice or habit. Indeed, in the name of 'evidence-based practice', clinicians are enjoined to justify their practice scientifically in just this way.

The publication of books on psychology and health care has grown to a torrent recently. This is itself evidence of a cultural change in health care. It has also been a stimulus to this change. The torrent needs to be continually fed by new books and I hope that this book will play its part. However, the book is not offered simply as another version of what has gone before. Broadly, there seem to be two main types of book in this field. Some are manuals: they show that—and how—specific clinical problems can be addressed in psychologically informed ways. These are written primarily for clinicians who do not need to know psychological principles. Other books are primarily textbooks in that they present detailed accounts of psychological evidence and theory that are relevant to health care. These are written for people who need to know about psychology, first, and how it might be applied, second.

This book is an attempt to do something different. Like the manuals, it is written primarily for clinicians. So whether I have included a topic depends on whether it offers a clinician any purchase on clinical problems. Like the textbooks, however, this book is written for people who are not looking for instructions to follow but want to know about psychological principles so that they can decide their own responses to complex clinical problems. In other words it is written primarily for the growing number of clinicians, from different professions, who seek to improve their patients' care by understanding psychological principles, ideas and concepts. That is, the book is a guide, rather than a manual or a conventional textbook, and it is for all clinicians for whom psychological factors matter to their work. It is aimed, therefore, at medical, nursing and counselling professions as much as psychologists. Writing for non-psychological professions risks falling into one of the two traps that await the psychologist who tries to write in a way that is understandable by, and relevant to, non-psychologists. One is the trite and trivial style of the psychologist who states the obvious on a radio or TV programme. The other is the psychologist who uses so much jargon as to appear obscure and out of touch. I have tried to tread a fine line between these caricatures.

As well as practising clinicians, this book is for those in training and those who are training them. There are, of course, already many excellent textbooks, particularly for medical students and nurses. However, many of these are geared to traditional curricula in which students pass exams by demonstrating clinically applicable psychological knowledge. Curricula are changing, however, and exams are evolving with them. I hope that this book will help students who need to pass exams in a different way: by demonstrating psychologically informed clinical practice.

The book has developed out of several areas of my own work. I make no apology for drawing heavily on my own teaching, research and clinical practice. This is not because my work is any better than anyone else's, but just because it is my book. In reality, none of it is *my* work. All of it has depended critically on the work of others. Therefore, while the book has developed from several areas of my own work, there are many people in each area whose contributions I must acknowledge. Medical and nursing students have provided sceptical, critical and rewarding audiences that have helped to identify what psychology contains that is relevant to clinical practice. Undergraduate and postgraduate psychology students have helped to show how leverage on clinical problems and theoretical development go hand in hand. Research collaboration with colleagues in other disciplines has helped to develop and clarify many of the ideas in this book. The best collaborators are those who demonstrate that exciting psychological insights into health care are not the preserve of psychologists but transcend disciplines. Amongst recent collaborators, I acknowledge my debt to non-psychologists—George Hall, Carl May and Clare Stanford in particular.

The final, and most important group of people who have helped to develop this book are patients. In my experience it is rare that they have complained or suffered because their clinicians have been poorly informed of the latest findings or latest theories in clinical or health psychology. Instead, their suffering of illness has very often been compounded by clinicians who have not listened to them, who did not understand what they said or who, without knowing it, were attending to their own emotional needs rather than their patients'. I acknowledge my debt to these patients who have helped to identify the psychological factors to include in this book.

I am grateful also to Barbara Jones for expert secretarial assistance, and to my Wiley Editor Michael Coombs for his patience and his thoughtful advice. My thanks and apologies go to colleagues in Liverpool and elsewhere for tolerating my distraction from the work in hand while this book was being written.

Peter Salmon
Liverpool 2000

Part I

APPLYING PSYCHOLOGY TO HEALTH CARE

Chapter 1

PSYCHOLOGY KNOWLEDGE: ITS RELEVANCE AND LIMITATIONS

KEY CLINICAL ISSUES

- What kinds of clinician is this book for?
- What kinds of evidence will it provide?
- How can the evidence be used? Will it show exactly how to manage patients?
- What's special about a psychological approach?

1.1 WHAT IS PSYCHOLOGY?

Psychology is the scientific study of the way people behave, think and feel. Its scope is therefore as large and varied as human nature itself. It has grown at a remarkable rate during the twentieth century from its beginnings in philosophy and physiology. It has become a popular university subject and is even becoming a popular school subject. However, its success has not relied on a capacity to provide easy answers to human problems. Indeed, interviewing panels for psychology courses often watch out for those who look to psychology to provide simple answers to complex problems of living—so as to direct them elsewhere. Psychology does, of course, provide some answers. More importantly, however, it identifies questions and offers ways to ask them. It also points to assumptions about human behaviour that are false and which must be replaced by the results of careful enquiry.

1.2 WHAT DOES PSYCHOLOGY OFFER CLINICIANS?

Which clinicians need to use psychological ideas and information? The answer is not difficult. It is all clinicians who, in the course of their work, need to interact with patients or their families, or need to use information or make decisions. In other words, all clinicians need to use psychology. The emphasis in this book is on psychological aspects of clinicians' interactions with patients and families. For some clinicians, this interaction is the backdrop to treatment or advice, such as when a patient visits the GP or primary care nurse, or when a patient is visited by an anaesthetist before surgery or by a health visitor after childbirth. For other clinicians, the interaction is the core of the job; these include the growing number of counsellors in primary and hospital care, as well as clinical psychologists who work in physical health care and health psychologists who work with patients. Psychological factors are central to all these clinicians' work, whether or not a clinician chooses to be aware of them. There is no such thing as a psychology-free interaction; psychological factors are always present. Unfortunately, when not thought out they are often harmful influences.

Different kinds of research about psychological factors in clinical relationships have been focused on different professions. For instance, research on adherence to instructions has been focused on doctors whereas research on relationships with patients has focused on nurses. This reflects the very different roles that these professions have traditionally had: doctors giving patients information and deciding treatment, with nurses looking after patients and forming closer relationships with them. These boundaries are blurring now so, except where it is necessary to identify a specific profession, the generic term 'clinician' will be used throughout this book.

1.3 USING PSYCHOLOGICAL EVIDENCE

It is generally accepted that clinical practice must be scientific: i.e., 'evidence-based'. Therefore clinicians who wish to be informed about their interactions with patients seek from psychology an 'evidence base' for their practice. As a slogan, 'evidence-based practice' appears quite simple, but the complexities of how to use psychological evidence are rarely considered. Let us examine two examples.

1.3.1 Example 1: The Experts' Questionnaire

In the first example, an oncologist wishes to evaluate the effects of a telephone support service, run by specialist nurses for some of her patients. There are now several books that detail questionnaires to measure quality of life in patients with cancer and she buys one of these. She finds a questionnaire that she recognizes because she has seen a number of published studies that have used it. She has also heard conference presentations from eminent researchers in which it has been used to demonstrate treatment effects. The book says that it is a valid and reliable measure of quality of life. However, she looks carefully at the items on the questionnaire and is uneasy. She realizes that her uneasiness is because most of these items concern symptoms—physical and emotional. Her own conversations with patients have raised other issues, including patients' fears of death and their worry about how their families will manage if they die. Many of her patients have even come to see their cancer as having positive effects on how they view life. The oncologist thinks that these reactions might be important, but using the recommended questionnaire will mean ignoring them. How should she ensure that her decision is based on evidence? She decides to devise, with appropriate advice and collaboration, her own questionnaire. It will incorporate what she finds best in the experts' questionnaire. It will also use principles of questionnaire design to capture other ways of adjusting to cancer that she thinks the telephone support service might facilitate but that the experts' questionnaire seems to miss.

1.3.2 Example 2: The Randomized Controlled Trial

1.3.2.1 The Researcher's View

The second example is chosen because most psychological research—like medical research in general—uses statistics. That is, it relies on demonstrations that variables of interest are related to other variables at a greater level than could plausibly have occurred by chance. The randomized controlled trial is an example. In this procedure, patients are randomized to be treated in one way or another. Then statistics are used to test whether any difference that is seen between the groups of patients after treatment could plausibly be a random or 'fluke' finding, or whether it has almost certainly arisen because of the different ways that the groups were treated. Of course, statistical information of this kind is important information. Such findings are essential building blocks in testing theories and evaluating treatment. However, in practice, the amount of variability that is explained by the treatment (i.e., the difference *between* the groups) is often very small by comparison with the background variability (i.e., the differences between patients *within* the groups).

The validity of the statistical approach is based on the assumption that background variation is 'error'. That is, were our observations and theories to be more precise, this variation would disappear. In practice, that view is rarely tenable. Researchers are often aware of many factors that would explain some of that variability, but that cannot be measured. The techniques might not be available, or the necessary questionnaires might overload the patients.

The researcher who is interested in pursuing a particular theory can afford to ignore these problems. For example, the researcher who examines the (fictitious) data in Box 1.1 will be content with the significant effect that this randomized controlled trial reveals. It shows that Bloggs et al found less pain after surgery in patients who had been given detailed information about what to expect in comparison with a control group who received only the peremptory preoperative information that was routinely given. The researcher will be pleased because this finding supports the theory from which the 'analgesic' effect of information was predicted—a

---

Box 1.1   Using statistical evidence

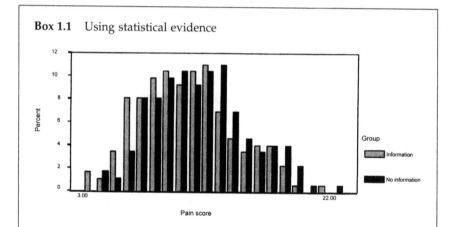

Pain score

Bloggs et al measured pain two days after hip replacement (by asking patients to answer a simple questionnaire) and used this measurement to test whether pain was reduced when the anaesthetist gave patients, before surgery, detailed information about what would happen to them. They randomized patients to two groups of 170. The group that was informed in detail had less pain than the patients who were treated routinely. Scores ranged from 3 to 22 and the graph shows the percentage of patients in each group with each score. Statistical analysis showed that this difference was significant at the $p = 0.01$ level. This means that a difference of this size between the groups had only a 0.01 (or 1%) chance of arising purely by chance. Therefore it is 99% certain that it was not a chance or 'fluke' finding and that it was actually caused by the groups' different psychological treatment.

theory that the researcher wishes to develop further. Now consider this finding from the point of view of a clinician—a senior nurse who is thinking about setting up a programme of preoperative preparation for hip replacement patients for whom she is responsible. She sees this report differently from the researcher.

1.3.2.2 The Clinician's View

Clinical significance versus statistical significance. First, the nurse notices that, although the statistics confirm that information was better than no information, they also reveal that only 2% of the variability in pain scores was accounted for by whether or not patients had been given information. Looking at this another way, she sees that around 40% of those without information have less pain than 50% of those with information!

Generalizability. The nurse then notices that this evaluation comes from a country where only relatively articulate and prosperous individuals tend to have access to the university clinical facilities where this work was done. It is not clear how well the intervention would generalize to her own patients. They are from a fairly deprived population in an area of high unemployment and from an age and socioeconomic cohort which left full-time education at the age of 15. Then she notices that the evaluation was published 10 years ago, so the work was probably done 12 or more years ago. The world has changed since then: ideas about informed consent have changed and more information is available to ordinary people. People have become more sceptical of clinicians. Treatment has changed, too. Partly because of similar randomized controlled trials, anaesthetists have changed their anaesthetic technique and analgesic medication, and surgeons have changed aspects of their procedure. Also political and economic changes have led to patients being admitted to hospital only the day before surgery and being discharged home after four to five days. This contrasts with the more relaxed times of the published study, when patients were admitted at least two days before surgery and remained for at least two weeks postoperatively. The nurse wonders how the intervention would interact with these changes in treatment. She wonders, too, how much of the effect that Bloggs et al found reflected the personality and status of the person providing the intervention—a male anaesthetist. Would the nurse command the same impact?

1.3.2.3 Using Evidence in Practice

The nurse still wishes her practice to be informed by this piece of scientific evidence, but wonders how. Broadly, there are two ways in which she might achieve this. She could provide her patients with detailed information, because that is what this study says is best. This would be the approach of a 'technician–practitioner'. Alternatively, she could weigh up all these factors, use her judgement to select out the aspects of the intervention that she has confidence in and apply this intervention to her own patients, but in such a way that she can evaluate its effects for herself. For instance, she could assess the level of pain in her patients for a few weeks beforehand, then during her intervention. A reduction when the intervention is introduced would encourage her to feel that she is on the right lines. If there is no change, interviews with patients might help her to improve the intervention. This approach would be that of a 'scientist–practitioner'. That is, although being informed by what others had done before her, she would want to discover the right response for her particular time and situation. Some would criticize her pragmatic approach as compromising the 'real' methods of science, such as randomized controlled trials. Alternatively, her approach might be seen as all the *more* scientific for being grounded in a willingness, faced with the hard reality of clinical practice, not to be bound by conventional assumptions and methods (Feyerabend, 1975).

Because a scientifically minded clinician does not unthinkingly extrapolate psychological evidence gathered at one time and in one place to the clinician's own practice at a different time and place, caution is needed in this book about citing evidence. Strictly, evidence in this field should not be cited as if it demonstrates a universal truth. It should be made clear that it was true only for that time and place. It is, however, tedious and unnecessary to be quite so cautious. It is easier and often more helpful simply to read that something is true. In this book, judgement has been used to decide how to extrapolate published evidence to contemporary clinical settings. On occasion it is better to observe cautiously that a certain finding has been reported. Often it is possible to be confident in extrapolating general assertions from specific findings.

1.3.2.4 The Need for Non-Statistical Evidence

Statistical evidence tells us much about processes that would otherwise remain masked by the variability of routine practice. However, it is not the only kind of evidence. Indeed, the nurse in the example above wishes that Bloggs et al had provided more description of their intervention and that they had provided information, too, about how the patients responded to it. To read some of the words that the anaesthetist used and with which the patients responded would bring the evaluation to life and help the nurse to develop her own intervention. Interviews with patients afterwards might have revealed what use they made of the intervention.

Did they remember the information or were they simply flattered that the doctor had taken the trouble to spend time telling them things? The problem that the nurse has identified is that psychological interventions are often reported as if they were drugs; that is, as if what was 'given' to the patients was what was 'received' (Peerbhoy et al, 1998). She knows from talking to patients who have been visited by an anaesthetist before surgery that their view of the interaction is often very different from the anaesthetist's. Psychological interventions are not standardized capsules, but invariably amount to interactions between people. The anaesthetist in Bloggs et al may have thought that he was 'giving information', but the patients may well have 'received' something different, like the feeling of being respected as individuals—or of being put in their places by being told what was going to happen and who was in charge!

1.3.3 The Evidence in this Book

1.3.3.1 Types of Evidence

Useful evidence can therefore come from various sources. As well as **statistical findings**, this book will draw on **qualitative research**. This describes the details of interactions between patients and clinicians, or exposes the patients' perspective. It is a short step from qualitative research to **clinical observation** and this, after all, is where medicine began. Clinical observations still have their value as scientific evidence. Cases can add depth of understanding to abstract concepts, and cases that defy expectations can point the way out of accepted, but erroneous assumptions. Finally, there are important areas where evidence is lacking or contradictory but where clinicians are required to make judgements about psychological matters. In these areas, intuition or **informed specu-lation** in this book will be preferable to offering nothing. At many points, this book will argue that the necessary evidence cannot be provided by this or any book. It can be gathered by the clinician who needs it, simply by **asking the patient**.

1.3.3.2 Sources of Evidence

The book will draw mainly upon psychological ideas and research. However, a great deal of psychological research is not done by psycholo-gists. Research by other professions and disciplines has often focused on psychological variables (such as satisfaction or fatigue) which have been selected for clinical or service-related relevance rather than theoretical interest. Qualitative work by psychologists was thin on the ground until recently and for this it is often necessary to look to the work of anthropologists or sociologists whose careful observations have provided important insights about the ways that people think about their bodies, illness and treatment. Whichever source of evidence is being drawn upon, the book will avoid using theoretical terms or jargon that are understood by only one discipline.

1.3.3.3 Selecting the Evidence

The test for material to be included in this book is that it should have important implications for a clinician in routine clinical practice in physical health care. This is a harsh test. Therefore the book will be partial and selective in what it draws from health psychology and other disciplines because much of current literature does not lend itself to being applied by individual clinicians at the clinical coalface. However, even clinically important psychological research into health problems has grown so remarkably that no single volume can provide more than a fraction of the evidence that is available. In some areas, extensive research has converged on similar findings, so only one or two illustrative studies need to be cited as evidence. In other areas only one study is available. Even so, there is more material than can be included in this book.

The situation is not hopeless, however. A clinician who wishes to make scientific and informed judgements does not have to know every single piece of research in the field. Instead, the clinician needs a framework within which to make these judgements, and which will structure thinking about the issues that are likely to be important. This book presents four elements of such a framework. These elements will be developed by chapters that, in general, follow the patient's journey through health care, from developing symptoms, through consulting a clinician and being hospitalized and treated. Many specific areas of health care will be neglected for no better reason than the finite length of this book. It is hoped that clinicians will apply the framework that the book provides to their own specific areas of clinical work.

1.4 ELEMENTS OF A PSYCHOLOGICAL FRAMEWORK

1.4.1 Holistic Care

1.4.1.1 Holistic Understanding of Illness and Treatment

The first element of a psychological approach to health care is holism: an awareness of the indivisibility of mind and body. This means escaping the grip that dualism has over the way that psychological issues are considered in health care. Chapter 2 will examine the origins of dualism and the forces that have led to more holistic approaches to undertanding illness. Chapter 3 will develop the holistic approach by introducing the relationship between factors that we normally think of as 'psychological' and those that we normally regard as 'physical'. Knowing about this relationship allows us to go on to consider how psychological factors can help to cause major physical disease (Chapter 4). On the basis of this, we can then examine how psychological factors might be recruited to treat those illnesses (Chapter 14) and how psychological factors are important in assessing effects of disease and health care (Chapter 15). We shall also look in detail at the special needs of a large group of patients who are casualties of dualism in health care. These are patients who present physical symptoms without any 'physical' disease process (Chapter 13). Because their presentation is physical but their needs are psychological, they fit into neither of the 'physical' or 'psychological' arms into which health care systems are usually divided.

1.4.1.2 Holistic Delivery of Health Care

Dualism has shaped research into psychological aspects of physical health care. This has often been carried out by psychologically minded individuals separate from the health care team. Therefore psychological factors have been viewed as 'additional' to the normal processes of care. For instance, there is a large amount of evidence from psychologists and others that special programmes for giving information to patients can be helpful to them (Chapter 11). There are complex studies that try to evaluate the effects of giving different sorts of information, in different ways. Applied literally (i.e., by a 'technician–practitioner'), this evidence might be used by a nurse or other clinician to design a formal programme of information giving, perhaps based on leaflets or videos. However, there is also evidence that clinicians do not know enough about what their patients think and worry about and that this is, essentially, because they do not ask them or do not let patients tell them (Chapter 10). For clinicians, a more holistic response to the evidence that information is beneficial would be simply to learn to let patients say what concerns them and to learn to provide the answers. Therefore this book will argue that psychological principles are best incorporated into routine clinical practice rather than being added on as an 'optional extra'.

1.4.2 Managing Challenge

The second element of the psychological approach in this book is an appreciation that people are rarely passive and accepting in the face of events that challenge. Instead, we actively respond to challenges in ways that manage them or help to protect us from being harmed by them. Illness and treatment are formidable challenges for most patients. Therefore, understanding how people respond to challenge in general (Chapter 3) will help us to understand patients' responses to illness and treatment (Chapters 7 and 8). Without this approach, some of these responses seem to defy explanation, such as when rejecting clinicians' advice or when failing to adhere to life-saving treatment (Chapter 9). Patients' illness can, of course, challenge clinicians, too. Understanding how clinicians deal with this kind of challenge will help to explain apparent 'failures' in their own behaviour (Chapter 10).

1.4.3 Making Sense of Disease and Treatment

The third element of this book's psychological approach is the appreciation that people think. Surprisingly, a great deal of clinical practice has been based on the contrary assumption: that patients just accept what they are told to believe and do what they are told to do. Because they do think, patients try to 'make sense' of what they are told by clinicians and what they experience in illness and health care. The book will examine how the symptoms that they take to clinicians arise from this process (Chapter 5). Understanding things is not just an intellectual game. What we *do* about a problem depends on what *sense* we have made of it. Therefore understanding the 'mental representations' that patients construct of their symptoms, illness and treatment is essential to understand their responses to these challenges (Chapter 6). Thinking is shaped by experience, and clinicians and patients have very different kinds of experience of illness and treatment. Therefore, it is not surprising that patients and clinicians can have very different ways of understanding the same symptom or treatment. These differences help to explain why patients often behave in ways that clinicians find puzzling, exasperating or destructive (Chapters 9 and 10).

1.4.4 Reflexivity: Sauce for the Gander

There is a tendency amongst clinicians to assume that psychological factors apply mainly to patients and that clinicians' behaviour is free from psychological influences. In clinical and health psychology, most theories and most research are, indeed, about psychological factors in patients. However, the interaction between patient and clinician is the main vehicle of psychological care. Therefore the psychological influences on the clinician that affect this relationship are also important. The book will therefore take a 'reflexive' approach. That means it will apply psychology to clinicians as well as patients. Indeed, the book will not, in general, advocate psychological techniques that can be applied to patients. Instead, it will emphasize the need for clinicians to examine and modify their own behaviour with patients.

KEY POINTS

- Psychological processes are central to health care.
- Psychological factors are always present, even though many clinicians do not appreciate that they are.
- When not thought about carefully, psychological factors can harm care.
- Psychological aspects of practice should be based on psychological evidence.
- Different sorts of evidence include:
  — information from questionnaires
  — statistical information such as from randomized controlled trials
  — qualitative descriptions of clinician–patient interactions and patient experiences
  — clinical observations.
- The clinician can use evidence as a 'technician' or 'scientist'.
- The 'scientist–clinician' uses evidence critically to develop a response to each specific, new problem and then evaluates the result.
- A psychological approach is different from usual clinical practice because it assumes that:
  — body and mind are not separate
  — people do not just accept challenges but actively manage them
  — people think about what happens to them
  — psychological processes affect clinicians as well as patients.

Chapter 2

THEORIES, MODELS AND OBJECTIVES IN HEALTH CARE

KEY CLINICAL ISSUES

- Why has dualism such a grip on health care?
- What is 'holism' and is it just a passing fad?
- How has consumerism affected health care?
- Do any of these 'isms' matter to a clinician in practice?

2.1 DO 'ISMS' MATTER TO CLINICAL PRACTICE?

Chapter 1 showed some of the difficulties that the nature of psychological research presents to the writer of a book of this sort. Further difficulties arise from the divergence—and sometimes contradiction—that exists among the goals and practices of health care itself. The term 'model' in health care is often used to refer to a coherent set of assumptions and associated goals and practices concerning health care. It is not, though, an abstract term. Alternative models mean tangible alternatives for management. When a GP prescribes an antibiotic for a patient with a sore throat, when a nurse counsels a distressed patient or when a hospital manager carries out a patient satisfaction survey, they are each allowing particular models to guide their work. Different models mean different ways of judging success also (Box 2.1). Depending on which model is being used, a successful clinical intervention could be one which removes disease, helps the patient cope with disease, stops the patient returning or sends the patient away satisfied. This chapter sets the scene for those that follow by distinguishing between the models that Western clinicians can choose. It also examines the different requirements that they lead to for psychology. These are the requirements that later chapters will address.

Box 2.1   Models of health care

Different models of health care have different underlying assumptions that lead to different criteria for judging quality of care. Therefore they lead to diverging requirements from psychology.

Model	Assumption	Criteria for judging care	What is required from psychology?
Biomedical dualism	Physical illness can be understood without reference to psychological factors	'Real' physical illness is separated from 'psychological' problems Pathology is removed	Ensure patient adheres to treatment
Holism	Physical and psychological factors interact	Illness resolved or reduced Patients' adjustment improved Patient's psychological needs met	Identify psychological needs Understand how psychological and biological factors interact in aetiology and treatment Use psychological treatment to improve adjustment or control pathology
Consumerism	Health, illness and treatment are the responsibility of the individual Patient decides his/her needs	Patient takes responsibility Patient is satisfied	Help patient to feel in control Help identify what patients seek Measure and enhance satisfaction

2.2 BIOMEDICAL DUALISM

2.2.1 The Origins of Dualism

2.2.1.1 Mind and Body at the Beginning of Western Medicine

It will soon become clear to the reader that this book reflects the view that mind and body are intimately connected. It is easy to mistake this idea as a recent or radical one, promulgated by specialist researchers and clinicians on the fringes of conventional medicine. In reality, it is the separation of mind and body by Western medicine that is historically aberrant. The longevity of the scientific view that physiological events and emotional experience are intimately bound together is seen in the theory of temperaments, attributed to Hippocrates around 400 BC. In this theory, the (im)balance of different kinds of body fluid was the key to understanding, not just physical disease, but individuals' personality. We still call upon this theory, two and a half millennia later, whenever we call someone phlegmatic, sanguine or melancholy because these terms evoke the names of the critical fluids (Box 2.2).

2.2.1.2 Mind and Body in Ordinary Experience

It has not just been experts who have been aware of links between mind and body. The everyday language of ordinary people uses *bodily* events to convey *emotional* feeling. Some of this language refers to real events

---

Box 2.2   A physiological theory of temperament

In Hippocrates' theory, people's temperament depended on the balance between bodily fluids. The names of the critical fluids are still important. Terms that we use to describe personality and mood today are derived from the names of these fluids.

Personality	Fluid
Choleric	Yellow bile
Melancholy	Black bile
Sanguine	Blood
Phlegmatic	Phlegm

that are associated with emotion (e.g., scared shitless, pain-in-the-neck). Others are bodily metaphors for suffering (e.g., gutted, broken-hearted). Ordinary experience and wisdom are captured in aphorisms, too, such as 'a healthy mind in a healthy body', which have spanned the centuries. Ordinary people's explanations of illness have also integrated physiological and psychological factors (Blaxter, 1989). For instance, present-day beliefs about effects of 'stress' and 'nerves' describe the power of emotional events to influence physiological ones. The unity of mind and body is seen in similar beliefs in many cultures (Helman, 1994).

2.2.1.3 The Separation of Mind from Body by Science

The separation of mind from body by Western medicine can be dated to the European Renaissance, when the objective principles and practices of the natural sciences were being developed. The mind, or soul, was regarded as subjective and not amenable to scientific study. The philosopher Descartes systematized the separation in his 'dualist' theory that mind and body were largely independent, parallel systems, such that the mind could not directly affect bodily processes. It was a short step from regarding mental processes as beyond objective study, and as having no relevance to bodily processes, to viewing them as having no reality at all, let alone any relevance to medicine. Therefore one unfortunate legacy of the dualist model has been the distinction between illnesses that are physical (and therefore 'real') and those that are psychological, psychosomatic or 'in the mind' (and therefore 'unreal'). Patients are keenly aware of the dualist model that lies behind this distinction (Chapters 5 and 13). This helps to explain the strenuous attempts of some patient groups (such as those with chronic fatigue) to establish that their *disease* is *physical*. This can better be seen as a need to establish that their *suffering* is *real*.

2.2.2 What does Biomedical Dualism Demand of Psychology?

Dualism has dominated mainstream medicine and has allowed a biomedical model to develop which has been astonishingly successful— whether measured by the understanding of physical disease that has been gained, or the respect and social position that its associated professionals have earned. Nevertheless, it is now generally accepted that this biomedical model cannot operate efficiently without attending to psychological processes. At the minimum, it is appreciated that patients often fail to comply with treatment recommendations of their clinicians. Attention to the psychological aspects of clinician–patient communication is therefore necessary to ensure adherence to treatment and to achieve the full potential of the biomedical model (Chapter 9).

2.3 HOLISM

2.3.1 Rediscovery of Holism

2.3.1.1 Psychological Factors Influence Physical Disease

The developing scientific basis of nursing, in particular, has been based on a more holistic view of patients and their problems than has been traditional in medicine. Moreover, the grip of dualism over *medical* thinking has been weakened by convergence of several independent developments whereby Western medicine has rediscovered the indivisibility of mind and body. One arose at the start of the twentieth century from the work of an Austrian physician, Sigmund **Freud**. He treated patients who presented physical symptoms, such as paralyses or sensory deficits, which neurology could not explain and which conventional medicine could not help. Freud showed that these apparently inexplicable *physical* problems could be understood as effects of unconscious *psychological* processes (Chapter 5). Freud was concerned with physical *symptoms*. Half a century later an endocrinologist, Hans **Selye** (1956), demonstrated that psychological factors affected physical *disease processes*. Each of these insights released a torrent of clinical research and treatment which has continued to the present. The legacy of Freud's insight is seen in Chapter 13. This shows how purely psychological techniques are used to treat symptoms which, although physical, seem not to be linked to any physical disease process. Selye's approach is the basis of Chapters 4 and 14, which describe psychological procedures that can reverse physiological disease processes.

2.3.1.2 Physical Disease Leads to Psychological Needs

Just as *psychological* factors were seen to cause *physical* symptoms or to set in train physical disease processes, it became obvious that *physical* disease had *psychological* effects. The background to this was the discovery, in 1905, of the spirochaete responsible for syphilis and its attendant psychological symptoms. This launched many attempts to find physical causes for other psychological illnesses. Some optimistic researchers still hope to find a single physical cause—and cure—for diseases such as schizophrenia or depression. This approach can amount to simplistic reductionism. That is, very simple explanations are sought for very complex problems, and physical explanations are seen as more 'fundamental' than psychological ones. A second consequence of this way of thinking is, however, more enlightened. This has been the growth of a view that is now regarded as an obvious fact. Whereas a disease process, or *pathology*, can be recognized in a specimen in a test tube, *illness* is a property of the whole person and, indeed the family or social group. It is therefore now accepted that the clinician's role is to treat *illness* rather than just *pathology*.

2.3.1.3 New Scientific Methods

The reintroduction of psychological factors into medicine requires a fresh look at the kinds of scientific methods which are acceptable. Although psychological factors once seemed beyond the reach of scientific methods, these methods were exclusively those of the natural sciences, so they emphasized objectivity and experimental control. Many of the insights upon which this book is based have not been gleaned from these methods. Qualitative research focuses on the subjective meaning and experience of events rather than their objective characteristics. Another departure from methods of the natural sciences is that complex statistical techniques have been devised to examine cause and effect where sheer complexity or ethical and practical problems have precluded controlled experiments.

2.3.2 What does Holism Demand of Psychology?

The holistic model clearly makes greater demands on psychology than does biomedical dualism. Holistic clinicians need to know how psychological factors might have contributed to a presenting physical problem, how the problem affects the person and the family, what their psychological needs are and how a psychological approach might help meet these needs as well as reverse the disease process.

2.4 CONSUMERISM

2.4.1 Clinical Paternalism versus Patient Autonomy

2.4.1.1 Patients' Control over Health Care

Because dualism was founded on highly technical and experimental scientific method, it clearly required highly qualified experts to understand it and put it into effect. It followed that ordinary people lacked the expertise to understand or question these experts' behaviour. The model is therefore the basis of the paternalistic or authoritarian attitude that has pervaded health care: that 'doctor (or 'nurse' or 'physio' or other clinician) knows best'. Many clinicians adopt this attitude automatically and, as we shall see, many patients expect and value it. However, we shall see also that there are often sound psychological reasons for patients to feel involved where possible (Chapter 11). There are professional reasons too; the emphasis on informed consent recognizes the need to protect both the patient and clinician from decisions that the patient might be unhappy with.

2.4.1.2 Patients' Control over Health

There are parallel changes in ordinary people's ideas about health that also emphasize autonomy. As health has improved in the West, so the view has grown that it can be controlled by the individual. The corollary of this is the belief that illness is always preventable and that, when it occurs, it represents a personal failure to keep healthy. Therefore the constant reminders of illness, particularly in the media, motivates strenuous efforts at control (Brownell, 1991). Obvious examples are dieting, including weight reduction or avoidance of 'additives', and the use of 'health' clubs and exercise. This book will present some evidence that health and illness are, indeed, affected by psychological factors, in particular stress, over which people can exert control (Chapters 4 and 14). Moreover, there are damaging behaviours, such as drinking alcohol and smoking, over which people also have control. Nevertheless, these factors merely change the *risks* of disease, not the certainty of it. Most illness remains stubbornly beyond individuals' control.

This view of autonomy over health and illness is therefore something of an illusion. Nevertheless, once illness strikes, the view shapes what some patients expect from health services. In conventional health care, the patient who demands control will be unhappy with clinical paternalism, and might even come to be seen as a 'bad' or complaining patient (Chapter 12). 'Alternative' therapies or self-help groups might offer more feeling of involvement and control than conventional health care offers. The down side to patient autonomy is the responsibility that patients can feel when illness takes hold, or when it is clear that the fight against an incurable illness is lost (Chapter 14).

2.4.2 The Culture of Consumerism

At a wider cultural level, too, a shift of responsibility for individuals' well-being from the state and its agents to the individual has been a feature of

UK political change during the last 15 years, as it has approached a USA-style view of the importance of personal responsibility. Therefore changes in health care have converged with cultural and political change to produce a growing consumer orientation to health care—as to other services. Rail or bus 'passengers' find themselves renamed as 'customers', a label that health care has not yet routinely adopted. Nevertheless, 'patients' are sometimes termed 'clients', even in publicly provided health services. This is not a trivial change. Being a 'patient' carries rights (to have one's needs met) as well as obligations (to accept what is given). By contrast, a provider is under no obligation to take on 'clients' or 'customers' and meet their needs although, once this contract is agreed, there is the presumption that the customer must be satisfied.

2.4.3 What does Consumerism Demand of Psychology?

Autonomy is as much a subjective psychological feeling as an objective state (Chapter 11). Therefore, this view of health and health care makes major demands upon psychology. For instance, psychological techniques might be used to encourage feelings of autonomy. However, patients differ in their attitudes to autonomy, so psychological techniques have been used to distinguish between individuals (Chapter 11). Where the clinician knowingly or unwittingly challenges the autonomy of a patient for whom it is important, the relationship can be irreversibly damaged (Chapter 9). Avoiding this danger requires intricate attention to psychological aspects of the communication between clinicians and patients.

The widespread use of patient satisfaction as a way of evaluating health care reflects the increasing grip of the consumer model. Satisfaction is commonly advocated as 'fundamental' to quality care. We shall see in Chapter 15 that, although satisfaction may be straightforward when applied to service in a shop or restaurant, its validity is highly questionable when applied to medical care. For the present, it is sufficient to note that satisfaction with any service—medical or otherwise—depends heavily on psychological aspects of the service.

2.5 CONCLUSION

Modern Western health care is a blend of dualism, holism and consumerism. Of course, it is rare that any clinician's work could—or should—all be encompassed within a single model. It is not even likely that a clinician's management of a single clinical problem could be con-

---

Box 2.3   Models of health care in practice

Think of two patients with whom you recently worked. Choose one with whom you think that you were successful. Choose another with whom you think you were unsuccessful. For each one, tick which of the following applies.

	'Successful' patient	'Unsuccessful' patient
There was clear physical pathology		
There was no clear physical pathology		
Patient followed my advice		
Patient did not follow my advice		
Patient took responsibility for managing the condition		
Patient left me with responsibility		
Medical condition improved		
Medical condition did not improve		
Patient adjusted to the condition as much as possible		
Patient seemed not to accept the condition		
Patient was satisfied with me		
Patient was dissatisfied with me		

Does the pattern of ticks say anything about which model(s) you used to decide whether you succeeded or failed? Might your feelings about success or failure have looked different from the perspective of a different model?

---

fined tidily within one model. Instead, different aspects of management will reflect the influence of different models (Box 2.3). Sometimes, a model will be applied that should not be applied—for instance, when a treatment approach is aimed at satisfying a patient whose management might be better served by a different response, or when a doctor aggressively treats pathology in an incurable patient who would be better helped to adjust to the inevitability of death (Chapter 8).

The models that clinicians work with can lead to contradictory targets for treatment. For instance, effective psychological management of a patient's problem can be incompatible with satisfying the patient. Clinicians' requirements of psychology are correspondingly complex. The clinician cannot look to a psychological approach for rules which can be followed blindly. Instead, the clinician can use this approach to help understand clinical problems and to deduce psychological responses. However, the choice between available responses will often be made on clinical or ethical grounds, not psychological ones.

KEY POINTS

- Models, or 'isms', are coherent sets of assumptions and expectations about health care.
- Different models make different demands on psychology.
- According to dualism, physical illness results from physical processes that can be understood only by technical experts. Its paternalistic clinicians need psychology to improve patients' adherence to their decisions.
- Holism accepts that psychological processes cause physical illness and physical illness causes psychological needs. Holistic clinicians need psychology to help explain and treat disease and its effects.
- Consumerism emphasizes patients' choice. Psychology is needed to improve and measure customer satisfaction.
- Clinical practice is a mixture of different models, which sometimes point to contradictory goals.

Part II

BECOMING ILL AND BEING ILL

CORNWALL COLLEGE
LEARNING CENTRE

Chapter 3

CHALLENGE, STRESS AND COPING

KEY CLINICAL ISSUES

- What is stress?
- Is everyone stressed by the same things?
- Does everyone show stress in the same way?
- What can people do to reduce stress?
- Is denial a bad way of coping with a challenge?
- Why do some patients make life even more difficult for themselves than it needs to be?
- Do friends protect against stress and disease?

3.1 STRESS

3.1.1 What is Stress?

Being 'under stress' is part of everyday language. In general, the word 'stress' is used to describe the toll that life can take on emotional and physical health. Being 'under stress' is one of the commonest explanations that patients give for their symptoms (Chapter 6). For scientists, too, stress has become a key concept for understanding the costs that are entailed in meeting the psychological challenges of daily life. These challenges differ for different people. Moreover, some people take in their stride things that other people see as overwhelming. Therefore recognizing whether someone is stressed just by knowing the challenges that are present is difficult. Instead of this 'stimulus-based' approach to defining stress, stress can be recognized from the *effects* of challenges (a 'response-based' approach to defining stress). These effects can be counted in just about every area of life, from emotional disturbance and relationship problems, through absenteeism and poor performance at work to physical ill health. Health care imposes particularly severe challenges, and the stress that patients are under can be manifest in ways that compromise their care, such as intense anxiety or non-compliance.

3.1.2 The Alarm Reaction

Faced with this bewildering range of effects that could be regarded as indicating stress, we shall focus initially on physiological changes. This view of stress is therefore at the heart of the holistic model introduced in Chapter 2. The germ of current understanding of physiological aspects of stress was the work of the physiologist Cannon (1929), who described the physiological changes that we now know as the 'alarm' reaction. Stimulated by any significant challenge to the individual, the autonomic nervous system rapidly mobilizes resources that the body needs to deal with the challenge. Heart rate rises so as to pump blood more rapidly to the muscles and provide the fuel that they need for an energetic response to the challenge. Respiration quickens so as to increase the oxygen available in the muscles for producing energy. There are other relatively rapid responses, too. Sweat glands are activated on the palms of the hands, perhaps to increase tactile sensitivity. Muscle tension increases, which might also be a preparation for a muscular response. When prolonged, this muscle tension can lead to muscle pain in different parts of the body. Stomach and bowel motility increases. Each can even evacuate its contents as the body concentrates its resources on responding to the challenge.

3.1.3 From Alarm to the Present Day

Cannon's description of these rapid responses was followed by the discovery by the endocrinologist, Selye (1956), of physiological and metabolic changes that follow the alarm reaction. He termed these the 'general adaptation syndrome'. In this way he signified that, like the alarm reaction, these changes mobilize resources that the body needs to respond to challenge. In particular, the glucocorticoid hormone, cortisol, is released from the adrenal cortex and this, in turn, increases blood sugar levels and so provides more energy to the muscles. In parallel with this, the catecholamine hormones (adrenaline and noradrenaline) that are released from the sympathoadrenal system (to fuel the alarm reaction) mobilize fats into the circulation, which also provide energy. The resulting model of stress is illustrated in Box 3.1. Both Cannon and Selye knew that challenges that are purely psychological, such as fear, can stimulate these responses. Indeed, later evidence suggested that Selye's work applied specifically to pychological challenges (Mason et al, 1976).

Box 3.1   The stress response

This simplified view of the stress response combines elements of Cannon's 'alarm reaction' and Selye's general adaptation syndrome.

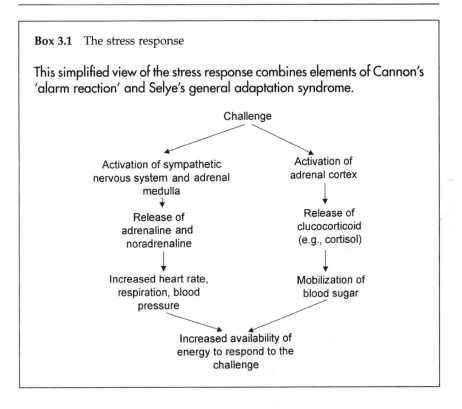

In the evolutionary past, mobilizing energy to respond to challenges made sense because most required energetic muscular responses to deal with them: typically fight or flight. In modern Western life, including medical care, challenges can rarely be coped with so energetically. We cannot run away from the doctor who has given us a frightening diagnosis. Neither can we fight the nurse who has arrived to carry out a painful dressing. Therefore it is the *maladaptive* nature of these stress responses that will concern us.

Although greatly modified, Cannon's and Selye's ideas have stood the test of time as a framework for understanding potentially harmful physiological effects of psychological challenges. However, research has led to two broad modifications of these ideas. First, additional physiological stress responses have been found. In particular, there has been a steady accumulation of evidence that the immune system also responds to emotional challenges (Bachen et al, 1997). These include challenges that are part of medical treatment: for instance, being diagnosed as HIV-positive

Box 3.2 The buffering of stress responses

Challenging events are not necessarily experienced as stressful. The extent to which they are depends on intervening psychological and social processes.

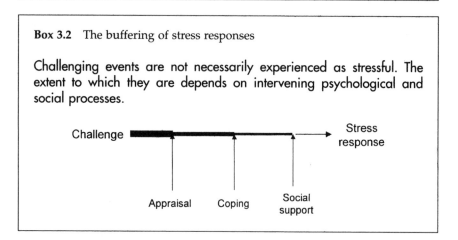

suppresses aspects of immune function (Antoni et al, 1991). The second modification is to the view that a challenge inevitably gives rise to the whole constellation of stress responses. This view has given way to a more complex picture (Box 3.2), explored later in this chapter, in which the strength and patterning of the stress response depend on intervening psychosocial factors. Clinically, this difference is very important. It is often unrealistic to protect patients by preventing challenges, but they can be protected instead by exploiting these intervening factors.

3.1.4 Patterning of Stress Responses

It has been known for a long time that different individuals respond to stress in different parts of the body (Malmo and Shagass, 1949). It has also been suspected that this could lead to clinical problems in particular organs (Fahrenberg, 1986). This scientific view echoes popular ideas that people have, for instance, a 'weak stomach' or 'weak chest' (Helman, 1994). However, cause and effect have been hard to pin down. A tendency to show stress responses in a particular part of the body *might* cause clinical problems there. However, the reverse is equally possible: i.e., having clinical problems in a part of the body might make it more sensitive to stress.

In clinical practice, this distinction hardly matters. Most general practitioners are aware of patients who reliably respond to life stresses with symptoms in a certain part of the body, such as bowel symptoms, migraine or stomach pain. Often these patients are frightened by these symptoms. Everyone knows that increases in heart rate, or clammy palms, can be stress responses, but many affected patients do not appreciate that muscle pain, headaches and bowel or stomach problems can also be stress responses. Therefore a simple explanation of stress can provide relief (Chapter 13).

3.1.5 Reversing Stress Responses

Just as the nervous system is geared to mobilize a coordinated stress response, it can organize an opposite, **relaxation response** (Benson and Klipper, 1975). It is claimed that the minimum conditions for eliciting this are quite simple: emptying of consciousness and a passive attitude to the thoughts, feelings and images that then drift through consciousness. Unsurprisingly, these conditions have been discovered by different cultures in different ways. Therefore the response is elicited equally by Western techniques of **relaxation training** and Eastern techniques of yoga and meditation (Benson and Klipper, 1975; Box 3.3). These techniques can reduce various signs of physiological arousal, including oxygen consumption, heart rate and blood pressure. Focusing on more specific components of individuals' stress responses can often achieve the same effect. In biofeedback, patients learn to relax by focusing on a specific biological variable, such as heart rate or blood pressure. The focus need not be on physiological responses: teaching hostile subjects to reduce their speech rate has decreased cardiovascular responses to stress (Siegman et al, 1992). In practice, an important advantage of simple techniques of relaxation training is that clinicians can easily teach them effectively, and so influence psychological mechanisms without having to address psychological issues directly (Patel and Marmot, 1988).

3.2 APPRAISAL

Box 3.2 shows three important factors that influence how much stress a challenge produces. The first is appraisal. This can be thought of as the reason why events that severely challenge some people are shrugged off—or even welcomed—by others. For instance, a sudden pain in the chest would probably be disregarded by a healthy person who has just eaten a strong curry, but the same sensation would be distressing to another who has recently left hospital after being treated for a myocardial infarction. Similarly, when a public figure dies from breast cancer, most women would give this only passing interest. For the woman

---

Box 3.3   The relaxation response

Eliciting the relaxation response is no mystery. It simply requires a passive attitude and a mental device for emptying the mind of distracting thoughts. Many people can achieve this by practising the following instructions. Audiotaped instructions are not necessary but they can help reduce distraction.

1. Sit or lie quietly in a comfortable position. Make sure there are going to be no distractions for 20 minutes or so and close your eyes.
2. Relax the muscles in each part of your body, starting with your hands, moving up to the head and down to your feet. Start like this.
   — Spend a few minutes just thinking about your hands, and all the feelings you can notice in them—the position of them, the pressure of your palms against the chair or bed. Think of the temperature of the skin of your hands. Notice feelings of warmth or coolness. Notice other sensations, such as slight tingling feelings. Notice any tightness or tension around your wrists and over the knuckles. As you notice the tension, let your hands feel heavy and loose. Let them sink heavily by your side.
   — Do the same with your arms, shoulders, your neck, scalp, then your chest, tummy and so on down to your toes.
3. Do not worry about whether you are successful in relaxing.
4. When you have finished, continue relaxing for a minute or two. Breathe slowly, quietly and calmly. Think about your breath; notice it on your upper lip as you breath in, and again as you breathe out. Continue like this until you would like to stop.
5. Open your eyes and rest until you want to get up.

---

who has just discovered a lump in her breast, it is a major challenge. Clearly, whether an event is challenging is a subjective matter: it depends on the judgement of the individual. It is this judgement that has been termed 'appraisal' (Lazarus, 1999). It is normally an immediate, unconscious process which identifies events that disturb our view of the world or our future. How people appraise challenges obviously depends on their beliefs. The individual who believes that intense pain in the centre of the chest must be coming from the heart will be more likely to appraise the after-effects of the previous night's curry negatively. In consequence, appraisals can be modified by changing beliefs (Chapters 13 and 14).

3.3 COPING

3.3.1 The Concept of Coping

Once appraised as such, a challenge leads not only to stress but to attempts to cope with it. Coping is therefore another 'buffer' of the link between challenge and stress (Box 3.2). Technically, 'coping' refers to actions which have the function of reducing the stressfulness of a challenge. In practice, this function is often hard to define and the term is usually used loosely to refer to any response to a challenge. Normally these arise unconsciously—and can simply amount to 'automatic' reactions like running away or crying for help. Alternatively, coping can be a conscious, considered process.

Coping has become one of the most influential concepts in health psychology. However, many uses of the concept are pure tautology. For instance, there are many reports that people who cope with a challenge by trying to avoid thinking about it are more distressed. This leads some researchers to argue that 'avoidant coping' *makes* people more distressed. However, avoidance is an *aspect* of distress: that is, people who are frightened often try to stop thinking about the thing that frightens them. Therefore the apparent association of coping with distress amounts simply to a description of the syndrome of distress: nothing has been discovered!

Another problem with the concept of coping is that people often do not see themselves as *coping with* a challenge. They see themselves as *experiencing* a challenge, and as *responding* to it, but do not recognize themselves as actively *managing* it. They might only begin to think in terms of coping once a psychologist or a clinician has asked them about coping, or given them a questionnaire about coping! This is part of the general problem in psychology that one can often not find out about someone's way of thinking without changing it. In this problem, however, lies the power of psychology, too, and the value of the concept of coping in particular. Introducing patients to the idea of coping can help them to think differently. It can therefore be a powerful way of helping patients to free themselves from existing ways of thinking so that they can identify new opportunities for responding to challenges. First, however, a convenient way of distinguishing different sorts of coping is needed.

3.3.2 Classifying Coping

There are many overlapping schemes to divide up coping. A useful starting point is to distinguish problem-focused and emotion-focused coping (Lazarus and Folkman, 1984). **Problem-focused coping** addresses the problem itself. It includes behaviour that manages the problem or finds out more about it. For patients, the opportunity for **behavioural problem-focused coping** is often restricted by enforced passivity in the face of disabling illness or clinical procedures. However, opportunities can usually be found for purely mental activities that constitute **cognitive problem-focused coping**. For instance, surgical patients can 'rehearse' mentally the physiotherapy exercises which will be important postoperatively, or they can engage in 'self-talk' to control distressing thoughts that make them anxious (Chapters 11 and 12). Problem-focused coping of these kinds can reduce physiological stress responses, particularly adrenocortical responses (Box 3.1), in both clinical and non-clinical situations (Dantzer, 1993; Manyande et al, 1995).

In contrast, **emotion-focused coping** deals with the emotional feelings caused by the challenge. Because of this, it is often called **palliative coping**. It includes many coping strategies which, in the short term at least, can be helpful, such as relaxation or distracting oneself by thinking of other things. For many people, palliative coping of this kind can be an effective way of managing brief clinical challenges, such as minor invasive procedures (Suls and Fletcher, 1985). Certain types of palliative coping are important in adjusting to the longer-term challenge of chronic disease, also. For instance, downward social comparison—i.e., seeing oneself as better off than other people—is a common way of reacting to chronic illness and might help emotional adjustment (Helgeson and Taylor, 1993).

However, palliative coping also includes **psychological defence** mechanisms. These include potentially destructive responses such as venting frustration on other people, or becoming angry with other people instead of focusing on one's own problems (Box 3.4). They also include **denial**, which appears in various guises. For instance, it can emerge in behaviours which at first sight seem to be lapses of memory, such as forgetting a mammogram screening appointment (Box 5.9). In other situations denial can arise in apparent failures of understanding, such as when a patient insists on going home from intensive care shortly after myocardial infarction. In each of these situations, denial means an unconscious attempt to protect oneself against the emotional challenge associated with illness. These illustrations point to a big clinical problem. Behaviours which, for patients, are ways of coping with severe challenges can be seen by clinicians in a very negative way. They can be seen as rejecting help, as provocative or even as revealing problems with the patient's personality.

Box 3.4   Varieties of defensive palliative coping

Patients often behave in ways that confuse, annoy or distress clinicians. Sometimes, these are attempts to cope with challenges of disease and treatment.

Patients' problem behaviour	What type of coping does it represent?
A 50-year-old man insists he is well and discharges himself from a coronary care unit where he was taken after a suspected heart attack	**Denial**: not accepting reality
A 25-year-old woman having a termination of pregancy is angry with her boyfriend, saying he made her have the abortion. She refuses to see him when he visits. Her mother says she cannot understand this because her daughter was adamant that she did not want the baby	**Projection**: placing the blame for one's own difficulties on others
A 60-year-old man with lung cancer denies any recollection of the consultation at which he was told his diagnosis. He maintains that he has a bad dose of bronchitis	**Repression**: keeping threatening memories or thoughts out of consciousness
A 14-year-old boy in hospital for major orthopaedic surgery irritates staff and other patients by boasting about his 'toughness'. After surgery he cries a great deal	**Reaction formation**: emphasizing the opposite to how one actually feels
A 55-year-old woman who was persuaded by her husband to go to her GP because of chest pains has been referred to hospital. Six weeks later, no appointment has arrived. She says she will not phone to chase them up because they must be very busy with more seriously ill people than herself. They will send her an appointment once they have a time for her	**Rationalization**: providing a logical explanation for events that avoids having to confront a problem
A 45-year-old man suffered physical abuse while in a children's home between the ages of 10 and 12. He is currently under the care of three different hospital specialties and has a reputation for becoming angry and abusive with the doctors for failing to help him	**Displacement**: directing emotional feelings to symptoms, people or objects that are less threatening than the problems which actually gave rise to the emotion

3.3.3 The Coping Process

If coping changes the severity of a challenge or the emotional response to it, then the kind of coping that is needed should itself change over time. Therefore, ways of coping that, at first sight, seem unhelpful can be a bridge to more adaptive responses. For instance, when it is prolonged, denial compromises adaptation to chronic disease and adherence to treatment. However, it has a key role in helping people through the early phase of adaptation to traumatic life changes, including bereavement and serious illness (Chapter 8). That is, by mitigating the initial intense emotional reaction, it can help to make it possible for people to use problem-focused coping later.

However, coping is also dynamic over a longer timescale. Ways of coping with a challenge reflect experiences of coping with challenges in the past. Clinically, it is evident that individuals who have coped with many serious adversities in life can draw on that experience in coping with the challenge of physical illness in themselves or someone close to them. Even experience of previous illness can increase resilience in this way. For instance, developing a chronic disease such as diabetes is a profound challenge that requires extensive problem-focused coping to manage the self-care that is needed and to reorganize life around the illness and its management (Chapter 7). Patients who have previously learned to manage diabetes are therefore better equipped to cope with the challenge of a new condition, such as renal failure, than are previously healthy patients (Blackburn et al, 1978). However, the way that an individual coped previously is probably crucial. The patient who coped previously by denial may be ill equipped to cope with a serious illness that requires major readjustment to the way of life (Box 3.5). Whether coping was successful in managing the previous challenge or its effects is also important. A challenge can be so intense that it is beyond effective coping. Experience of this kind can sensitize patients to a worse reaction to diagnosis of serious illness and can render them unresponsive to conventional psychological help (Box 3.5; Baider et al, 1997).

3.4 SOCIAL INTEGRATION AND EMOTIONAL SUPPORT

3.4.1 The Importance of Social Integration

The environment is not simply a source of challenge. It contains resources that protect the individual against challenges. Important physical

Box 3.5 Coping with illness depends on previous experience of challenge and coping

The response of these two patients to a diagnosis of cancer can be understood once their previous experience of challenges and coping is known.

Patient X

X was diagnosed with bowel cancer seven months ago. She initially seemed to respond well, but then became withdrawn and depressed and was referred for counselling. She said that she lacked energy to do the things that she used to enjoy and that it would have been better if the cancer had killed her.

X described several previous major challenges. Her mother died when she was 15, but she got on with looking after her younger brothers and her father and 'never had time to stop and feel sorry for myself'. After marrying, she had two miscarriages and then a son who caught (and recovered from) meningitis as a baby. She did not become upset: 'It's no use to anyone, crying all around the place, is it?' When her husband was seriously injured in a traffic accident, she 'didn't brood on it', but 'just got on with life'. She was positive and cheerful after diagnosis of cancer, too: 'It was nowhere near as bad as having flu. She laughed and joked with the nurses and doctors before surgery and supported other patients who 'were much worse off than I was'. She worked (as a teacher) until the day she went into hospital and returned to work just two weeks after leaving hospital.

Analysis. Her habitual way of coping was by denial; she did not acknowledge or express distress and attended largely to others' needs rather than her own. This worked well with short-term challenges, but was unsuited to the enduring effects of cancer. These include fears of disease recurrence and death and ever-present reminders of the disease in magazines and on TV.

Patient Y

Y was referred to a psychologist because she was 'failing to cope' with her breast cancer. Five years before her diagnosis she had married a businessman whose home was in the Middle East. She returned there with him, learned the language and settled into life as a woman in an unfamiliar culture. Then war came to the country. Her husband 'disappeared'. She was arrested when trying to escape, was imprisoned

Continued

in squalid conditions for three months and was brutally raped and assaulted. Soon after being deported to her home country she was diagnosed with breast cancer and underwent mastectomy. When seeing her doctors she was mute, relying on a friend to speak for her. She did not address the psychologist during the first two meetings, and then only spoke a few words: 'It's all terrible, terrible.' Only after many meetings could she begin to provide any more detail.

Analysis. Y's experience in prison had overwhelmed her. Being investigated and operated upon by (male) doctors evoked feelings that had been elicited by the assaults in prison and that were too intense for her to cope with.

resources obviously include good housing and clean air, and the lack of these helps to explain why the poor are iller and die earlier than the rich (Carroll et al, 1993). However, a less tangible resource is also important. A clue to this is revealed by comparing life expectancy amongst Western countries: it is longest, not in the richest, but in those with the the most equal income distributions: e.g., Sweden and Norway rather than the USA (Wilkinson, 1992). One explanation is that, beyond a minimum level of prosperity, health reflects social integration rather than absolute wealth. This view fits the evidence, from smaller-scale studies *within* countries, that having friends and being integrated into social networks helps to preserve health, prolong life and to speed recovery from illness (Berkman and Syme, 1979; Rosengren et al, 1993).

3.4.2 The Importance of Emotional Support

3.4.2.1 What is Support?

For the clinician, a patient's social integration is normally fixed and can rarely be modified clinically. However, social integration is the vehicle for an important process which the clinician *can* influence and which is the third 'buffer' between challenge and stress (Box 3.2). This is social suport. Some of the components of **material support** are obvious: someone to look after the children, do the shopping or drive the patient to hospital. However, the aspect of social support that concerns us here is **emotional support**. Simply, this refers to the availability of people to whom one can disclose important feelings and problems.

Merely expressing feelings about upsetting or traumatic challenges reduces physiological arousal and helps to reduce damaging physiological effects (Pennebaker and Susman, 1988; Pennebaker, 1993). It is the disclosure that is important, rather than advice received in return. Therefore, even just writing about one's feelings has physiological benefits (e.g. improving aspects of immune function) and reduces people's need for health care consultation. Writing about one's problems in an insightful, analytical way is particularly helpful (Pennebaker et al, 1997). Therefore, one reason why disclosure helps might be that it occasions the opportunity to *think* about problems.

3.4.2.2 Effects of Emotional Support in Illness

The benefits of emotional support are more extensive and more powerful than many physical treatments. Very simply, in major physical illness, such as coronary artery disease (Williams et al, 1992) or breast cancer (Waxler-Morrison et al, 1991), patients with better support recover faster or live longer. The effect, although extensive, is not universal and appears not to influence survival from lung or colorectal cancer or from advanced stages of breast cancer (Ell et al, 1992). Nevertheless, the protective effect of support is also seen in less serious physical conditions, as diverse as upper respiratory infection (Cohen et al, 1997) and pregnancy (Collins et al, 1993). The mechanisms that link support to health are complex. Well-supported patients are more likely to comply with treatment (e.g., Kulik and Mahler, 1993). Support reduces emotional distress which can, itself, impair treatment and recovery. Support probably also directly influences some of the physiological mechanisms that are affected in stress (Berkman, 1985).

3.4.2.3 Complications of Support

Because of its clinical significance, it is important to be clear about how emotional support can be recognized where it exists, and how it can be provided where it does not. Unfortunately, it cannot be recognized simply from whether a friend, relative or other supporter is available. The spouse's role illustrates this.

Having a spouse (or other close confidant) appears to protect men against premature mortality (House et al, 1982). Similarly, men who are visited most frequently by their wives after cardiac surgery recover the most quickly (Kulik and Mahler, 1989)—regardless of how good or bad the marriage is. By contrast, being married is a *risk factor* for mortality in women with breast cancer (Ell et al, 1992; Waxler-Morrison et al, 1991).

Perhaps, for these women, the presence of a spouse who himself needs support is an extra burden (Chapter 7), whereas men who are ill can simply continue to receive the support which the marriage has provided premorbidly. In practice, the extent and direction of support within a marriage will depend on the nature of the relationship before illness. For instance, where partners have adopted very traditional masculine and feminine roles, this can complicate adjustment to changes in the balance of dependency between them (Helgeson, 1993).

There are other reasons why potentially supportive relationships are often not supportive in practice. Clinically, a common finding is that the relationships are strained by illness to the point of being unsupportive. Again, the direction of support is often not what would be expected. Family or friends may themselves be so upset by patients' suffering that *patients* have to support *them.*

Therefore, the availability of support is not an objective phenomenon. It is a subjective matter. A patient is not necessarily receiving support just because there is a spouse, friend or even clinician available. Support occurs where the patient *feels* that someone is available who understands and respects his/her concerns. For clinicians, therefore, the focus should be on whether support is available from someone who facilitates disclosure and *listens.*

3.4.2.4 Support by Clinicians

Clinicians, by definition, provide material support. Additionally, however, they face two responsibilitities in relation to emotional support. The first is to assess how good a patient's support is, and we have seen that this cannot simply be equated with the presence of potential supporters. The second responsibility is to provide emotional support. Unfortunately, many common clinical responses to patients' disclosures do not achieve effective listening (Box 3.6). Evidence that clinicians do not detect patient worries further suggests that their ability to support patients is limited (Chapter 10). They are hampered by many of the same factors that restrict the support that family and friends provide. Displaying distress is an important way in which a patient elicits support. Displaying too much, for too long, can burden or repel clinicians and family alike. Clinicians, like other carers, may themselves be upset or even emotionally disturbed by patients' suffering, so that they use psychological defences to distance themselves from it (Chapter 10). Finally, we shall see that, even where clinicians are available to provide support, their ability to do so is severely constrained by patients' belief that staff should not be burdened with patients' worries and that the *patients* should support *them* (Chapter 10).

Box 3.6 Clinicians' failures to provide emotional support

In each of the following instances, nurses or doctors failed to provide emotional support. Alternative responses are shown which would have indicated that the clinician understood the patient's concerns and was ready to hear them.

Scenario and actual response	Alternative response
A 16-year-old girl about to have a termination of pregnancy says that she feels worried. The nurse tells her 'It'll soon be over now.'	'I can see you're upset. Would you like to talk to someone about how you feel?'
A man about to have a minor operation tells the anaesthetist that he is worried about the anaesthetic. The anaesthetist says 'We do hundreds of operations like this every month, and we have never had any problems. There's really no need to worry.'	'It's natural to worry about an anaesthetic even when it's for a safe and routine operation like yours. Tell me what frightens you about it most.'
A woman attending a diagnostic clinic after finding a lump in her breast tells the nurse that she doesn't think she will cope if she finds she has cancer. The nurse tells her that 'Cancer's not so bad these days. Treatment is much better than it used to be.'	'I can see you're frightened about what might happen. Many women are when they come here—even though it's usually a false alarm. If you do have cancer, we'll talk together about how we will treat it and how you will cope.'
A 10-year-old boy is recovering from an appendectomy. He is crying and wailing that he wants to go home. The nurse tells him 'There's nothing to worry about. You're better now."	'The operation's over, but you're still unhappy aren't you? Tell me what's frightening you.'
A 35-year-old man attends his GP for results of blood tests which were done because he complained of tiredness and lack of energy. The GP tells him 'The tests are all normal so there's nothing to worry about.'	'Physically you're OK and there's nothing to worry about there, but you're obviously not feeling well in yourself, are you?'

3.5 CONCLUSION: HELPING PATIENTS TO MANAGE STRESS

Specific applications of this account of stress, coping and support are developed in later chapters. For the present, it should be appreciated that it provides a new way of looking at many patient behaviours that challenge clinicians. Often, these behaviours are results of patients' attempts to cope with challenges arising from illness or treatment. Some of the most natural of clinicians' responses to patients who are coping in this way will magnify the challenge or its emotional effects, and so exacerbate the problem. For instance, avoiding distressed and complaining patients restricts their opportunity to use emotional support. The result will be a patient who is more distressed and complains more. Encouraging patients to adhere to treatment by re-emphasizing the seriousness of their condition only adds to their fear. It might therefore further intensify the denial that was behind their non-adherence. Instead of responding automatically to behaviour of this kind, the clinician's response should be based on a careful assessment of the nature of the challenge that the patient is experiencing, the availability of emotional support, and the patient's ability to use different ways of coping (Box 3.7). The dynamic

---

Box 3.7   Assessing challenge, coping and support in practice

X was the eldest daughter of a large family whose mother died when she was 15, leaving her to look after her siblings and father. She has been married for 12 years. A year ago she underwent mastectomy and reconstructive surgery for breast cancer. She describes no fears about the future and says that the cancer has all been removed. However, she was unhappy with the reconstruction and angry with the doctors and breast nurses for leading her, she says, to expect a better result. A further reconstruction was carried out, but she complained that it was still unsatisfactory. She became even angrier with the surgeon because of further scarring. He told her that her reconstruction was better than many women's. Her specialist nurse has told her that it's now time to put the problem behind her. Her problems can be analysed in terms of stress and coping by answering four questions.

What does she appraise as challenges?

The first challenge that she describes is not having an adequate reconstruction which she feels is essential for her to get back to normal life. When talking at more length, she reveals that the sight of her uneven figure in the mirror is a reminder of the cancer and of the possibility that she might not see her children grow up. There are concerns about her marriage, too. Because she dislikes her appearance, she thinks her husband must, too. She also feels taken for granted because her husband does not help out more in the house since her illness and because he does not show any understanding of how she feels.

How does she cope at present?

Emotion-focused coping. Anger with doctors and preoccupation with needing a perfect reconstruction may be defensive coping. They help her avoid more threatening challenges including the need to learn to live with reminders of her disease and with her changed body image. Her confidence about the effects of surgery on her cancer suggests denial.

Problem-focused coping. She seems not to be doing anything that will solve the challenges that she has identified.

What are her sources of support?

BN does not feel that the surgeon or nurses are supportive. She does not tell her husband her worries. She thinks it would be unfair because his work is so demanding. She also keeps her worries from friends, fearing that she would become tearful, which would annoy them.

Are any of these factors changing?

There is no reason to expect any improvement over time. Indeed, the relationships with her husband and the surgeon are likely to deteriorate further and exacerbate her difficulties.

and changing nature of coping with stress must also enter into the assessment. In some situations, the correct response will simply be to wait while the natural time course of coping unfolds (Chapter 8). In others, quick action will prevent continued deterioration. In Chapter 7 we examine how the patient in Box 3.7 might be helped.

KEY POINTS

- 'Stress' refers to the physiological, emotional and other costs of meeting psychological challenges—including illness and treatment.
- Physiological responses to challenge gear the body for 'fight or flight', but are poorly adapted to managing the challenges of modern Western life.

- Different people show different physical effects of stress, but often do not realize that these *are* stress responses.
- Therefore many people consult clinicians with symptoms that are stress responses.
- Whether something is challenging depends on how the individual appraises it.
- People can respond to challenges by managing the challenge (problem-focused coping) or managing its emotional effects (emotion-focused coping).
- Patients' emotion-focused coping with disease and treatment often entails reactions that confuse and challenge clinicians.
- Having someone to disclose one's feelings to protects against stress.

Chapter 4

PSYCHOBIOLOGY OF DISEASE PROCESSES: HEART DISEASE AND CANCER

KEY CLINICAL ISSUES

- Does stress cause heart disease?
- Can people's personality put them at risk of cancer?
- Can patients 'fight' cancer?
- What should patients be told about psychological influences on disease?

4.1 WHY DOES PSYCHOBIOLOGY MATTER TO CLINICIANS?

This chapter will focus on heart disease and cancer, not only because they are so important in Western health care (they are the two biggest killers in Western countries), but also because the psychobiology of these diseases has been so intensively studied. Therefore they provide models for how psychological factors might, in future, be successfully implicated in other diseases where the evidence is at present only very preliminary. Behavioural factors (such as smoking, diet and exercise) increase the risk of these diseases, but will not be considered here because they are more relevant to prevention than to treatment. Instead we shall return to the psychological processes introduced in Chapter 3. There are three reasons why these are important for a clinician.

4.1.1 To Inform Patients

First, patients are increasingly exposed to popular literature and mass media in which they are told that 'stress causes heart disease' or 'cancer-can be fought'. Some patients receive these messages from poorly informed clinicians, too. Others are equally unfortunate in meeting clinicians who are principled sceptics of the role of psychological factors. Because these clinicians cannot conceive of a mechanism whereby psychology could influence biology, they are sensitized to disbelieve any evidence that it does. They will therefore disappoint the patient who sees in psychological processes an opportunity to exert some control over the illness: i.e., to engage in a special kind of problem-focused coping (Chapter 3). A growing role for clinicians is to provide authoritative advice to patients and, by answering their questions, to clarify misunderstandings. Therefore clinicians need to know how far the evidence goes and they need to be able to recognize claims in popular or scientific literature, or hopes expressed by patients, that go beyond what evidence supports.

4.1.2 To Understand Psychological Treatment

The second reason for returning to the psychobiological processes in Chapter 3 is that psychological treatments are available that are claimed, not merely to help the patient cope with disease, but to reverse or oppose the disease processes themselves. Whereas psychological approaches of this kind are now becoming routine in treating heart disease, they are still speculative and controversial in cancer. Nevertheless, for a scientifically minded clinician in either area, understanding psychological processes that *cause* disease is essential to make sense of the psychological techniques that are claimed to *treat* it.

4.1.3 To Understand Effects of Clinicians' Behaviour

A third reason for knowing the psychological processes that have been linked to disease is to help clinicians to appreciate that their own behaviour can recruit these processes. We shall see that, in trying to protect cardiac patients from stress or in reassuring patients with cancer, clinicians can unwittingly promote the very psychological processes that have been implicated in those diseases.

4.2 PSYCHOBIOLOGICAL PROCESSES IN HEART DISEASE

4.2.1 Psychological Effects on the Cardiovascular System

4.2.1.1 Acute Effects

Scientific evidence is much more complex than the popular idea that 'stress causes heart attacks' (Box 4.1). Brief mental stress can cause

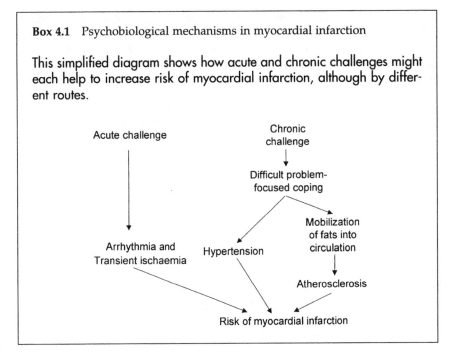

Box 4.1 Psychobiological mechanisms in myocardial infarction

This simplified diagram shows how acute and chronic challenges might each help to increase risk of myocardial infarction, although by different routes.

arrhythmia or transient ischaemia that is not normally clinically apparent, and intense psychological stress can impose a demand on the heart that is as large as that of physical exercise. Major cardiac events, including sudden deaths or ventricular arrhythmias, therefore sometimes follow intense emotions or major challenges, particularly bereavements (Steptoe, 1993). These short-term, acute or catastrophic effects of stress are probably only clinically important when the cardiovascular system is already compromised. The following section shows that psychological factors can be involved in that compromise also.

4.2.1.2 Long-Term Effects

Although the cardiovascular system is stimulated rapidly by challenges in general, it is the individual's way of reacting to stress which determines whether cardiovascular activation is sustained. This can be studied in laboratory experiments in which subjects are exposed to a challenge, such as electric shock or loud noise, and provided with different ways of coping, such as different psychomotor tasks that can reduce or avoid the shock. It turns out that it is those who are given a difficult but just-possible task who show a sustained 'alarm' response of the sympathoadrenal system (Chapter 3) and consequent cardiovascular activation (Obrist, 1981). In subjects who have an easy—or impossible—task, the response is only transient. This finding indicates that cardiovascular responses to challenge are promoted by attempts at active, problem-focused coping, but which circumstances make difficult.

There are several ways in which repeated excitation of the cardiovascular system by circulating and neuronal catecholamines in this way can increase the risk of disease (Bohus and Koolhaas, 1993). The coronary arteries can become damaged and inelastic. This, in turn, can lead to hypertension. Damage also promotes the accumulation of fatty deposits that eventually occlude the arteries. This process, called atherosclerosis, is probably also increased by one of the effects of the catecholamine component of the stress response: release of fats into the circulation. Resulting occlusion of the coronary arteries can cause angina pectoris (pain associated with psychological or physical challenge) and it increases the risk of myocardial infarction (Box 4.1).

Poor integration into a supportive social network is a risk factor for having exaggerated cardiovascular responses to challenge. It is a risk factor, too, for developing coronary heart disease and hypertension (Steptoe, 1993). We shall see also that, once a myocardial infarction has occurred, support can make the difference between life and death (Chapter 7).

4.2.2 Who is at Risk?

4.2.2.1 Exposure to Coping Demands

This analysis helps to understand why and how certain groups of people are at particular risk of heart disease for psychological reasons. One group comprises those who, because of their occupation or socioeconomic or domestic status, are repeatedly exposed to requirements for difficult, problem-focused coping. Although this includes certain successful professional groups such as air-traffic controllers, the image of the stressed executive or politician is something of a myth. Much more important numerically are those at the opposite socioeconomic extreme. These are the people in occupations or life situations where high demands require effortful problem-focused coping but where the opportunity for choosing effective coping responses is much less than is enjoyed by the 'stressed' executive. Therefore those at risk include low-status groups such as manual workers (Karasek and Theorell, 1990) and migrants (Poulter et al, 1990). In women, the increased risk of heart disease that is attached to working outside the home and having many children can be explained in the same way (Haynes and Feinleib, 1980).

4.2.2.2 Hostile Appraisals

A second set of individuals with an increased risk of developing cardio-vascular disease are those who, although not subjected to *unusual* demands, show exaggerated cardiovascular responses to *normal* challenges. To some extent, this is an inherited physiological tendency. However, as we have seen, the response to a challenge depends on the individual's appraisal of it. Anger and hostility, which are more common in individuals who develop hypertension and cardiovascular disease (Steptoe, 1993), probably have a key role in forming threatening appraisals. A hostile attitude means feeling devalued or misunderstood by other people, or fearing that other people cannot be trusted (Box 4.2). It means being driven to compete against people for fear of being beaten by them. Because of these appraisals, the hostile person probably feels challenged by situations which less hostile people would not see as challenges at all (Benotsch et al, 1997). This increases the demand on the individual for active coping and leads to greater cardio-

---

Box 4.2   Recognizing hostility

Hostility is not the same as aggression. An individual can be hostile without displaying aggressive behaviour. Hostility can be recognized in resentful or antagonistic appraisals of everyday situations. These appraisals make the individual feel alienated from others. This type of appraisal is illustrated by examples of items from a questionnaire that is often used to measure hostility (Cook and Medley, 1954). Agreement with each signifies a hostile appraisal.

'I often meet people who are supposed to be experts who don't know as much as I do.'

'I often find people jealous of my good ideas just because they hadn't thought of them first.'

'Some of my family have habits that bother and annoy me very much.'

'People often disappoint me.'

'No one cares much what happens to you.'

vascular responses to interpersonal situations (Suls and Wan, 1993). The result is that being hostile increases the risk of heart disease (Whiteman et al, 1997).

This analysis takes us a long way from the idea that 'stress causes heart disease'. Instead, it emphasizes individuals' appraisal of challenges and their way of coping with them. Fortunately, modifying these factors is a much more realistic clinical goal than is the common, but mistaken instruction to patients with heart disease to 'avoid stress'. In Chapter 14 we shall see how these factors can be exploited to treat heart disease psychologically.

4.3 PSYCHOBIOLOGICAL PROCESSES IN CANCER

4.3.1 Science Versus Wishful Thinking

Although psychological mechanisms do seem to be implicated in cancer, their nature and importance are controversial. Correspondingly, we shall see in Chapter 14 that the power of psychological treatment to influence the disease process in cancer is highly speculative. Nevertheless, the possibility that the sufferer might be able to slow or reverse the development of cancer by the power of the mind alone is a recurrent theme in popular media and in modern folklore. Belief in this possibility connects with many patients' desire for autonomy; that is, for a feeling of control over their health and illness (Chapter 2). The belief connects also with some clinicians' belief in the value of 'fighting' cancer—a belief that is impressed on many patients. Given that, in reality, cancer remains largely uncontrollable by the patient, Chapter 14 will show that there can be emotional costs to believing—or being led to believe—that it *is* controllable. In practice, the clinician needs to be able to advise and support those patients who wish to feel in control, without burdening them with responsibility for 'failing' to halt disease progression. Therefore it is important that the clinician is aware of the extent of the evidence that links psychological factors to the development of cancer—and of its limitations.

4.3.2 Linking Coping to Cancer

4.3.2.1 The 'Cancer-Prone Personality'

Extensive research over 50 years has identified personality features that are most common in people who develop cancer or in those who die from it. These results have been summarized in the concept of the 'Type C' personality (Temoshok, 1990). This revolves around a distinctive and habitual way of coping with challenges: being stoical, self-sacrificing, cooperative and compliant. It means also failing to express negative emotions, particularly anger. The tendency to focus on others' needs rather than their own means that such people tend to cope with challenge or conflict by 'rationalizing' (Chapter 3); that is, by emphasizing the other's point of view, rather than reacting emotionally in their own interest. People with this personality are said to feel hopeless or helpless in the face of challenges.

From a clinical point of view, linking cancer to personality is not, at first sight, useful: personality is very hard to modify clinically. Nevertheless, the cancer-prone personality offers clues to psychological factors that might be modifiable. These include the ways in which patients cope with challenges and whether they express their emotional distress. Attempts to modify these factors have given rise to tantalizing hints that the disease process might be susceptible to psychological intervention. These are considered in Chapter 14. The corollary of the Type C personality is that two psychological features have been identified which seem to indicate that people are protected against cancer.

4.3.2.2 Fighting Spirit

The most influential concept of a protective factor that has emerged from research into survival following initial diagnosis and treatment is 'fighting spirit'. The language of fighting is common in talking about cancer (Sontag, 1978), and is a natural response to the way that people separate disease from themselves and regard it as an alien and threatening external entity (Chapter 6). One patient stated that 'I was determined I was going to beat the cancer. If it came to a competition sort of thing, I thought, well, I am going to win this one.'

There is some evidence that patients who live longer after breast cancer are those that respond to diagnosis by viewing cancer as a challenge, not to be dwelled on, but over which they can exert some control and which can be overcome (Moorey and Greer, 1989). This is the attitude that has been called 'fighting spirit'. It seems, at first sight, to be a kind of problem-focused coping. However, in some respects, it means denying the severity of the disease, which is a form of palliative, emotion-focused coping (Chapter 3). Indeed, breast cancer patients who reacted either by denial or fighting spirit have lived longer than those who accepted their diagnosis fatalistically (Moorey and Greer, 1989). The evidence is, however, much less clear for poorer-prognosis cancer and

Box 4.3 Cause and effect

Research linking psychological factors to disease often produces correlational evidence. For instance, women who react to breast cancer with
fighting spirit survived for longer (Pettingale et al, 1985). This observation is often taken as evidence for the simple causal model (a).

However, the direction of cause and effect cannot be decided from this
type of evidence alone. The evidence is equally consistent with models
(b) and (c). In these models, the relationship is entirely the product of
an unmeasured variable which influences each observation. The evidence also fits models (d) and (e). In these models, the association is
caused by an intervening variable.

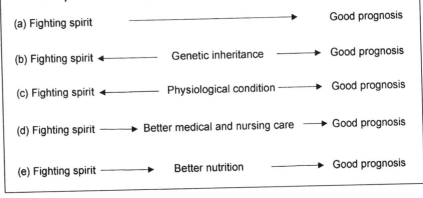

even the evidence in breast cancer is contradictory (Watson et al, 1999)
and open to several explanations (Box 4.3).

Nevertheless, there is an important warning here for clinicians who care
for patients with cancer. Those whom psychological factors put at greatest risk from cancer are those whom clinicians are likely to regard as 'good'
or 'cooperative' patients (Chapter 12). That is, they do not complain and
they do what they are told. Indeed, patients who go on to survive longest
have been regarded by their physicians around the time of diagnosis as
poorly adjusted to the illness and with *negative* attitudes towards their
doctors (Derogatis et al, 1979). The implications of this point are pursued
in Chapter 14 when psychological treatment of cancer is examined.

4.3.2.3 Emotional Expression

It seems that people who are emotionally expressive are at a smaller risk
of developing some cancers or dying from them. This can explain the

otherwise paradoxical finding that recurrence-free survival after mastectomy was longest in breast cancer patients who were overtly emotionally disturbed around the time of surgery (Dean and Surtees, 1989) or when beginning outpatient treatment for metastatic breast cancer (Derogatis et al, 1979). It can explain also why survival and freedom from recurrence after malignant melanoma were longest in patients who were most distressed at the time of referral (Fawzy et al, 1993).

4.3.3 Emotional Support

The importance of *expressing* emotional feeling indicates that having people who will listen should be important, too. There are, indeed, many reports that implicate social support as a protection against cancer in several different respects. Lonely people are more likely to develop cancer, are more likely to delay going to the doctor and to delay starting treatment after first noticing symptoms of cancer, and they have shorter survival after diagnosis (Bloom et al, 1991). As we saw in Chapter 3, these broad generalizations mask some important complexities in the evidence. For example, in general, married cancer patients tend to survive longer than unmarried ones (Goodwin et al, 1987). However, Chapter 2 showed that there is some evidence that marriage is a risk factor for *poorer* survival from breast cancer. This does not, of course, mean that emotional support is bad for women with this condition, because support from *outside* the marriage is associated with better survival (Ell et al, 1992; Waxler-Morrison et al, 1991). Instead this paradoxical finding points to the fact that marriage means, for many women, being enmeshed in a relationship that is geared to meeting others' needs rather than their own.

4.3.4 Psychobiology of the Immune System

It is easier to accept the evidence that implicates psychological factors in cardiovascular disease because several specific links have been established with physiological processes that are known to be important in heart disease, such as hypertension or atherosclerosis (Box 4.1). In the same way, the importance of psychological factors in cancer would be more compelling were links of this kind to be identified. Many biological systems bear on the risk of developing cancer, and on the speed of succumbing to it or recovering from it. Nevertheless, the obvious starting point is the immune system. Its known sensitivity to the catecholamine and corticosteroid components of Selye's stress response (Chapter 3) provides one way in which it might be influenced by psychological factors. Indeed, Chapter 3 has already shown that stress responses are seen in the immune system. The obvious question is whether psychological factors influence immune function in a way that is consistent with the findings in cancer.

The complexity of the evidence reflects the complexity of the immune system and the diverse challenges that have been studied. These have included major real-life challenges such as unemployment, bereavement or caring for a dependent relative as well as exams and mental tasks in a laboratory. In general, however, immune function is compromised by challenges (Bachen et al, 1997). There are specific findings on the human immune system which are consistent with the evidence in cancer. One is that people with emotional support are somewhat protected from immune stress responses (Bachen et al, 1997). Another is that emotional expression about severe challenges can improve aspects of immune function (Christensen et al, 1996; Esterling et al, 1994). One key prediction from the clinical research is that immunosuppression should be promoted preferentially by passive, stoical or helpless attitudes to challenge. There is now some support for this (Brosschot et al, 1998). Moreover, the corticosteroid stress response, which might contribute to immunosuppression (Riley, 1981), is already well known to be largest where the challenge meets with a passive, helpless response (Steptoe, 1983). However, human research is still more limited than animal research and the proposed links remain speculative.

4.3.5 Caveats

It is important to appreciate limitations of the evidence that has shaped present views of psychological risk and protective factors in cancer. First, generalizations gloss over many inconsistencies and contradictions. In particular, evidence is much clearer in relatively good-prognosis cancers—particularly breast cancer—than in more aggressive cancers. Secondly, although findings are large enough to be statistically significant, psychological factors explain only a small part of the variability in incidence or prognosis (Chapter 1). Thirdly, the evidence is, of necessity, correlational. This means that, for instance, many findings show that aspects of the cancer-prone personality are found more often in people who have cancer or who have a poorer prognosis. This does not mean that the cancer-prone personality *causes* cancer. Indeed, cause and effect cannot be distinguished from one another with this kind of evidence. It might be that, contrary to the usual inference, the presence of a tumour leads to the so-called cancer-prone personality. There is now some evidence that aspects of the cancer-prone personality do *predict* incidence of cancer, even when people are assessed years before any sign of illness (Persky et al, 1987). Even here, it remains possible that the findings do not reflect a carcinogenic effect of personality. They might result from an unsuspected factor in the environment, or in people's behaviour, physiology or genetics, that causes *both* the cancer-prone personality *and* cancer (Box 4.3).

A more insidious problem is that cancer has been attributed to deficits of patients' personality for 50 years in medical journals—that is, since long before systematic evidence became available to support these claims (Cassileth, 1995). This should be a warning that the continued enthusiasm for this link might represent clinicians' way of coping palliatively with their inability to cure such a dreadful disease—by 'blaming' patients for developing it.

4.4 PSYCHOBIOLOGY IN OTHER DISEASE CONDITIONS

Even the brief account of the psychobiology of stress in Chapter 3 shows that psychological challenge influences physiological systems that have widespread effects on the body. It is therefore not surprising that psychological factors are implicated in many other diseases as well as heart disease and cancer. In one study, measuring patients' experience of major challenges over their lifetimes, as well as recent challenges, accounted for 32% of the variance (variability) in current health status (Leserman et al, 1998). It has been suspected for many years that psychological effects on immune function help to explain some of the variability in who develops infectious disease and how long it lasts (Kiecolt-Glaser and Glaser, 1995). More recent evidence that psychological challenges slow the healing of minor wounds (Marucha et al, 1998) suggests that psychological factors might, in the future, prove to be important in the healing of large wounds such as leg ulcers or surgical incision (Kiecolt-Glaser et al, 1998).

In chronic disease, also, psychological factors probably influence disease processes. For instance, it has been suggested that stress responses exacerbate the disease process in inflammatory bowel disease and rheumatoid arthritis. There are better-understood effects of stress in insulin-dependent diabetes (Bradley, 1988). By reducing insulin production, enhancing glucose production and reducing glucose use, the catecholamine and glucocorticoid components of the stress response are geared to maintaining blood glucose levels. This fits the idea of a response that has evolved to provide the energy needed to cope with challenges. However, in diabetes, this stress response could be disastrous.

4.5 CONCLUSION

The model of stress that was introduced in Chapter 3 provides a framework for understanding widespread effects of psychological factors on physical disease. It therefore provides a basis for designing and applying psychological treatments. There is a tendency to imagine that psychological treatment is simply a matter of reversing stress and that it is always beneficial to do so. Therefore relaxation training (Box 3.3), in particular, tends to be offered as a panacea. For example, stress reduction methods including relaxation have been applied in diabetes, with some success (Bradley, 1994). However, Chapter 3 showed that individuals vary in their stress responses. Therefore 'blanket' approaches to stress reduction might often be unnecessary and wasteful. Diabetes illustrates the need for more careful evaluation of psychological treatment: interfering with a finely balanced control of glucose levels in diabetic patients might even risk hypoglycaemia (Bradley, 1994).

In heart disease and cancer, sophisticated psychological treatments have been investigated in particular detail. They focus on changing the psychological characteristics that this chapter has shown to be associated with those diseases. These treatments are considered in detail in Chapter 14.

KEY POINTS

- Clinicians need to be able to inform patients about psychological influences on disease, without burdening them with responsibility.
- The popular idea that 'stress' causes disease is too simplistic.
- Physiological disease processes are affected by people's ways of appraising and coping with challenges.
- Some people are at risk of heart disease because they are exposed to challenges that are hard to cope with.
- Others are at risk of heart disease because they appraise challenges in ways that make them seem hard to cope with.
- Cancer has been linked to stoical and emotionally suppressed ways of coping with challenges.
- 'Fighting spirit' and emotional expression have been controversially linked to better outcome from some cancers.

- Recovery from cancer and heart disease is sometimes better when patients have emotional support.
- Because psychological factors influence physiological disease processes, psychological treatment of some physical diseases is possible.

Chapter 5

PSYCHOLOGY OF PHYSICAL SYMPTOMS

KEY CLINICAL ISSUES

- Are physical symptoms a reliable guide to what is going on in the body?
- What is an 'illness template'?
- If a physical symptom has no physical cause, must it be psychological?
- Why have so many adults attending some hospital clinics been abused as children?
- Why do some people delay consulting with symptoms that need urgent treatment?
- Why do others consult persistently with symptoms that need no treatment?

5.1 THE FALLIBILITY OF PERCEPTION

We tend to assume that, when we see something, we necessarily see a direct and faithful representation of the real world. The truth is not so simple. Seeing is an active process of interpreting information about the world. That is, it is not an automatic reaction to a visual stimulus, but depends on three intervening factors. The first of these is attention. This is not simply a matter of whether we turn our eyes away from or towards the object. Attention includes unconscious psychological mechanisms that switch the brain's limited processing capacity to one stimulus or another. The second and third factors are the context and our past experience. Normally, these influences guide perception accurately. However, they sometimes mislead (Box 5.1).

It is natural to assume that knowledge of our own bodies is more direct than our perception of the outside world and therefore more reliable. Indeed, a patient bringing physical symptoms to a doctor can be convinced that 'something must be wrong', even where the doctor

---

Box 5.1 Perception depends on interpretation

Present just the row or column of the following pattern to someone that has not seen it before. Most people will see a row of letters or a column of numbers. That is, they will unconsciously make sense of, or interpret, the ambiguous shape at the centre. What they see depends on the surrounding cues and previous experience of seeing series of numbers and letters together.

12

A 13 C

14

---

can find nothing in the patient's body that could be causing the sensations. However, where the accuracy of bodily perception can be assessed by objective measurements (for example, heart rate or nasal congestion), it is very poor (Pennebaker, 1982). In fact, as we shall see, bodily—or 'somatic'—perception depends on the same interpretative, and therefore fallible, processes that guide visual perception.

5.2 ATTENTION TO BODILY SENSATIONS

Whether a certain bodily sensation is noticed depends on the degree of attention to it. This, in turn, depends on the balance between attention commanded by other stimuli and the 'salience' of the sensation in question. A trivial illustration is that people cough more during boring than interesting parts of films (Pennebaker, 1982), presumably because they are more likely to notice previously disregarded sensations when they are less distracted by the screen. A more serious example is that the symptoms of repetitive strain injury (pain or fatigue in the wrists and hands in the absence of any obvious pathology) are more common in boring and unsatisfying work environments (Hopkins, 1990).

In general, any experience or thought that directs attention internally is liable to increase the probability that a bodily sensation is noticed. Conversely, drawing attention outwards will make this less likely (Pennebaker, 1982). This is one reason why being unhappy increases the experience of physical symptoms (Watson and Pennebaker, 1989). Clinically, every general practitioner knows patients who have so little else in their lives that bodily sensations dominate. The converse are the patients whose consultations with symptoms of serious physical disease are delayed because they have been too busy to attend to the early symptoms. Personality differences arise here. 'Monitors' are those who generally respond to signs of danger—internal or external—by giving attention to them and doing whatever they can to find out about them. Unsurprisingly they are more likely to attend doctors with minor problems than are their converse, the 'blunters' (Miller et al, 1988).

5.3 MAKING SENSE OF BODILY SENSATIONS: ATTRIBUTION AND MISATTRIBUTION

Attention means that a somatic sensation is *noticed*. It does not determine what is *experienced*. This depends on a process of interpreting, or 'making sense' of, the sensation. This process is sometimes called 'attribution'. Using this term highlights the fact that we typically make sense of a sensation by attributing it to a cause. Therefore a view of cause is central to the way that a sensation is experienced.

5.3.1 Attributing Sensations to Emotion

Sensations of physical arousal (such as those that a stress response can give rise to; Chapter 3) can be attributed to—i.e., experienced as— emotional excitement. This has been shown in experiments where people have been physiologically aroused by such varied methods as adrenaline injection (Schachter and Singer, 1962), physical exercise (White and Knight, 1984) or hyperventilation (Salkovskis and Clark, 1990). Different clues have been provided to guide the participants in these experiments in making sense of what they experienced. For instance, healthy people asked to hyperventilate after a negative cue (being told that there was a risk of passing out) found it an unpleasant experience. Those with a positive cue (being told that it might give rise to symptoms of a higher level of consciousness that indicate good adjustment) found hyperventilation pleasant (Salkovskis and Clark, 1990).

5.3.2 Attributing Sensations to Illness

The attributions that people make are, of course, not only to emotions. Attributions to illness can also make sense of physical sensations. For instance, following strenuous exercise (to produce feelings of arousal), a conversation in which flu was mentioned led people to feel that they had more flu-type symptoms than people who had missed out on either the exercise or the conversation (Pennebaker, 1982). Although this kind of research has focused on diffuse sensations of physiological arousal, similar processes probably influence how somatic sensations in general are experienced (Cacioppo et al, 1986). It is easy to see how misattribution can lead people to consult doctors with fears of serious illness when their symptoms have, in reality, mundane explanations such as diet or stress.

5.3.3 Failing to Attribute Sensations to Illness

Misattribution can work in both directions. It also leads people to attribute symptoms of serious disease to trivial causes so that they do not seek the care that they need. For instance, ambiguous symptoms that arise at times of stress are liable to be attributed to stress rather than physical illness (Benyamini et al, 1997). Previous illness can also shape misattribution. Having angina or diabetes increases delay in seeking attention for symptoms of myocardial infarction (Dracup and Moser, 1991), presumably because such patients already have a way of making sense of their symptoms as familiar and not immediately serious.

Attributions clearly depend on people's beliefs. Many beliefs are culturally based. Therefore cultural stereotypes of illnesses influence how people interpret somatic sensations (Lalljee et al, 1993). An example of a cultural stereotype is the common misconception that heart disease is a purely male affliction. The woman who believes this will be more likely to attribute her own chest pain to exertion or indigestion. Similarly, an elderly man will delay consulting a doctor with urinary retention if he attributes this to inevitable problems of ageing.

Misattributing serious illness as something less threatening is not simply a matter of making mistakes. It can also be a type of defensive, palliative coping motivated by deep-seated fears. This is likely to be one reason why early symptoms of cancer are sometimes viewed in non-threatening ways. Such attributions protect the individual from the anxiety that cancer arouses (Cacioppo et al, 1986).

5.3.4 Clinical Reattribution

Clearly, the sensitivity of attributions to experience and to illness cues means that errors are common. Nevertheless, this also means that attributions are open to relatively simple approaches to modifying them (Box 5.2). Unfortunately, clinicians often fail to exploit this possibility and fail to provide explanations in ways that make sense to patients (see Box 11.2). The malleability of symptom attributions forms the basis of the psychological treatment of patients with 'functional', or unexplained, symptoms that is described in Chapter 13.

5.4 PERCEIVING PAIN

Pain is critically important in health care. In practice, the modern availability of effective analgesia means that the most important psychological factors in managing acute pain are those that influence patients' use of analgesia (Chapters 9 and 11). However, a huge clinical and research literature has developed to help understand and treat pain psychologically. Many specialist techniques have been devised and these are described in detail elsewhere (e.g., Skevington, 1995). This section cannot describe the psychology of pain. Nevertheless it will show that, like other somatic symptoms, the experience and report of pain result from processes of attention and attribution. That is, perception of pain reflects the processes that influence bodily perception in general, and these are the processes that can be recruited in psychological treatment for pain.

5.4.1 Attention to Painful Sensations

Perceiving pain normally requires attention to the bodily sensation that gives rise to it. Therefore, acute pain (lasting no more than a day or two) can be relieved where sufferers focus attention on things other

---

Box 5.2 The meaning of pain: changing attributions

Some patients, for example with back pain, become trapped in a vicious circle in which they avoid exertion and mobilization. They are frightened of the pain and other symptoms because of the misattributions that they make about pain. The result is that they become 'deconditioned'. Exertion hurts even more, so the fear escalates. Crook et al (1998) wanted to encourage strenuous exercise in a group of patients like this. One patient illustrated the kind of thinking that prevented exercise:

'It's no good. I can't do this. When I got home last time [after a training session] I felt terrible. I couldn't do anything. I hurt all over. I was so scared. I said to my husband "They've overstretched my spine with those exercises." It wasn't right, was it, hurting like that? I mean, you don't hurt for nothing, do you? It means you've gone too far.'

The physiotherapist helped her to reattribute the sensations in the following way:

'Pain is a warning from the body. Sometimes that warning means that something has been damaged. But it doesn't always mean this—just as fire alarms often go off when there's no fire. In these cases the body is signalling that something is happening that it's not used to. In your case, you should expect a bit of pain as your body's way of warning you that muscles are being used and tendons are being stretched that have become 'deconditioned'. So, in a way, a little pain is a good sign. When you feel some discomfort and perhaps a little pain you know you are exercising at the right level. Too much pain means you are doing too much too quickly, but none at all might mean your muscles aren't being asked to do anything different.'

---

than the source of the pain (Suls and Fletcher, 1985). By the nature of pain, it is usually very difficult to direct attention away from it. Nevertheless, the attention available for a painful sensation, for example during medical procedures, can sometimes be reduced by distraction (Johnson et al, 1998) or by flooding patients' attention by giving them demanding mental tasks (Morley, 1997). This approach can be particularly useful in helping children to cope with painful procedures.

5.4.2 Attributing and Misattributing Pain

In some situations, cues that are provided can determine whether a sensation is experienced as painful or in some other way. For instance, laboratory study has shown that it is possible to change the attribution of a single tactile sensation between pain and pleasure, just by changing the cues that are given to subjects as to what they are experiencing (Pennebaker, 1982).

There is non-clinical evidence that surrounding cues also influence whether a sensation arising from injury is perceived as painful. Historically, the turning point in appreciating this was a study of soldiers who suffered traumatic wounds during World War II. Many apparently experienced very little pain by comparison with what would be expected from comparable injuries in civilian surgical patients (Beecher, 1956). The suggested explanation was that, for the soldiers, pain 'meant' *escape* from danger (because they were removed from battle) whereas, for surgical patients, it 'meant' the *beginning* of danger.

Providing sufficiently compelling clues to change the attribution of intense painful sensations is, of course, difficult for clinicians in practice. Nevertheless, pain can sometimes be eased in this way. Techniques can include imagining that the pain is something different, or that the context is different. A child, in particular, can sometimes be helped to imagine being a character from a TV series in a daring and exciting situation while a painful procedure is carried out. Adherence to mobilization exercises in chronic pain and other sedentary patients is often impaired because patients become worried about the pain and discomfort that the exercises produce. They view these symptoms as signifying that the exercises are damaging them. Adherence can therefore be improved by helping the patients to view the pain positively, for instance as a sign that they have worked hard enough to begin reconditioning deconditioned muscles (Crook et al, 1998; Box 5.2).

Whether someone finds a sensation painful does not, though, just depend on what is happening at the time. Just as with the perception of bodily sensations in general, the perception of pain depends on people's previous experience and beliefs (Skevington, 1995). For instance, people with a history of chronic pain are more likely than others to perceive sensations of various kinds as painful.

5.4.3 Placebo

The sensitivity of pain perception to psychological variables is seen in the power of placebo treatment. This occurs where a completely inert treatment (usually an inert pill or capsule) relieves pain. Some of the therapeutic effect of analgesics in routine use probably reflects this power of suggestion rather than their pharmacological action. Although variable between individuals and generally short-lived, placebo effects are often substantial (Skevington, 1995). There are many different explanations for placebo effects on pain. Essentially, however, a placebo's action depends on a clinician's suggestion that treatment will alleviate pain and on the patient's acceptance of this suggestion. Therefore placebo effects should not be seen as a 'special case'. They are instances of a process which has wide implications for health care: people's perception of their bodies depends on a combination of information from inside the body and from the outside world. Unfortunately, dualism lives on in the belief of many clinicians that pain that responds to a placebo is not 'real' pain (Lander, 1990).

5.5 PSYCHOLOGICAL CAUSES OF PHYSICAL SYMPTOMS

5.5.1 Escaping Dualism

So far in this chapter, we have assumed that, at the centre of the experience of a somatic sensation or symptom lies a real physical stimulus, as the germ of grit to the pearl. As a scientific position, this presumption has the dubious advantage of preserving the dualism described in Chapter 2: i.e., that psychological processes merely modify the effects of physical factors. Of course, the nature of bodily function is such that physical stimuli exist continually, ready to be turned into conscious sensations—or even symptoms—by the right conditions that draw attention to them. The outbreak of coughing that follows a single cough in a cinema illustrates this. If proof is needed, Pennebaker (1982) described experiments in which people who were unsuspectingly minding their own business were induced to scratch (and, presumably, to itch) merely by an experimenter sitting down—and scratching—next to them. Perhaps the reader is now beginning to notice an itch on the skin or a tickle in the throat and thereby illustrating the point that somatic stimuli are always there for attending to. However, it is easier if we set aside the view that psychological factors merely modify the way that a 'real' physical sensation is experienced. Instead, let us simply accept that what are usually regarded as *physical* experiences and symptoms can be entirely products of processes and events that are usually regarded as *psychological*. The following sections examine three psychological factors that can give rise to physical symptoms.

5.5.2 Illness Templates

5.5.2.1 Illness Templates as Products of Health Care

Because patients try to make sense of what clinicians do in response to their complaints, the process of treatment and investigation can change the way that patients think about their symptoms. Therefore clinical care can—unwittingly or deliberately—build up an 'illness template' (Shorter, 1992). This is organized set of *expectations* about symptoms that guides an individual's *experience* of symptoms. The development of a powerful illness template can give rise to a largely iatrogenic 'illness' (Box 5.3).

5.5.2.2 Transmission of an Illness Template: The Example of Mass Psychogenic Illness

Every few years, mysterious outbreaks of illness are reported which defy doctors' attempts to treat them and scientists' attempts to explain them physiologically. Often, but not always, they are triggered by an event that challenges a whole community, such as the announcement that a town's water supply had been accidentally contaminated (Box 5.4). The symptoms are typically subjective and diffuse, such as fatigue, concentration difficulties or pain. Often, they might be based on sensations that arise from stress responses (which could, indeed, have been caused by the triggering event).

An explanation for some of these episodes has been termed 'mass psychogenic illness' (David and Wessely, 1995). The central factor in this is the illness template which is transmitted from person to person or, in recent years, to a whole community by mass media. A vicious spiral develops whereby, as more people display the symptoms, the template becomes more and more compelling and so more people become afflicted (Cooper, 1993). Attention from scientists and media accentuates the process.

5.5.2.3 Medical Ideas in Illness Templates

Many illness templates are cultural phenomena. That is, they reside in the language that people use and the beliefs that they have. They are shaped by the permeation of medical ways of thinking into ordinary culture and language. There they help to mould people's experience of their bodies. Therefore they also mould the symptoms that people experience and take to their doctors (Shorter, 1992). Medical thinking, and therefore illness templates, change over the years. In Victorian times, these

---

Box 5.3   Disabling effects of medical intervention

For some patients, a history of medical investigation and treatment has a major role in shaping their symptom experience, disablement and dependency on medical care. The following patient was described by Valori (1993).

Mr X started noticing itching in his armpits around the time that he lost his job and his marriage hit the rocks. He thinks he could better cope with putting life back together again if he did not have to keep scratching, so he goes to see his general practitioner (GP). He thinks that she (the GP) would not want to know about the challenges he faces, so he just explains about the itching. He receives a prescription and is told to return if the problem does not resolve. It does not. He assumes that the GP must be concerned, else she would not have asked him to return. At his next appointment, the GP notices that he is very strained. She thinks that he must be very worried about his armpits so she sends him to the hospital. There a registrar is fascinated by the problem and orders lots of tests. Nothing turns up, so he prescribes some more drugs that do not help. X is more worried now. Something must be wrong, otherwise he would not have been sent for all those tests. But the doctors cannot find the problem. The itching is getting worse. He notices itching in his groin, too, and fears that the problem is spreading. Meanwhile, his marriage has broken up and he has left his wife and children. Because of his concern to have the problem sorted out he is referred to another specialist. This consultant has seen other patients with this problem and believes that he has identified a stress-related syndrome of 'irritable armpits'. He carries out some more tests, involving ambulatory monitoring of armpit hair movement and sweating. These confirm his diagnosis. X is at first relieved and reassured to have a diagnosis, but then disappointed at being told that there is no treatment and that he has to learn to live with the syndrome. He feels let down by the doctors and begins to search the Internet for any information about his syndrome and for support groups that might help him with it. Meanwhile, his wife has started divorce proceedings and his itching is growing worse.

templates included paralyses or sensory deficits of the sort that attracted Freud's interest (Chapter 2). Now, however, these conditions no longer interest doctors so much because improved knowledge of the nervous system makes it clear that they do not have a physical basis. Currently,

Box 5.4   The power of an illness template

Camelford is an English town of 12,000 residents. In July 1988, 20 tonnes of aluminium sulphate were, in error, dumped in a reservoir feeding its water supply. For a few days, drinking water was acidic, discoloured and contaminated. Nausea, rashes and mouth ulcers were reported immediately, although very few people consulted their general practitioner about them. Later, however, cognitive symptoms were reported by many people, including memory loss, concentration difficulties and fatigue. These symptoms focused media interest. They also underpinned a campaign by residents which included public meetings, press coverage and litigation against the water company. However, objective studies in Camelford and existing literature on such poisoning provided no clear evidence of long-term effects. David and Wessely (1995) identified the factors, other than biological effects of the poisoning, that might have maintained these symptoms.

1. Early attempts to reassure the residents were delayed and were not presented sufficiently clearly to help them make sense of their own symptoms as self-limiting effects of contamination and perhaps stress responses.
2. Symptoms of the kind that came to dominate complaints exist normally at a high level in any community. Anxiety associated with the incident might have exacerbated the symptoms or increased attention to them.
3. Illness templates were available from continued media involvement. Residents supplying information to media were self-selected, and might therefore have had a greater tendency to report such symptoms generally. The template of cognitive impairment was fed by a completely separate report around that time which linked long-term aluminium consumption to Alzheimer's disease. There was also publicity about the link between Jakob–Creutzfeldt dementia ('mad cow disease') and ingestion of a previously innocent substance—beef.

We cannot disregard the *possibility* that poisoning led to long-term symptoms. However, it is clear that we do not need to assume this because sufficient alternative causes are available.

there is a great deal of medical interest in finding physical causes for fatigue and pain. Therefore current illness templates emphasize these symptoms.

The power of illness templates is most striking in the so-called 'functional syndromes' (Chapter 13). These are disorders such as chronic fatigue or fibromyalgia, in which patients have physical symptoms, typically fatigue and pain, but in which no physical pathology is reliably found (Box 5.5). Even a syndrome with a clear biological basis, premenstrual syndrome, turns out to have the properties of a template. Women who were led to believe that they were premenstrual reported having psychological and physical premenstrual symptoms, even though menstruation was, in

---

Box 5.5 Functional syndromes

Functional problems are physical symptoms or syndromes which are unexplained by physical pathology. Sometimes the fact that they are unexplained is masked by a medical label or diagnosis. The following are examples of terms in common use to describe such syndromes.

Systemic syndromes. Symptoms are diffuse and not identifiable with specific organ systems.

    Chronic fatigue/myalgic encephalomyelitis
    Gulf War syndrome
    Total allergy syndrome

Abdominal syndromes. These syndromes are defined by pain localized to specific regions of the body.

    Atypical chest pain
    Irritable bowel syndrome
    Non-specific abdominal pain
    Non-ulcer dyspepsia
    Pelvic pain
    Menstrual pain
    Premenstrual syndrome

Musculoskeletal syndromes. These are characterized primarily by pain and stiffness

    Lower back pain
    Fibromyalgia
    Repetitive strain injury

reality, a week away (Ruble, 1977). Recall of symptoms is biased in the same way so that symptoms on menstrual days are recalled as more intense than they were (McFarland et al, 1989).

This is a controversial area. There is heated debate between two sets of protagonists. On the one hand are the patients and clinicians who believe that psychological mechanisms, such as illness templates, are central to understanding this sort of syndrome. On the other are patients and clinicians who believe that a virus, pollution, neurological or muscle damage or other physical cause exists. The vehemence of the debate, particularly on the side of some patients' groups, shows the grip of the dualist way of thinking introduced in Chapter 2. According to biomedical dualism, if symptoms are not explained by physical pathology, then they do not exist. The holistic view is much simpler. We can simply accept that symptoms exist that are as real and disabling as those that arise from organic pathology, but that are products of a complex set of processes among which psychological factors, including illness templates, are critical.

5.5.3 Emotional Distress

5.5.3.1 Emotional Disorder

It is sometimes assumed that, if physical pathology is absent, psychological pathology must be present. In a sense, this is an attempt to preserve the 'reality' of symptoms by finding another kind of pathology to explain them. However, the dualist legacy means that many patients view the suggestion that symptoms are caused by psychological problems as meaning that they are 'all in the mind'—that is, they are imaginary (Chapter 13). In fact, physical symptoms that are unexplained by physical pathology do not necessarily indicate emotional disorder. The processes of misattribution described previously are clearly sufficiently powerful to create disturbing symptoms in the absence of any psychological problem. Therefore, although some surveys of patients with functional symptoms have found evidence of emotional disorder, many have not. Even in surveys that have found relatively high levels of depression or anxiety, this *average* result belies many patients without emotional problems (Stanley et al, 1999).

5.5.3.2 The Somatic Language of Emotional Distress

Nevertheless, it is undeniable that physical symptoms *are* an integral part of emotional distress and, in some cases, they do signify emotional disorder. In Chapter 3, we saw that specific organs are particularly sensitive to stress in certain individuals. Moreover, as noted in Chapter 2, real and metaphorical physical sensations provide much of the language of unhappiness. We are used to hearing complaints of being 'worn out', having 'no energy' or feeling 'gutted' or 'broken-hearted' as revealing a speaker's emotional state. However, complaints of other symptoms, such as back pain, migraine, bowel symptoms or fatigue, can often also be seen in this way. Amongst people who go to their GP suffering depression, as many complain only of physical symptoms of this kind as complain of emotional problems (Craig and Boardman, 1990). Unfortunately, when depression is presented in this way, it is highly likely to go unnoticed by the GP. Complaining of physical symptoms in these instances can be thought of as a metaphorical way of complaining of unhappiness. Therefore the details of the somatic metaphor can provide further information about the patient's emotional feelings (Guthrie, 1992; Chapter 13).

5.5.4 Childhood Adversity

5.5.4.1 Childhood Sexual Abuse

Patients' descriptions of persistent, functional symptoms sometimes show that they regard the symptoms as signifying an alien and threatening entity with a reality of its own (Peters et al, 1998; Box 5.6). Given

---

Box 5.6 Disease as an alien force

These statements were made by patients experiencing persistent symptoms in the absence of any evidence of physical pathology (Peters et al, 1998). They describe a disease entity which:

Can exist outside the patient's body	'It just come on me and never left me.'
Invades the body	'The glandular fever left a scar on the lung. I assume that's where the [ME: myalgic encephalomyelitis/chronic fatigue] virus got in.'
Moves through the body	The migraine starts here and moves to here.'
Changes its form	'That [ME] started from glandular fever and it just turned into the ME.'
Resists attack	'I'd beaten it and it came back.'
Evades capture	'It's never got caught when you've gone for tests'

that the symptoms are, in reality, a part of themselves, the patients are, in this way, separating themselves into two elements. It has been suggested that this is a defensive form of palliative (i.e., emotion-focused) coping. Undesirable or unacceptable aspects of history or personality are separated off so as to preserve a view of the self as basically sound (Cassell, 1976; Helman, 1985). This phenomenon is considered further in Chapter 6.

One traumatic aspect of people's history that can be understood in this way is childhood abuse. This is surprisingly common in Western society. Depending on how abuse is defined (usually as forced sexual contact before around 16 years old), around 10–20% of children experience at least one episode of sexual abuse involving physical contact with an adult. Unsurprisingly, many go on to receive psychiatric care as adults. More surprisingly, many go on to receive disproportionate amounts of *physical* health care. The scale that this care can reach is illustrated in Box 5.7, which details the enormous amount and variety of health care that was received by one sample of abused women. It is implausible that most of the investigations and treatments that they received were justified by physical pathology. In fact, childhood abuse is *more* common in patients with 'functional' symptoms; that is, where there is no physical pathology (Fry, 1993).

Box 5.7 Adult sequelae of childhood sexual abuse

Arnold et al (1990) identified seven female psychiatric patients (mean age 31 years) who had disclosed penetrative sexual abuse as children. Review of medical history revealed the extraordinary extent of lifetime hospital health care that they had received.

	Range	Mean
Number of non-psychiatric consultant teams involved	8–35	18
Number of non-psychiatric hospital admissions	9–28	18
Number of operations	1–10	8
Thickness of case notes (cm)	4–17	10

The main specialties seen were gastroenterology, general medicine and general surgery (seen by all patients), gynaecology (6 patients) and orthopaedics (4 patients). In only 30% of operations was physical pathology confirmed.

5.5.4.2 *Linking Abuse to Symptoms*

Of course, this kind of evidence does not confirm that sexual abuse *causes* symptoms. Occasionally, the form that symptoms take reflects the specific nature of the abuse, such as vaginal or pelvic symptoms in a woman who suffered penetration as a child (Levis, 1991). However, this close link is not the rule. Symptoms in diverse parts of the body, from headaches to back pain, are associated with abuse (Fry, 1993). Sexual abuse might therefore cause a general tendency to experience many types of somatic symptoms (Leserman et al, 1998), or to express distress somatically. Alternatively, perhaps the early experience of abuse leads people to seek further 'abuse' through medical treatment.

A further possibility is that sexual abuse is linked only indirectly to adult physical symptoms. It might be a marker of other factors which are more directly involved. For instance, sexual abuse is often associated with physical and psychological abuse, and these are also more common in functional patients (Reilly et al, 1999). Additionally, parenting that exposes a child to abuse is typically disturbed in other ways (Fry, 1993), and adult symptoms might be the result of a failure to form secure attachments during childhood (Stuart and Noyes, 1999). Clinicians should be open to the possibility that functional symptoms might signify, not just childhood sexual abuse, but previous adversity or trauma which is sufficiently intense that the patient copes palliatively by focusing concerns on a different problem—symptoms and health care (Box 5.8).

5.6 FROM SYMPTOM TO CONSULTATION

Consulting a clinician is not the usual response to symptoms. Most symptoms that people experience never lead to consultation (Scambler et al, 1981). Clearly other factors than symptoms explain why patients consult. However, identifying why patients seek health care is not straightforward and many patients find it hard to say what led them to consult at the time they did. Obviously the intensity of the symptom is one factor (Ingham and Miller, 1986). Living near to the surgery or health centre also makes consultation more likely. However, many psychological and social factors are also important.

5.6.1 Beliefs

It is obvious that whether people consult depends on what they believe about their symptoms. They are more likely to consult when they believe

---

Box 5.8   A memory of abuse

Insistent demands for health care in the absence of pathology are sometimes a clue that a patient has emotional traumas to disclose.

X is a 58-year-old lady who persistently attended her GP, mainly with irritable bowel syndrome. She also had chronically painful osteoarthritis in her hips. She was referred for psychological help because the GP was aware that further investigation and treatment were not helping her. She had a powerful sense of humour and used this to field any question about herself. She was well practised, too, in asking people about themselves. People mistook this humour for happiness. They mistook her interest in them for a sign she was at ease with herself.

After she was encouraged to talk about herself, she disclosed major traumas in her life: a violent marriage, now ended, and a son and family who severed contact with her five years ago. Discussing these traumas with the psychologist made it easier for her to acknowledge and disclose another. She said that she had rembered something very important that she wanted to tell someone. When she was 16, she had been raped by a friend of the family. She could not tell anyone then because she thought she would not be believed.

Her habits of complaining of physical symptoms have built up over 40 years and will not be quickly lost. Indeed, they will be fuelled by her developing osteoarthritis. Nevertheless disclosing these traumas, and being able to make sense of her symptoms by linking them to her experiences, reduced her anxiety and reduced her frequency of consultation with the GP.

---

symptoms reflect physical illness or when they do not have an explanation (Ingham and Miller, 1986). Their beliefs also influence what they seek from the consultation and how they respond to it. Therefore beliefs are considered in detail in Chapter 6.

5.6.2 Stress and Distress

Fear about symptoms will normally make consultation more likely (Conroy et al, 1999). Given a certain level of symptoms, patients are more likely to consult if they are emotionally distressed in general or if they have other, quite separate, problems (Drossman et al, 1988; Lydeard and

Jones, 1989; Smith et al, 1990). Therefore life stress and emotional distress are important factors that lead to consultation (Tessler et al, 1976) and help to explain why some patients become 'frequent attenders' (Baez et al, 1998).

However, fear about symptoms can have paradoxical effects. Too much fear may well delay or prevent consultation (Box 5.9). Life stress also acts in complex ways. First of all, it increases consultation most in people whose symptoms are unlikely to be caused by physical pathology (Miranda et al, 1991). Indeed, some of these symptoms are likely to be stress responses (Chapter 3). One report suggests that the relationship of life stress to consultation with these symptoms is more complex still. Where people have life stress of recent origin, they are *less* likely to consult. Where there is stress that has been going on for a long time, consultation becomes *more* likely (Cameron et al, 1995). These observations could not be explained by whether or not patients attributed their symptoms to stress. Perhaps acute stress distracted people from consultation. Perhaps, also, as stress becomes more prolonged people simply feel more need for help. This pattern of findings has an important implication for clinicians, in particular general practitioners. Consultation with functional symptoms by patients who are under stress often indicates a need for support rather than for investigation or treatment (Chapter 6, Box 5.3).

Box 5.9 Fear of disease does not always lead to consultation

Mrs Y had attended a routine breast-screening mammogram two weeks previously. She received a letter from the hospital asking her to attend for an appointment for further tests. Having read the letter she put it in her handbag. When the day of the appointment came, she threw it into the waste-bin and did not attend her appointment. Her husband found the letter, read it and found out from his wife what had happened. She said that it was bound to be a mistake and she felt quite well and could not have cancer. He persuaded her to make another appointment and took a day off work to attend with her. She was diagnosed with breast cancer and had a mastectomy. She became depressed afterwards and received counselling. It soon became clear that she was terrified of cancer. Her aunt had died from it 20 years earlier and she feared that she would soon die also. She had also feared that she 'couldn't cope' if she did turn out to have cancer.

CORNWALL COLLEGE
LEARNING CENTRE

5.6.3 Social Networks

Social networks also have complex effects on whether people consult. In a study of women's use of networks, there were 11 times as many lay consultations about symptoms as there were medical ones (Scambler et al, 1981). However, different parts of the networks had different effects. The women were *more* likely to consult their general practitioner after discussing their symptoms with *relatives*; consultation was *less* likely after discussions with *friends*. Perhaps, whereas friends 'normalized' the symptoms and reduced anxiety about them, relatives amplified their concerns. In fact, the social network can trigger consultation in several ways; for instance when a partner or employer 'sanctions' consultation, or when a relationship is threatened by the symptom (Zola, 1973; van de Kar et al, 1992; Box 5.10).

Generalizing about the effects of social networks is of little value to the clinician. Instead, the clinician needs to appreciate that whether or not an individual consults at a particular time is normally the outcome

---

Box 5.10   Triggers to consultation

By interviewing patients visiting an outpatient clinic in the USA, Zola (1973) found that it was rare that any of them consulted when they were most ill. Instead, it was generally when something happened that threatened the way that they had coped with the symptoms. There were five of these 'triggers'.

Interpersonal crisis	e.g., I was irritable because of my headache and we had a big row.
Perceived interference with personal relationships	e.g., I keep having to ask people to repeat what they say [because of deafness]. It's getting embarrassing.
Sanctioning	e.g., My husband said that I *had* to come and he rang up and made the appointment.
Perceived interference with functioning	e.g., It's stopping me doing my job properly.
Recurrence or persistence	e.g., I'll give myself till the end of the week. If it's no better by then, I'll go to the doctor.

of a sequence of lay consultations. Therefore, large changes in the frequency of consultation might not signify any change in level of symptoms. They can be caused entirely by changes in the social network (Dowrick, 1992).

The social network contributes in other ways to decisions to consult. It establishes subjective 'norms' for which behaviours are appropriate (Fishbein and Ajzen, 1975). Just being part of a network of people who rarely consult a doctor will tend to make consultation less likely. It also establishes norms for levels and types of symptoms that are normal. Symptoms that are shared with other people in the network will seem less threatening and will be less likely to lead to consultation. This is probably one reason why elderly people often do not consult with symptoms that are signs of serious disease. They wrongly regard them as normal signs of ageing.

5.7 CONCLUSION

Consulting with physical symptoms is the end result of a long chain of psychological and social processes. Whether physical symptoms are brought for health care is therefore only loosely related to whether there is physical pathology that needs to be treated. Serious symptoms that need urgent investigation and treatment are ignored or managed at home. Symptoms that indicate no physical illness at all are urgently and persistently brought for help. Many clinicians will wish only to treat physical pathology and will not wish to be concerned with psychological needs (Chapter 2). Nevertheless, even a clinician of this kind has the complex task of interpreting patients' presentation in the light of the psychological processes described here. Other clinicians will see their role as extending beyond the strict confines of physical pathology. When their patients bring physical symptoms, these clinicians will want to understand the psychological factors that explain why they have attended. They will therefore not only ask about the symptoms. They will ask what led to the patient consulting with them when they did.

KEY POINTS

- Experiencing a physical symptom depends on two psychological processes:
  — attention
  — attribution.

- Whether a symptom is attended to depends on what else competes for attention.
- Symptoms are often misattributed to the wrong causes.
- Physical symptoms can arise without physical pathology or psychological disorder.
- Physical symptoms can result from psychological processes, including:
  — illness templates
  — emotional distress
  — childhood trauma.
- Most symptoms do not lead to consultation. Whether they do depends on the symptom, beliefs, the patient's other problems and who else they have consulted.

Chapter 6

THE PATIENT'S AGENDA: BELIEFS AND INTENTIONS

KEY CLINICAL ISSUES

- Do patients and clinicians think about the body and its problems in the same way?
- How should patient's beliefs about their symptoms be assessed?
- Do adults have more mature beliefs than children?
- Do patients always know what they want when they consult a clinician?
- Does it matter if a clinician has no time to find out what a patient thinks is wrong?

Chapter 5 showed that diverse factors determine whether a patient experiences a symptom and then whether the patient consults with the symptom. It follows that different patients have very different needs when they do consult, even with the same symptom. This chapter focuses on two areas which are central to understanding patients' needs when they consult clinicians. They are important whether the consultation is with a general practitioner, practice nurse, or a hospital clinician. They are: what does the patient believe about the symptom or illness; and what does the patient want to be done about it?

6.1 WHAT DO PATIENTS BELIEVE ABOUT THEIR SYMPTOMS?

6.1.1 Theoretical Approaches: Assessing Properties of Beliefs

The process of attribution described in Chapter 5 can obviously lead to highly idiosyncratic beliefs. How, then, can a clinician or researcher assess and compare the beliefs of different patients? One approach is to identify very abstract properties of their beliefs that can be measured in all individuals, whatever their specific beliefs.

Box 6.1   Assessing properties of patients' beliefs: the Health Belief Model

Patients' responses to a symptom or illness often do not fit the objective characteristics of their problem, but can be understood by knowing the patients' *beliefs* about the problem. In particular, the clinician needs to know what a patient thinks about: whether the problem is severe; whether the patient is vulnerable to it; whether treatment might help; and whether there are barriers to accepting or receiving treatment.

These patients each delayed consulting their GP with symptoms of serious illness. For each patient, the X shows the belief that was critical in this delay. The GP needs to identify these beliefs because, if unaddressed, they might compromise the patients' acceptance of treatment, too.

	Is the problem severe?	Am I vulnerable to it?	Will treatment help?	Are there barriers to treatment?
X has noticed signs of dark blood in his faeces and his bowel habits have changed. He thinks this is probably just 'piles' or something he has been eating. So it will probably stop if he ignores it. His wife says he should go to the GP. But he thinks that the GP will be annoyed to have his time wasted by such a silly complaint	X			X
Y noticed a lump in her breast just after her 40th birthday. Her aunt and her mother both died of breast cancer more than 10 years ago and she thinks that her lump may be a tumour. She remembers that both had treatment (surgery, radiotherapy and chemotherapy) that made them very ill and tired and made them bald			X	X

	Is the problem severe?	Am I vulnerable to it?	Will treatment help?	Are there barriers to treatment?
Z recently retired from her job as a care assistant. She has been feeling breathless at times, and has begun to have pains in her chest. Her husband wants her to have her heart checked but she says that women don't get heart problems and, besides, they are caused by stress and now she's retired she doesn't have any		X		

6.1.1.1 The Health Belief Model

A simple theoretical approach to assessing patients' beliefs has been termed the Health Belief Model. According to this model, the beliefs that matter in relation to a specific disease or condition are: how **vulnerable** the person thinks they are to a condition; how **severe** he/she thinks it is; the **benefits** that he/she thinks will come from different ways of responding to it; and the **barriers** that they think stand in the way of each of those responses. Barriers include beliefs that a treatment will be painful or degrading or that it will worsen quality of life (Safer et al, 1979). The critical point is the emphasis on what the *patient* thinks on each of these points, not the objective characteristics of the condition or what the clinician might think.

The Health Belief Model assumes that an individual decides a course of action rationally, on the basis of a kind of cost–benefit analysis of the different possible responses—including doing nothing. At many points in this book it will be clear that patients' decisions in relation to illness and treatment are not always rational. That is, they are influenced by emotional factors as well as cognitive ones. Nevertheless, these beliefs do help to explain aspects of patients' behaviour (Janz and Becker, 1984). Therefore the model provides a simple framework that can be used to assess relevant beliefs of any patient about symptoms or disease (Box 6.1). It can also be used to target attempts to modify patients' beliefs. For an example, consider a patient who has been told that she has a life-threatening disease, such as breast cancer. She is offered treatment, but she decides to reject it. She knows that her condition is severe and that she is highly vulnerable to dying from it. Therefore there is no point in the clinician re-emphasizing those facts. However, the key to her decision lies in her beliefs about treatment, and it is here that the surgeons' and nurses' efforts should be directed. She thinks that the benefits will be small: a slight increase in the chances of survival. She also envisages major barriers to treatment: disfigurement (because of mastectomy) and debilitation and sickness (because of radiotherapy and chemotherapy).

Where individuals' own management of their conditions is at issue, their belief in the ability to deliver this has been called **self-efficacy**. Believing that self-care could deal with a minor problem will not prevent a consultation if there is insufficient self-efficacy. For instance, a patient might feel under too much pressure from long-term family or work problems to carry out self-care activities. Whether individuals consult a clinician therefore reflects the balance of their beliefs in the clinicians' and their own ability to manage their needs (van de Kar et al, 1992).

This kind of approach to patients' beliefs often remains quite far removed from how patients actually think about their symptoms. It can, though, be helpful clinically. It provides a simple structure for clinical assessment of patients' beliefs. It also emphasizes the need for explanation to be tailored, not just to the objective features of the patient's condition but to the patient's subjective beliefs about it. Just emphasizing this point to clinicians can improve their patients' care and outcomes (Innui et al, 1976).

6.1.1.2 Illness Representations

A different approach has been to build a theory on the basis of descriptions of how people's beliefs about disease are organized in practice. There is not universal agreement about the best theory of this kind. At a very general level, people distinguish illnesses along just two dimensions: how contagious they are and how serious they are (Bishop, 1991). More detailed studies have suggested that patients' beliefs can be described according to five key questions (Box 6.2): **How long will it last? What is it? What caused it? What effect will it have? How can it be treated?** An individual's 'explanatory model' (Kleinman, 1980) or 'mental representation' (Leventhal and Benyami, 1997) of a disease is regarded as the sum of that individual's answers to these questions. Knowing this 'mental representation' can help to explain whether a patient consults and how they respond to the clinician's instructions when they do (Chapter 9).

Box 6.2   Assessing properties of patients' beliefs:
mental representations

What a patient believes about an illness (the 'mental representation' of it) can be thought of as made up of answers to five broad questions. A questionnaire to measure these beliefs has been devised (Weinman et al, 1996). Patients answer several *specific* questions that address each broad question. Examples are shown here.

What is the illness like?
How frequently do you experience an upset stomach as part of your illness? How often do you experience fatigue as part of your illness?

What caused the illness?
Did a germ or virus cause the illness? Was stress a factor in causing the illness?

What is the time course of the illness?
Will the illness last a short time? Is the illness likely to be permanent?

What are the consequences of the illness?
Does the illness affect the way others see you? Is the illness serious?

Can the illness be controlled or cured?
Will the illness improve in time? Can what you do determine whether the illness gets better or worse?

6.1.2 Asking the Patient: Assessing the Content of Beliefs

Both the approaches above are somewhat theoretical and abstract, in that they look for general *properties* of the specific beliefs that can be found in any individual. They are not so concerned with the specific *content* of the beliefs that people have. They also emphasize beliefs about illness rather than symptoms. When asked directly about their symptoms, patients reveal a wide variety of beliefs, many of which do not directly relate to those theoretical approaches (Woloshynowych et al, 1998; Box 6.3). However, some consistent themes do seem to emerge in these beliefs in both Western and non-Western cultures (Helman, 1994).

6.1.2.1 Disease as an 'It'

An interesting change happens as part of the process whereby a sensation is turned into a symptom of disease (Cassell, 1976; Chapter 5). Whereas

---

Box 6.3   What do patients believe about their symptoms?

Before they saw their GP, patients with physical symptoms were asked what they thought had caused their symptoms. Their responses were used to form a questionnaire which 406 similar patients completed (Woloshynowych et al, 1998). Some of the causes are listed here, with the percentage of patients who thought that it probably or possibly caused their symptoms.

Beliefs	%
Weak spot in my body	56
Stress	55
Part of body inflamed	46
Part of body wearing out	46
Moods and emotions	45
Germ or infection	45
Not looking after myself	42
Overwork	42
Body lacking something it needs (e.g., vitamins)	41
Warning to change the way I treat my body	34
Weather or temperature changes	34
Poor circulation	32
Job or housework	30
A blockage somewhere in my body	24
Damp or a chill	24
Pollution	25
Payment for something I have done	13

---

the sensation is likely to be experienced and described as a part of the person (e.g., 'feeling tired'), the symptom tends to be separated off as an entity distinct from the person (e.g., 'being overcome by fatigue'). Evidence of the process is seen in the impersonal language that patients often use to refer to 'the cancer' or 'the heart'. It is seen also in the way that symptoms are attributed to malevolent disease entities (Peters et al, 1998; Box 5.6). Yet another example is where a part of the body is seen as autonomous, as in haemodialysis patients' explanations of renal failure as the kidneys just 'deciding to pack up' (Krespi et al, 1999a).

Just as dualism separated mind from body (Chapter 2), this process fractionates the body. A part of it (the disease) is viewed as not belonging to the body, which remains basically whole and healthy. In some cases, of course, there *is* a localized disease entity, such as a tumour, that can be separated from the body. However, many illnesses, such as diabetes or hypertension, are not like this. They exist systemically in the way that the whole body functions. In other diseases, such as chronic fatigue, the only evidence of the disease is in the way that the individual behaves (Henningsen and Priebe, 1999). Nevertheless, patients and clinicians normally talk about even these diseases as if they exist separately from the individual.

The splitting of disease from the body in this way has enormous implications for how patients, clinicians and researchers think about disease. It becomes natural to ask how patients 'manage' their angina, how they have 'adjusted to' their cancer or how they 'cope with' their arthritis. By contrast, it would not be regarded as sensible to ask how they 'manage' their heart, 'adjust to' their immune system or 'cope with' their legs! Clearly this convention of splitting disease from the body is helpful for many purposes and it will be adopted in this book. However, viewing illness in this way, and feeling threatened by an external disease entity, shapes the patient's demands on the clinician. We shall examine this influence below and in Chapter 10.

6.1.2.2 The Different Types of Disease

People's beliefs about symptoms and disease show some other interesting themes (Box 6.4). A particularly widespread belief is that symptoms reflect an **imbalance** of bodily forces or substances. This was envisaged by Hippocrates (Chapter 2) and is seen also in the opposition of 'yin' and 'yang' in traditional Chinese philosophy and medicine. The belief in the importance of 'feeding a cold and starving a fever' (Helman, 1978) is a contemporary Western example. Imbalance appears also in the more medicalized beliefs that symptoms reflect a 'hormone imbalance', 'overloading of the immune system' or a need for vitamins.

Invasion, weakness and **degeneration** of the body are also common types of explanation for illness (Box 6.4). Different types of belief are linked to different types of symptom. For instance, gastrointestinal symptoms are particularly likely to be linked to a weak constitution, aches and pains are more likely to be blamed on the body wearing out, and respiratory problems are especially attributed to environmental dangers such as 'germs', damp or pollution (Salmon et al, 1996b).

In non-Western cultures ill health is sometimes blamed on other individuals or on supernatural forces. It would be a mistake to imagine that these are primitive beliefs that Westerners are free from. Westerners' readiness to blame illness on **stress** (Woloshynowych et al, 1998; Box 6.3) indicates a readiness to blame others, including family and employers who demand

---

Box 6.4   The content of patients' beliefs: cross-cultural themes

Several types of belief emerge in people's explanations for symptoms in Western and non-Western cultures. Some Western examples are shown here.

Imbalance	Hormone imbalance Too much acid in the stomach Not enough sleep
Invasion	Sitting in a draft or on a cold surface Germs Damage by chemicals or pollution
Weakness	Being 'run down' A weak chest Something that runs in the family
Degeneration	Body tissues stiffening with age Crumbling of the spine Joints wearing out
Other people	Being overworked Family being too demanding Being under stress
Psychological	Nerves My personality Being highly strung
Supernatural	Being paid back for behaving badly when I was younger Something to test me God's will

---

too much (Helman, 1994). Many haemodialysis patients blame their doctors for their renal failure (Krespi et al, 1999a), which reflects the same phenomenon. Belief in the importance of the **supernatural** is also not confined to non-Western culture. Western patients' beliefs in God, or fate, provide both hope and fatalism.

6.1.2.3 The Nature of the Body

Underlying these cultural beliefs about symptoms are a small number of very different ways of regarding the body. A popular one is as a system of **plumbing**. According to this view, the body contains various fluids (such as blood and phlegm), but also cavities (such as the chest) and orifices connected by pipes (such as bowels). Symptoms reflect excess or deficit in a fluid (e.g., 'full of catarrh') or interrupted flow (e.g., 'poor circulation' or a 'blockage'). The consequences of blockage are thought to be potentially very widespread and damaging. For instance many people believe that, without a 'good clear-out' (such as by laxatives or, for some modern individuals, colonic irrigation), retained faeces could pollute the blood and worsen health and complexion (Helman, 1994).

The industrial age has brought another view of the body: as a biological version of the **machines** that people see around them (Mabek and Olesen, 1997). This view has entered the language in many phrases, such as 'nervous breakdown', or 'recharging the batteries'. The body as a machine links naturally with changes in medical practice. It supports the belief in the ability of surgery to 'repair' and 'replace' parts of the body, in the manner of a mechanic fixing a car. It also connects with beliefs in the efficacy of technological support for the body, such as by haemodialysis or in vitro fertilization. In this way, the body is just one machine among many (Helman, 1994). These views of the body as a fixable machine probably contribute to many overoptimistic expectations of what modern medical treatment can, in reality, achieve.

Plumbing and machines provide patients with very tangible ways of talking about their bodies. At first sight these provide common ground with biomedical clinicians who also want to talk in very mechanistic ways. The problem is that the patient uses these models in ways that often make little objective sense (Box 6.5). Therefore understanding the content of patients' beliefs can help to explain problems in communication, such as non-adherence (Chapter 9). In general, it seems rare that clinician and patient share beliefs about the patient's condition. Before their two belief systems can be reconciled the clinician must first be able to identify the important elements of the patient's beliefs. Being aware of cultural themes in the content of people's beliefs will help the clinician to identify important beliefs in individual consultations. The clinician's task is then to ensure that what the patient is told makes sense in terms of the patient's way of understanding their illness.

6.1.3 Illness Beliefs through Childhood

6.1.3.1 Illness Beliefs and Cognitive Development

Obviously, people's ways of making sense of symptoms depend on how sophisticated their understanding of the body is. This, in turn, depends on their education. In the extreme, 'medical students' disease' describes the supposed tendency of medical (and nursing) students to seek— and find—evidence in their bodies of the diseases that they have been studying. However, ways of understanding symptoms and illness

---

Box 6.5   Patients' biomedical beliefs

Patients' mechanical way of thinking about the body can help them to understand some of the information that clinicians provide. However, allowing patients to describe what they think often reveals important discrepancies with what clinicians would think (Mabeck and Olesen, 1997). The following patients consider that they have understood their diagnosis or treatment, but their understanding is different from their clinicians'.

'The fish oil helps to lubricate the joints. It lubricates the stomach and the intestines and then the joints. So I just have to take enough of it to make sure there's enough between the joints.'

'I've got bronchitis—lots of fluid on my chest. It got worse when I stopped smoking. I think the cigarettes help to keep the chest clear. The smoke breaks up the fluid so that I can cough it up.'

'High blood pressure means that the blood vessels might burst. So I mustn't do anything that might make the pressure go up. So I don't think exercise would be very safe.'

---

also reflect normal cognitive development. Therefore these change dramatically through childhood (Bibace and Walsh, 1980; Walsh and Bibace, 1991; Box 6.6).

In children's 'prelogical' phase (before about seven years), their explanations for illness (as for other events) generally do not differentiate cause from effect. That is, they are **circular**. For instance, a simple view of 'contagion' develops whereby an event which is *associated* with an illness is seen as one and the same thing as the illness. This very simple kind of explanation extends to the idea that illness is a punishment for doing something wrong.

From ages of about 7–11 children's thinking becomes more **concrete** and **logical**. Therefore they can explain illness by a limited chain of cause and effect, typically linking contamination from the environment, such as cold temperatures or smoking, through to changes in the body and, ultimately, disease. After about 11, the ability for **abstract thought** combines with their growing biological knowledge. These children can describe the interaction of multiple causes and (unseen) bodily parts and processes.

These developmental transitions mean that the ways that children recognize illness in themselves change through childhood. Young children are

---

Box 6.6   Children's understanding of the common cold

As children's ways of understanding the world develop, so do their ways of understanding illness. These are revealed in what they say about illness (Bibace et al, 1994).

5–7 years: Prelogical thinking

Explanation is based on association, either with internal events (i.e., symptoms themselves) or external events:

- *Internal:* 'You get a cold when your nose runs.'
- *External:* 'It's from being outside when it's cold.'

7–11 years: Concrete thinking

The child can link the cold to events that are beyond direct sensory experience. Again, explanations emphasize internal or external events:

- *Internal:* 'The germs get into your nose and block it up.'
- *External:* 'When you're out in the cold or the wet, it gets into your body and stays in your chest and your head.'

11+ years: Abstract thinking

Abstract concepts are used. Chains of cause and effect can be formed, using lay or medical concepts:

- *Lay concepts:* 'You catch germs. Then the body fights them off. You cough to get rid of them. Your nose runs to wash them out.'
- *Medical concepts:* 'It's what happens when the immune system fights off a virus.'

---

liable to see themselves as ill because of events which are actually *responses* to the illness—such as going to bed or having their temperature taken. Older children are more likely to decide that they are ill because they have specific symptoms (Hergenrather and Rabinowitz, 1991).

6.1.3.2 Clinical Assessment of Children's Beliefs

Clinicians' responses to children's beliefs must be sufficiently subtle to take account of children's level of understanding (Chapter 11). Merely restating what, to the adult clinician, is obvious will not work. Instead, the child's way of thinking must first be found out. The younger child's understanding can often be elicited by drawing or through play. For example, the clinician and child can pretend that a doll has the child's illness. Explanation or reassurance can then be provided in ways that make sense in terms of the child's understanding, not the adult's.

Knowing the stages through which children's thinking passes can guide the clinician in making this kind of assessment. However, stage theories are, by their nature, simplistic (Chapter 8). In reality, different children pass through stages at different ages. Another danger of stage models is that they imply a pattern of development that cannot be altered. In reality, children's understanding of different illnesses varies (Sigelman et al, 1993). Much of this variability is probably caused by varying exposure to different illnesses (Paterson et al, 1999). Therefore the clinician who cares for children must appreciate, not merely children's *general* level of reasoning, but their *specific* understanding of the illness, injury or procedure in question.

6.1.3.3 Child-Like Beliefs in Adults

It is also inaccurate to assume that adults are free from the ways of thinking that children use (Woloshynowych et al, 1998; Box 6.3). Beliefs in which illness is attributed, for instance, to punishment for not looking after oneself properly or to other people being too demanding reflect a prelogical way of thinking. Yet others are highly concrete in attributing symptoms simplistically to invasion of the body by a single external factor, such as weather or pollution or, in the case of breast cancer, to a fall or injury. Adults frequently copy children in conveying the existence or severity of disease by describing the treatments. For example, one patient expressed the severity of her menstrual problems by saying that 'I had to have an extreme D&C'. News reports often describe people as being so badly traumatized that they 'needed counselling'. Therefore adults are not free from immature ways of thinking about illness. They differ from children only in the greater variability of ways of thinking. Even within a single adult these can encompass both child-like and abstract ideas (Bibace et al, 1994).

6.2 WHAT DO PATIENTS SEEK BY CONSULTATION?

6.2.1 Mindless Consulting

A large amount of everyday behaviour is 'mindless' (Langer et al, 1978) or habitual. It owes its existence to past learning rather than present needs. Illness behaviour is learned from parents (Whitehead et al, 1994). Therefore it is to be expected that people often attend the doctor in response to a symptom simply out of habit. That is, they have learned to do so and have no clear idea of what they seek. The following sections consider reasons for consulting that do reflect present needs. The first two are rarely made explicit and are often not appreciated consciously by either party to a consultation.

6.2.2 The Sick Role

Going to the doctor is only one way of getting help and advice for physical symptoms. Therefore what the patient seeks from the doctor depends on what has been obtained from other sources. For some patients, these include other professionals, such as pharmacists, health visitors or community nurses. More generally important, however, are the lay people that are usually consulted before the clinician (Helman, 1994). Information is consulted also in books, mass media and on the Internet (Davison and Pennebaker, 1997) or through pressure groups. This process of lay consultation allows patients to work out a view of the problem before they see a doctor.

Doctors do, however, retain a special significance amongst these various consultation sources. As well as being a source of expert medical treatment, or a gateway to specialist services, they uniquely have the authority to sanction, or legitimate, the 'sick role' (Radley, 1994). This refers to the freedom from normal social and family obligations that only 'genuine' illness permits. It also includes the entitlement to certain privileges. The privileges can be financial, like sickness pay, but they also include receiving sympathy and support. Even for a minor problem like a sore throat, legitimation of the sick role for the family or employer is an important reason to consult a doctor (Little et al, 1997a). Providing a 'sick note' is the most obvious way in which the sick role is sanctioned. However, merely receiving a prescription, a diagnosis or an explanation is normally sufficient.

Sociologists' analyses of the sick role have assumed that it is permitted by society on the assumption that the sick person intends to return to normal life. It is therefore a privilege associated only with acute illness. In chronic illness the same role is not available (Chapter 7).

6.2.3 Alliance against Disease

In Chapter 5, and earlier in this chapter, it was explained that patients often view symptoms as indicating an alien disease entity (Blaxter, 1989;

Cassell, 1976). An automatic response to feeling threatened is to seek an ally. Therefore attending a doctor can be a way of securing an alliance against the threat, regardless of whether the doctor has anything tangible to offer. Patients with persistent and debilitating symptoms that doctors had been unable to explain or treat did not complain about the doctors' failure in these respects (Peters et al, 1998). Instead, they valued doctors who had simply taken the patient's side 'against' the symptoms; for example, the doctor who has 'not helped . . . , but tries everything . . . he's a good doctor'.

6.2.4 Patients' Intentions

Most patients will not be aware that they are consulting for the sick role, or to form an alliance. Therefore the clinician must be aware that, when patients consult, important aims in doing so are not expressed. Even with careful questioning it is unlikely that the patients could describe the importance of the sick role or of forming an alliance. Nevertheless, given the highly elaborate beliefs that patients have about their symptoms, it is to be expected that they also have clear beliefs about how they might be helped that they *can* express—at least when asked. In general, patients have most knowledge and experience of primary care clinicians, given their greater exposure to care at this level than in hospitals. When asked, therefore, they reveal clear expectations about some of the main responses that a general practitioner can make (Webb and Lloyd, 1994).

6.2.4.1 Expectations, Pressure and Intentions

Patients' **expectations** have been measured widely. However, the term is not very helpful because it tends to imply a passive patient, whose only role is to anticipate what the doctor might do, not to shape it. In fact, patients do not just *expect* care; they actively *seek* it.

One approach to understanding patients' active role has been to examine **patients' pressure**. This is defined by the subjective feeling of the doctor. Studies where this has been measured do provide some clues about what patients seek. For instance, general practitioners feel under most pressure to refer patients to hospital where patients seek reassurance (Armstrong et al, 1991). However, a concept defined according to clinicians' feelings is not very helpful in understanding what patients actually seek when they consult. Therefore the term **intention** has been used to reflect the active, consumer-oriented, role that patients can take. Surveys of intentions that patients have when they consult their GP have identified three broad types of help that they seek: **emotional support**; **information and reassurance**; and **medical investigation and treatment**. These intentions are independent of each other. This means, for example, that whether patients seek support is not related to whether they also seek medical investigation and treatment (Valori et al, 1996). Patients have clearly differentiated views as to which types of clinician can provide each of these kinds of help (Salmon and Quine, 1989).

To some extent, what patients seek from clinicians depends on social and cultural influences (such as media) over which clinicians have no direct influence. However, patients' intentions and expectations do also reflect what actually happens in consultations. For instance, the high level of prescription that patients anticipate from GPs accurately reflects the number of consultations that do lead to prescription (Webb and Lloyd, 1994). Moreover, treatment that is given at one consultation shapes patients' intentions at the next. For instance, many patients are prescribed antibiotics for sore throat, a minor condition that does not usually require treatment. Being treated in this way makes patients more likely to bring a sore throat to the GP in future and then to expect antibiotics to cure it (Little et al, 1997a, 1997b).

6.2.4.2 Recognizing Patients' Intentions

There is a discrepancy between what patients want from clinicians, at least in primary care, and what clinicians are trained to provide. Patients' main intentions are usually for support and reassurance, but the clinicians from whom they seek it have been trained, instead, to provide medical intervention. The potential for mismatch between what patients want and what clinicians provide is increased because it seems that general practitioners, at least, are probably not accurate in detecting what patients' intentions are (Salmon et al, 1994).

Misperception can have serious consequences. For instance, patients who are emotionally distressed seek more support than other patients, although they do not seek any more medical investigation or explanation (Salmon et al, 1994). Suppose that the clinician misperceives a distressed patient as seeking medical intervention, and provides this. The patient's important needs will be unmet, and the process of medical intervention could begin to feed the patient's concern and dependency and shape an 'illness template' (Chapter 5, Box 5.3). In this way, misperception of what the patient seeks can create problems that are iatrogenic—i.e., products of health care rather than patient needs.

Questionnaires have been devised that can measure patients' intentions in routine primary care consultations (Valori et al, 1996). However, the questions that are asked are so simple that they can easily be incorporated into consultation. Therefore, the most practical approach for the clinician who wants to know what the patient seeks is simply to ask.

6.3 CONCLUSION

Chapter 9 will show that some of the problems of communication that arise between patient and clinician can be explained by clinicians' neglect of the issues described in this chapter. In particular, patients' non-adherence to clinicians' recommendations can often be attributed to their clinicians' failure to bridge between the different beliefs that each party to the consultation has. This chapter has shown also that misreading the sort of help that a patient wants can lead to treatment that is unnecessary and fails to meet patients' needs. The reason that clinicians often do not appreciate patients' beliefs and intentions is not because they are obscure or complicated to assess. Most of the research described in this chapter has emerged from asking patients extremely simple questions. These questions can easily be asked by a clinician in routine practice. They are not, however, routinely asked. Instead, clinicians tend to overestimate the importance of their own beliefs and intentions and to underestimate the importance of the patients'.

KEY POINTS

- Clinical assessment should normally find out what patients believe about their condition and what help they want.
- *Properties* of beliefs can be assessed, such as beliefs about the seriousness of the condition, effectiveness of treatment and barriers to treatment.
- *Content* of beliefs can be assessed, such as attributing disease to an alien entity, imbalance of body processes, invasion of the body, or other people.
- Children's illness beliefs become more elaborate as cognitive development proceeds, but adults retain child-like beliefs.
- Some reasons for consulting a clinician are not acknowledged in con-

sultation: habit, sanctioning the 'sick role' and seeking alliance against disease.

- Simple questions reveal the main sorts of help that patients are aware of seeking: information, support and technical intervention.
- Clinicians commonly misperceive intentions, leading to treatment that is unnecessary, inappropriate or iatrogenic.

Chapter 7

THE PSYCHOLOGICAL IMPACT
OF PHYSICAL ILLNESS

KEY CLINICAL ISSUES

- Has modern treatment of chronic illnesses, such as renal failure or diabetes, removed much of the burden from patients?
- Should depressed patients be referred for specialist psychological treatment?
- Why do seriously ill patients sometimes claim that their illness is trivial?
- Does it matter if patients blame themselves for developing cancer?
- Why do some patients become housebound after myocardial infarction even though they are well enough to return to work?
- Should all psychological treatment be provided by psychologically trained staff?

One of the defining aspects of the holistic approach to health care (Chapter 2) is the appreciation that effects of physical disease processes extend beyond the traditional concerns of physical health care. This chapter will outline two broad areas within which the holistic clinician will wish to assess the psychological effects of illness. The first concerns the emotional challenge that illness imposes. This requires attention also to patients' ways of coping with the challenge and to how the social network helps or hinders the process. The second area concerns cognitive rather than emotional changes; that is, changes in the ways that patients seek and process information relating to illness.

7.1 THE CHALLENGES OF ILLNESS

7.1.1 Challenges of Acute Illness

Before clinicians can understand patients' emotional reactions to illness, they need to understand the psychological challenges that illness and treatment present to patients. A few phobic patients have an intense, **irrational fear** of hypodermic needles, blood or injury that has no basis in their own experience. More generally, challenge arises from the **uncertainty** that illness introduces into life. This uncertainty reflects the uncertain course of illness and treatment, but also the exposure to **unfamiliar people, procedures and environments** (Chapter 12). An additional source of challenge for many patients arises not directly from the illness and treatment, but from **disclosing suffering**, weakness or anxiety to others.

In general, however, specific concerns often reflect previous experience, or are based on knowledge that patients have acquired from family, friends or media. These fears can therefore reflect, not present reality, but recollections of relatives who have died in hospital, perhaps in a poorly managed and painful way, or recent media reports. For instance, Box 7.1 describes a patient in whom a minor diagnostic procedure aroused such intense anxiety as to prevent her undergoing it. Her anxiety seemed out of proportion to the procedure's objective characteristics. Neither did it fit with the small risk that cancer would be found. Instead, the procedure challenged the patient because of her own experience that linked hospital, and specifically anaesthesia, with death, and her own (mistaken) knowledge about risk factors for anaesthetic problems.

7.1.2 Challenges of Chronic Illness

There is not a rigid distinction between chronic and acute illness. Even acute procedures have enduring physical or emotional effects. Where there are major enduring effects of an acute illness or its treatment, or where disease is chronic, the scale of the challenge that confronts the patient can be much greater than that of an acute, time-limited, illness (Moos and Schaefer, 1984). In acute conditions, however frequent they may be in a patient's life, the patient can enter the 'sick role' on a transitory—or cyclical—basis. In this way, the patient is released from obligations of normal life (Chapter 6). The dispensations that this brings are accepted by all parties because the patient is trying to get better and the clinician is trying to make the patient better. When the patient cannot be cured, this role is not available. Therefore people with chronic illness find themselves expected to meet **continuing obligations** associated with being a normal member of the family or society.

There are important **new obligations** too because the management of chronic illness relies heavily on the patient (Box 7.2). Often patients'

Box 7.1   Making sense of a patient's fears

Mrs X had been asked to come into hospital for minor surgery (laparoscopy). She had tried to come on a previous occasion, but was in tears soon after reaching the ward and had demanded to go home. The surgeon and nurses had tried to reassure her by telling her that the procedure would not cause any pain, that the chances of finding anything seriously wrong were very low indeed. These attempts to calm her had not worked. An interview with her elicited the following fears. Each showed misunderstanding. Each was managed by explanation before the next admission.

1. Her father, aunt and brother had all died in this hospital, two of them while undergoing surgery. As a 12-year-old child, X had been told that her father was going to the hospital for a day or two, but she never saw him again. She was frightened that she would die under anaesthesia, too.
2. X had been told years ago that she should stop smoking before being admitted for a separate operation. Although she had been able to stop smoking for two weeks before that operation, she had resumed smoking three weeks ago (about 10 a day). She feared that this would make the anaesthetic dangerous.
3. X had seen a TV programme about someone who had a stroke under anaesthesia. Her father had a series of strokes and she thought she was at risk.
4. X felt that she would need sedation as soon as she got to the hospital—and perhaps before—but feared that she might be left alone for an hour or two after admission before anyone attended to her.
5. Finally, X thought that no one would be available to listen to her. She thought that her fears would be regarded as too silly for the doctors and nurses to take seriously.

No doubt the surgeon and nurses thought that they were reassuring Mrs X. Because they had not first assessed her fears, their words were irrelevant to her.

---

obligations include dietary and other lifestyle changes. They have to **learn about physical limitations** and **learn how to cope** with them (Charmaz, 1995). However, there is also often the **responsibility for treatment**, including highly technical procedures involved in monitoring physiological parameters or administering treatment, such as in insulin-dependent diabetes or continuous ambulatory peritoneal dialysis after renal failure.

Box 7.2 The burdens of chronic disease

Chronic disease brings numerous challenges. There are new obligations around managing the disease, together with continuing obligations to family and others that pre-dated the disease. These are challenges that one patient noted in her diary during a single week. She had recently experienced end-stage renal failure and had begun haemodialysis at a satellite unit.

Remembering to take my medication.
Remembering to check my potassium levels.
Remembering to measure out the fluids I drink.
Saying 'no' to a friend who wants me to have a drink with her.
Deciding whether to phone the doctor about recurring pains in my legs.
Finding a way to stop feeling bored and miserable while on dialysis.
Keeping up a 'brave face' for the children despite feeling miserable.
Finding a way of avoiding drinking when I feel hot and thirsty.
Finding different sources of self-esteem to replace being the breadwinner.
Managing reduced income after having to give up work.
Saying 'no' to family and friends when they try to help with things I can still do.
Learning to organize activities around the timing of dialysis sessions.
Not losing my temper with one of the nurses at the dialysis unit who annoys me.
Knowing how to tell friends that I can't eat something they have made for me.
Deciding whether to phone friends who have not contacted me since I became ill.
Coping with feeling guilty about the effects on the children.
Finding a restaurant that will cook food in a way that I can eat it.
Correcting husband without hurting his feelings when he has prepared food that I should not eat.
Deciding whether I should risk upsetting my daughter by not having a drink she made for me.
Wondering if my family would be better off if I were dead.

There is also the need to form long-term **relationships with clinicians**. These relationships have to encompass both the patients' dependence on the clinicians and the patients' responsibility for managing their illness independently.

Negotiating the new and continuing obligations is a challenge in itself, such as in trying to minimize disruption to work or family that is caused by treatment or clinic visits. Many patients continue to suffer physical or emotional effects of an illness that, in other people's eyes, has been successfully controlled or treated. This leads to an additional burden: keeping up the **appearance of normality** that they think other people expect. In any individual case, these and additional challenges combine into a formidable list (Box 7.2).

7.2 EMOTIONAL REACTIONS TO THE CHALLENGES OF ILLNESS

Illness, like other psychological challenges, triggers an array of emotional reactions (Lazarus, 1999). Even positive emotions, such as hope or relief, can be problematic where they are intense, prolonged or misplaced. However, it is negative emotions that normally require most attention from clinicians. Emotional changes are not just *reactions* to illness. They become part of the challenge that the patient has to cope with.

7.2.1 Anxiety

Anxiety is pervasive in illness and health care. Patients' anxiety is usefully divided into **outcome** anxiety, which refers to fears of what the results of illness and treatment will be, and **procedural** anxiety, which arises from fears about clinical procedures. Outcome anxiety is often unavoidable: illness is, after all, dangerous. By contrast, procedural anxiety should usually be regarded as evidence of a failure of clinical care where it results from inaccurate beliefs or fears about what is going to happen (Box 7.3).

Being anxious does not just mean that patients have disturbing beliefs. It also means that there are changes to the way that they think and the way that information is processed. In particular, there are changes to the perceptual processes of attention and 'making sense' of sensations (Williams et al, 1997; Chapter 5). First, **vigilance for threatening stimuli** is increased: that is, anxious people attend especially to signs of danger. Secondly, anxious people are also more likely to make **threatening interpretations of ambiguous information**. A third problem is that people tend to **recall memories** that are consistent with their mood. Therefore an anxious patient is likely to be attending especially to signs of present danger, and to memories about previous dangers. Because of this, an

---

Box 7.3   Fears of routine procedures

Procedures that are routine to clinicians can seem dangerous to patients. Patients rarely get the opportunity to state their fears. When they do, they often reflect misunderstandings which are readily corrected. These are some fears that patients have voiced.

Clinical procedure	Patient's fear
Inflation of blood pressure cuff on a child	'It's too tight. My arm is getting too full of blood. It'll burst.'
Morphine analgesia postoperatively	'Morphine is a dangerous drug. I'll become addicted if I have too much.'
Barium meal	'Radiation gives people cancer. Perhaps this is going to give me cancer.'
Colonoscopy	'I might dirty myself in front of everyone.'
Entering a hospice for palliative care	'Dying from cancer is painful. My uncle was in terrible pain when he died.'
General anaesthesia	'I've a strong constitution. I always need more painkillers than the proper dose. If they give me a normal anaesthetic I might wake up in the middle of the operation.'

---

anxious patient's view of a clinical procedure is very different from the clinician's. Managing any patient's anxiety therefore depends on a careful assessment of the basis of the anxiety, followed by explanation which will make sense to the patient. This is pursued in Chapter 11.

7.2.2 Depression

Depression has particularly complex and destructive effects. It will therefore be examined in detail.

7.2.2.1 Causes

Illness restricts the opportunity for familiar and rewarding activities. Where complete recovery is not certain, it threatens expectations or assumptions about future sources of reward and fulfilment. Therefore, becoming depressed is a common reaction to illness, particularly where

---

Box 7.4   Hopelessness after terminal diagnosis

A patient was told by his doctor that he had a terminal illness. He realized that nothing could be done to save him. He sat staring at the doctor. His skin became pale. His face crumpled. He tried to say something, but he just choked on his tears. He trembled and shook and had to be helped up and supported until he reached home. Once home he became very depressed and died within a much shorter time than expected.

This is one of many similar reports gathered by Cannon (1942). The language and details have been changed, as explained in footnote 1.

---

there is continuing illness or disability. Sadness, passivity, self-blame, feelings of hopelessness and helplessness and internal focus of attention are all part of being depressed. All these reactions are able to impair treatment effectiveness and compromise recovery and rehabilitation.

7.2.2.2   Effects

Effects of depression can be catastrophic. Overt suicide is more common amongst patients with cancer and AIDS than in the general population. However, it is likely that chronically ill patients' own decisions contribute to many other deaths that are not recorded as suicide. Patients' decisions account for around half the instances where long-term renal dialysis is discontinued (Neu and Kjellstrand, 1986). This might explain the findings that depressed renal failure patients are more likely to die than non-depressed patients (Christensen and Moran, 1998). The fatal power of hopelessness is well illustrated by the account in Box 7.4. It describes how one patient responded to being told that he had a terminal illness (details have been changed in the text to emphasize its relevance to the present time).[1]

Depression has many other, more insidious, negative effects on recovery from illness. Its effects in rehabilitation from myocardial infarction have

---

[1] In Cannon's (1942) original account, the 'doctor' was a witch doctor. He had cast a spell on the 'patient' to his face and had told him that he would die. Cannon documented the deaths of many people in this way and coined the term 'Voodoo death' to describe the phenomenon. Consider the meaning that the word 'cancer' has in Western society and the power that doctors are thought to have. Might there be any similarity between what Cannon described and receiving a diagnosis of cancer from a Western doctor?

been studied in particular detail. Depressed patients are much more likely to die during the first year after myocardial infarction (Frasure-Smith et al, 1999). Survivors go on to less successful rehabilitation, with more medical complications (Carney et al, 1995). Possible explanations are as diverse as are the components of depression (Carney et al, 1995). There may be physiological concomitants of depression that trigger further cardiac events. Motivation for adhering to treatment and rehabilitation is reduced. Feelings of passivity compromise the problem-focused coping responses that are needed. Negativity and inward focus of attention alienate the support network (including clinicians). Self-blame and low mood can lead to self-destructive behaviours.

7.2.2.3 Detecting Depression

Recognizing depression in someone who is physically ill is more difficult than in someone who is physically healthy. Therefore most depression in physically ill patients remains undetected. One problem is that, in physically healthy people, depression is often indicated by physical symptoms (Chapter 5). In particular, sleep and appetite disturbance are often important in diagnosing depression. In physically ill people, of course, physical symptoms of these kinds often arise from the physical condition or its treatment. Therefore physical signs of depression are often wrongly disregarded by clinicians who misattribute them to patients' illness. A widely used questionnaire for screening for depression is the Hospital Anxiety and Depression Scale (Zigmond and Snaith, 1983). It was designed to detect depression without the need to consider ambiguous physical symptoms, so it focuses on (low) mood and (lack of) enjoyment of activities. A questionnaire like this can be used for routine screening of groups at risk. However, no questionnaire can be 100% accurate (Chapter 15). Therefore, careful observation of patients and sensitive interviewing of patients and carers are more important in clinical practice.

7.2.2.4 Helping the Depressed Patient

Chapter 8 will show that depression can be a stage of adjustment to disease and often resolves without specialist help. Besides, there are not enough specialists available to treat every depressed patient. Therefore there are several decisions that have to be made in responding to the depressed patient (Box 7.5).

Specialist treatment. If the patient's safety is threatened by depression, the patient has a right to expert help. Similarly, where depression is preventing the patient from adhering to treatment, or preventing self-care, or

---

Box 7.5 Deciding how to meet the needs of a depressed patient

Depression in physical illness can be a dangerous threat to recovery, or a brief stage in adjusting to illness. Specialist treatment is not available for every patient and is often unnecessary. This diagram shows decisions that a clinician can make as an *initial* response to recognizing that a patient is depressed.

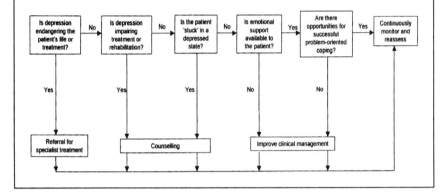

---

where the patient has become 'stuck' in a depressed state, there is also the right to receive specialist care. Specialist approaches to managing depression are beyond the scope of this book. They are also beyond the scope of most clinicians who are trained for physical health care. Therefore referral for specialist psychological or psychiatric help may be necessary, with a view to drug treatment or psychological therapy. However, there are barriers to specialist treatment. Specialists are often not available, or their waiting lists are too long. There are certainly not enough specialists to see every patient who meets these criteria. There is another barrier. Referral to a psychiatrist or psychologist risks allowing patients to feel stigmatized as 'mentally ill', 'reacting badly' or being 'disturbed'.

Counselling. Counselling is often more accessible than specialist referral. It is normally available in the treatment setting and avoids the stigma associated with being referred to a psychiatric clinic. Counselling can, in principle, be provided by clinicians that already work with the patient. Detailed guidance is available from many texts. Here, it is sufficient to emphasize that the primary aim of counselling is not to 'treat' the patient, but to provide the conditions in which a 'natural', but fragile, process of adjustment can unfold (Chapter 8). In addition, establishing an effective relationship of this kind can allow the counsellor and patient jointly to address the patient's problems (Box 7.6).

Box 7.6   Elements of counselling

Counselling is a special kind of conversation. The clinician establishes the conditions for a relationship and then uses the relationship to work with the patient. In this hypothetical case, a counsellor is working in a problem-focused way with a depressed patient who has been treated for cancer. In practice, counselling is often disrupted by clinicians' responses that suggest to the patient that the clinician cannot cope with the patient's distress, does not see the patient as an individual or does not understand the patient. Similarly, a problem orientation to the counselling can increase depression if it fails to lead to experiences of mastery.

What does the counsellor want to achieve?	Patient's presentation	Unhelpful response	Potentially helpful response
Make the situation feel safe for the patient; don't contradict what she says	'I look at the children and just think that I'll not see them grow up.'	'There's no need to feel like that. You'll live longer than I will.'	'It must be hard to really believe what you've been told, that the cancer isn't likely to come back.'
Allow patient to express emotion; give time and don't inhibit distress	Cries and apologizes for crying	'Don't worry. Here's some tissues. Let's wipe the tears away.'	'That's fine. It's what this meeting is for—so you don't have to keep everything bottled up. We'll go on talking when you're ready.'
Show respect for the patient as an individual	'I can't help thinking, life's just not going to be worth living with this hanging over me'	'That's normal. Everyone feels like that at first. But they soon feel better.'	'It's hard to think about the future, isn't it?'

continued

What does the counsellor want to achieve?	Patient's presentation	Unhelpful response	Potentially helpful response
Empathize with the patient's suffering	'All my hopes for the future have come to nothing.'	'Don't worry. There's lots you'll still be able to do.'	'I can see it's hard for you to see yourself achieving anything in the future.'
Help patient to identify and clarify important problems	'There's nothing I feel like doing any more. The housework is piling up and the house is a mess.'	'Let's see if we can get you back to doing a small amount of housework.'	'Maybe housework just isn't interesting any more. Maybe your illness has made you look at things differently from the way you used to. Let's see if there's anything that would be more important or fulfilling than housework, given the way you feel.'
Help patient to achieve realistic goals	'I go to bed telling myself I'll get up and do such and such. When the morning comes I just think, "I can't be bothered." '	'You've really got to push yourself. When you've succeeded once, it will be easier next time.'	'Perhaps you're still aiming to do too much. Let's make sure that, when you go to bed, you've something more realistic planned for the next day.'

Clinical management. If expert treatment or counselling is not indicated, that does not mean that depression should simply be tolerated as an 'understandable' or unavoidable reaction. On the contrary, it then becomes very important for the clinician to ensure that support and opportunities are in place that will allow the patient's adjustment to progress. Assessing **support** is central and this depends, not just on the presence of supporters, but on whether communication with them is open and effective (Chapter 3). It also means being assured that the supporters are, where necessary, receiving the support that *they* need. The patient's **opportunites for problem-focused coping** must also be assessed. Experiences of successful coping—sometimes called 'mastery' experiences—are important in overcoming depression. These can be unnecessarily restricted for many reasons. Care or advice is often inadequate; for instance, where there is insufficient physiotherapy advice as to how to begin and stage walking practice after hip replacement, or a lack of clarity in instructions about how to judge a safe level of exercise after myocardial infarction. Alternatively many patients are allowed to aim too quickly for unachievable or unrewarding targets that are demotivating and depressing. In this case, they need help to adopt realistic goals that provide the opportunity to develop feelings of mastery.

7.2.3 Anger

Although ostensibly a very different emotion from depression, anger can also be a reaction to the same experience of disempowerment by illness. Unfortunately, it is in the nature of anger that, whatever its cause, it is usually directed at whoever is available. At times of illness, this puts professional and lay carers in the line of fire. Moreover, many patients blame their illness on other people (Chapter 6), including clinicians who they think have failed to look after them (Krespi et al, 1999a). These attributions help to fuel their anger. Anger impairs outcome by complicating clinician–patient relationships, and by focusing patients' concerns on problems which are incidental to illness and its treatment. In general, persistent or extreme blame of others is associated with worse adjustment to life challenges in general, including illness (Tennen and Affleck, 1990; Turnquist et al, 1988).

7.3 COPING WITH THE CHALLENGES OF ILLNESS

7.3.1 Problem-Focused Coping

Successful problem-focused coping is central to patients' management of their own illness. Beneficial examples include careful self-medication in diabetes, titrating effort to capacity after diagnosis of angina or explaining to drinking partners why previous habits have to change during cardiac rehabilitation. However, problem-focused coping is not always beneficial. It can be counter-productive. Harmful problem-focused coping is seen in the patient recovering from myocardial infarction who insists on exercising to exhaustion to test out or prove the extent of his 'recovery', or the patient with operable cancer who intends to treat herself by diet and imagery (see Box 9.4). Similarly, the common strategy for anxious patients of finding out as much information as possible may be reassuring where the information source is balanced and understandable. The same coping strategy is damaging where the search for information leads to a confusing medical textbook, a dramatic media article, or an inflammatory Internet site.

To the clinician, who sees the *effects* of patients' coping, these ways of coping look very different. To the patient, however, they are all forms of problem-focused coping. Faced with a patient whose problem-focused response is counter-productive, the clinician's task is therefore to accept that such a patient wishes to engage in problem-focused coping and to steer this in a constructive direction. It is obviously important that coping is directed at the right problem. After myocardial infarction, for instance, efforts to control diet or exercise have much more potential for success than attempts to 'reduce stress' (Chapter 14). The popularity of complementary therapists shows the value that patients attach to opportunities for problem-focused coping that conventional medical care often seems to deny them.

7.3.2 Emotion-Focused Coping

Palliative, emotion-focused coping can also be either helpful or harmful. Relaxation is, at worst, a distraction and might even have beneficial emotional or physiological effects (Box 3.3). Imagery can be used to help patients feel more in control (Chapter 11). By contrast, pretending that a serious illness is trivial, using alcohol excessively, focusing disappointment and anger on clinicians or keeping suffering to oneself could all be destructive. Again, the implication for the clinician is clear. Having recognized that problem behaviour by a patient is an attempt at palliative coping, it will be counter-productive to try simply to stop that behaviour. Instead, the clinician must help the patient to find an alternative method of coping.

7.3.3 Defensive Coping

One variant of palliative coping, psychological defence, can be particularly problematic in the reaction to serious, life-threatening illness (Croyle et al, 1997). Patients sometimes claim that that their illness is not serious or that they have been cured; or they ignore treatment and rehabilitation advice. To understand this, consider a common way in which threatening information about oneself is dealt with in normal life: by minimizing its significance. For example, being criticized by a manager is much easier to bear if we choose to view that manager as a poor judge of people. Threatening information about health meets with the same defence. A striking example comes from research in which healthy people were told that they had high blood pressure or high cholesterol levels. Their defensive response was, in general, to think that high blood pressure or cholesterol levels were not so dangerous (Croyle, 1990; Croyle et al, 1993).

Rationally, one would expect that being told that a health problem can be treated should reduce the importance that a sufferer attaches to that problem. However, reassuring people in this way seems to reduce the defensive 'minimization' effect (Ditto et al, 1988). That is, knowing that a treatment exists means that people can acknowledge the seriousness of the problem. In Chapter 8, we see that even the importance of health itself is minimized in the face of serious illness.

Minimization is only one of several ways in which people can defend themselves against information about health problems. Additional ways include doubting the accuracy of tests that have produced the information, believing that a problem is quite common or, simply, 'remembering' having been told information that was less threatening than the information that was actually given (see Croyle et al, 1997).

7.3.4 Which Way of Coping is Best?

Generalization about this is unhelpful. The different demands that are associated with illness require different responses. Therefore it is probably the patients who are able to cope in a variety of ways that will fare best. The 'right' way of coping changes over time, too. Particularly with chronic or life-threatening illness, the demands unfold and develop (Chapter 8). The emotional distress that follows the shock of diagnosis might only permit defensive and other palliative coping at first. However, persistent palliative coping will compromise the patient's ability to manage the complex responsibilities which illness (particularly chronic illness) can bring. In insulin-dependent diabetes, for instance, avoidant patients are poorer in glycaemic control (Frenzel et al, 1988).

A great deal that is written about coping in health psychology implies that people are free to choose between different coping responses. This is unrealistic because ways of coping are *aspects* of people's problems, not just *influences* on them (Chapter 3). For instance, feeling helpless and unable to influence what is happening is a feature of depression. Therefore depressed patients' opportunity for problem-focused coping is severely reduced. There are material and social constraints on coping responses, too. In coping with heart disease, for instance, it is the patients with social contacts and financial security who can most easily cope by making changes to their lives. Without these resources, denial or resignation are more likely (Radley, 1988).

7.3.5 Improving Coping

7.3.5.1 Equipping Patients to Cope

Box 7.2 illustrated, for one patient with one chronic disease, the diverse range of challenges that occur over even a few days. Therefore, generalizing about the 'best' way of coping is obviously futile (Lazarus, 1999). The only generalization that is realistic in this area is that the variety of challenges that serious disease brings requires a corresponding variety of types of coping responses. Clinicians' role is therefore to ensure that patients are equipped to adopt the necessary coping responses.

Apart from material resources, appropriate information and training can broaden the range of **problem-focused coping** responses that patients can deploy. For instance, careful and precise information about diet and exercise are essential for effective problem-focused coping with rehabilitation after myocardial infarction (Box 11.4). Information is not always enough: training in blood sampling and testing is crucial to management of chronic illness such as diabetes or renal failure. Effective palliative or **emotion-focused coping** also depends on knowledge and skills. For instance, patients need information about how to use analgesia correctly (Chapter 9). Training in relaxation techniques may also be necessary to reduce negative emotions and physiological arousal.

Helping patients to match ways of coping to the precise nature of challenges in chronic illness has been formalized in an educational approach called 'coping effectiveness training', which teaches basic ideas about stress and coping over several sessions (Chesney et al, 1996). Helping patients to cope better can have large effects. In rheumatoid arthritis, for instance, educational approaches of this kind can relieve symptoms as much as common anti-inflammatory drugs (Hirano et al, 1994).

7.3.5.2 The Need for an Individual Approach

Challenges differ between patients. Their objective circumstances are different, and even the same circumstances are appraised differently by different people. Therefore there are limits to what can be achieved without attention to individual patient's needs. Box 3.7 showed how challenge, coping and support could be analysed in one patient who had undergone mastectomy for breast cancer. The analysis identified challenges concerning her illness and its effect on her marriage. There was no sign of effective problem-focused coping with these challenges. Her emotion-focused coping made the challenges worse by preventing her from learning to adjust to the disease and its effects and by alienating those who might support her, including clinicians and her husband. The types of help that are needed follow directly from this analysis.

First, she needs help to analyse some of her challenges (i.e., to engage in cognitive problem-focused coping) so that she appraises them more accurately. She needs to appreciate, for instance, that her husband's lack of awareness of her needs might result from her determination not to disclose them rather than from lack of affection! Then she needs to engage in more problem-focused coping. Specifically, she needs to discuss her fears with her husband (fears about marriage) and clinicians (fears about the cancer). Depending on what she finds out, she will face decisions about whether and how to change her life. She might want to wear different clothes because of her changed shape. She might wish to learn to talk openly about her illness so that she is not burdened by the need to hide the evidence of it from other people. It is not as simple as this, of course. Before she can dislose fears to her husband or clinicians, she needs to be helped to feel more comfortable with disclosing distressing material in a protected relationship with a counsellor or another clinician who will help her to do this.

7.4 THE SOCIAL NETWORK

7.4.1 Support and Challenge in the Social Network

Friends and family have a complex role in patients' adjustment to disease. In theory, and often in practice, they provide a buffer against the negative impact of the disease, as support does in relation to stress in general

---

Box 7.7   Support and challenge in the social network

The social network provides support with the challenge of chronic illness, but also contributes to the burden. This table shows the proportion of 156 haemodialysis patients who agreed with statements about their social network (Krespi et al, 1999b). Although almost all patients felt supported by people close to them, they were also troubled by the feeling that their illness burdens their carers.

Item	%
People close to me help me to do things I can't do	83
People close to me understand how my illness affects me	83
People who look after me let me do things for myself	80
People are affectionate to me	63
People close to me are under pressure because of my illness	62
I feel sorry for people close to me	58
I feel guilty about people who look after me	53
It upsets me to see people doing things that I can't do	23
I feel bitter at people close to me	19

(Chapter 3). Support can make the difference between life and death. For instance, after a first myocardial infarction, patients are more likely to suffer a reinfarction within six months if they live alone (Case et al, 1992).

However, the social network is not a reliable source of support. Those close to the patient can be too upset to provide support. They might even have adopted a 'conspiracy of silence' about the illness (Maguire and Faulkner, 1988). Moreover, the social network is potentially a source of burden as well as support. Box 7.7 illustrates the complex role that it plays in one chronic condition: end-stage renal failure treated by haemodialysis (Krespi et al, 1999b). As well as being a source of practical and emotional support, these patients' networks impose significant emotional burdens. Particularly important is the feeling of guilt about the effects of the illness on carers. Another common problem is feeling unable to meet the expectations of others, including family, friends and clinicians (Hatchett et al, 1997). In practice, some of the expectations that patients try to meet are imagined rather than real. Nevertheless, they are powerful influences. One of the most important perceived expectations is that family, friends and other carers need to be protected from being upset by the patient's illness. One patient with cancer explained that 'I couldn't bear what it [cancer] did to the children. That was the worst part' and another that 'I've got to keep strong for him [husband]. He'll go under if I do.' This perceived need to protect other people may be very important in influencing the course of adjustment, and is discussed in Chapter 8.

7.4.2 Clinicians as Supporters

Where support from the patient's own network is limited in these ways, support from clinicians is particularly important. There is no dose–response relationship between time in contact with a clinician and the support received. Even a brief consultation can be experienced as supportive and a long one can leave the patient feeling lonely. Nevertheless, the brevity of routine clinical consultations and the lack of privacy are not ideal for forming supportive relationships. Therefore, specialist nurses have a key role in allowing the patient to express the feelings they have been prevented from expressing to other clinicians. A trained nurses' support can help patients even where the informal support of a voluntary group is ineffective (McArdle et al, 1996).

Support is not merely an end in itself. A supportive relationship provides a vehicle for monitoring the patient's needs and ensuring that they are met. Regular contact by telephone can be sufficient to identify needs that arise. In this way, a nurse's telephone follow-up of survivors of myocardial infarction has been used as the basis of a programme of targeted support which reduced subsequent mortality (Frasure-Smith and Prince, 1989).

Chapter 10 describes how clinicians' support is limited by their attempts to protect themselves from patients' distress. However, a further impediment to clinicians' support is the discontinuity of care. Where care switches between different clinicians, the opportunity to develop a disclosing relationship with any one is limited. An example is transfer from a coronary care unit to a general medical ward. Objectively, this demarcates a stage in *recovery*. By contrast, it can be experienced by patients as a *rejection* by staff. It marks a new challenge, also: the need to learn about a new setting and new staff. Therefore continuity of care from specific clinicians between the two stages eases the transition (Klein et al, 1968).

7.4.3 Clinicians as Facilitators of Patients' Support

Despite these difficulties, periods of intense clinical care can, in general, be experienced as supportive. Not only the clinicians, but also receptionists, secretaries, ambulance drivers and fellow patients are available to listen and empathize. The end of this phase of treatment, such as when radiotherapy ends following treatment for cancer, is therefore a vulnerable time. In the longer term, therefore, the clinician's role should be to help the patient to use support networks that are not dependent on clinical care. Box 3.7 described a patient who felt embittered at receiving so little support from her husband or friends. However, she did not disclose her needs to them and probably conveyed an impression of strength, confidence and independence which deterred any attempts at support. A clinician who wishes to help this patient could achieve a great deal by providing support directly. Even more would be achieved if the clinician released support in the patient's network by helping her to communicate openly with her family and friends. A more efficient way of achieving open communication in routine practice is to involve the key individuals in treatment, information giving or counselling. An intervention that includes the spouse or partner is often more effective than one that is focused on the patient alone (Keefe et al, 1996).

7.5 COGNITIVE REACTIONS TO ILLNESS

By cognitive reactions is meant the changes that illness can produce in the ways that people seek or interpret information. The previous section showed that patients' emotional feelings about illness can influence how they interpret information about their illness. However, illness also directly affects patients' thinking. These 'cognitive' reactions can be important clinical problems in their own right.

7.5.1 Making Sense of Illness

7.5.1.1 Meanings of Illness

A common response to trauma of various kinds is the attempt to find some 'meaning' in it (Debatz, 1996; Janoff-Bulman, 1992). For most patients, the starting point in finding meaning in illness is to explain the illness in some way. Cultural ideas provide many of these explanations. For instance, patients commonly explain their breast cancer as an effect of stress or suspected 'carcinogens' such as oral contraception or nuclear waste. In a significant minority of women it is blamed on an accidental blow to the breast (Taylor et al, 1984). Similarly, myocardial infarction is typically blamed on stress, lifestyle factors or genetic inheritance (Petrie and Weinman, 1997).

The 'meaning' of an illness extends, for some patients, to the belief that it is a test or a challenge for them—or even a punishment for previous misdeeds. This is a striking feature in breast cancer (Luker et al, 1996), but is probably widespread. Nearly half of a sample of haemodialysis patients blamed their renal failure on their not looking after themselves better (Krespi et al, 1999a).

7.5.1.2 Blaming Oneself

The different explanations have complex effects. To the extent that causes, such as lifestyle or stress, are within the individual's control, attributing illness to them involves an element of self-blame or of feeling that illness is a punishment. One might expect that this would lead to feelings of guilt or depression and to preoccupation with the past. These reactions might, in turn, detract from a focus on self-management for the present and future. There is some support for this view (e.g., Kiecolt-Glaser and Williams, 1987).

Nevertheless, a study of the explanations that were adopted for spinal cord injury has supported the contrary view (Bulman and Wortman, 1977). The better-adjusted patients were those who felt some responsibility for causing their injury. Similarly, non-insulin-dependent diabetic patients who blamed themselves for causing diabetes tended to have better metabolic control (Hampson, 1997). Conceivably, self-blame might help by establishing a feeling of control in an otherwise disempowering situation. In reality, it is implausible to generalize about whether self-blame is constructive or not. Instead, it is important for the clinician to appreciate that it might well be a valuable way of making sense of illness and is not necessarily harmful.

7.5.1.3 Feeling in Control

Clinically, patients' more important beliefs concern the degree of influence that they feel they have over the course rather than cause of the illness. There is a great deal of evidence that better adjustment is promoted by feelings of having some control over illness—particularly chronic illness (Scharloo and Kaptein, 1997). However, the desire to feel in control often founders on the reality of disempowerment by illness and treatment (Chapter 11). This probably explains why it was those chemotherapy patients who preferred not to feel in control who were the better adjusted to their treatment (Burish et al, 1984). Unfortunately, the realities of illness are often compounded by the unnecessary difficulties that are imposed by staff attitudes (Chapter 12).

7.5.2 Changes in Perception of the Body

Chapter 5 showed that the perception of bodily sensations depends on an active process. Beliefs and information from several sources are brought to bear on the task. Having an illness, and being anxious about it (see above) are a major influence on this process. The influence is particularly important where the illness is chronic or where the patient views it as leaving a lasting vulnerability to further problems. Because patients are incorporating specific information and experience into their attempts to make sense of bodily sensations, the effects of different illnesses inevitably differ markedly. Therefore the effects will be illustrated by the ways that two kinds of disease influence perception of the body.

7.5.2.1 Cancer

Fears of disease recurrence are common in patients who have been treated for cancer (Lee-Jones et al, 1997). Therefore, whereas a lump under the skin would normally be disregarded, it can be a serious challenge to the patient who is in remission from cancer. It is not only the *interpretation* of sensations that is changed. Perception involves attentional processes also (Chapter 5), and these respond to fears and beliefs. Heightened attention, or vigilance, to signs of recurrence may extend to active and regular searching for sensations that might indicate disease recurrence (Lee-Jones et al, 1997). An example is the patient who, after being treated for cancer, regularly and exhaustively palpates the body surface searching for signs of unfamiliar lumps.

Patients' feelings of vulnerability to disease change in ways that do not necessarily reflect medical knowledge. For instance, concern that symptoms indicate cancer is increased by symptoms which, although unrelated to cancer, increase people's fears of vulnerability generally (Easterling and Leventhal, 1989).

7.5.2.2 Heart Disease

Similar processes occur after myocardial infarction, but with rather different consequences for patients' lives. Reflecting cultural beliefs about heart disease, many patients blame their heart attack on stress (Petrie and Weinman, 1997). Unfortunately, stress is widely misunderstood (Chapter 3). Therefore patients typically avoid any sensation of exertion or arousal because they perceive them as dangerous symptoms. The result can be a state of 'invalidism' whereby patients restrict their activities far beyond what is necessary or desirable. Indeed, the consequent boredom or frustration and focusing of attention on bodily symptoms further exacerbates stress.

It is not only the patient whose perceptual processes are influenced by illness. Those of the patient's family, too, are changed. For instance, the spouses of patients who have suffered myocardial infarction tend to share the patients' beliefs (Petrie and Weinman, 1997). Where these beliefs concern the dangers of exertion and stress, the spouse's fears reinforce invalidism. However, these culturally based beliefs can be countered by carefully presented clinical evidence (see Box 11.4). For instance, the spouse can undergo a supervised treadmill test along with the patient so as directly to experience the level of activity and exertion that the patient can safely manage (Taylor et al, 1985).

7.6 CONCLUSION

This brief analysis shows the diverse, and sometimes paradoxical, ways that individuals respond to illness. In particular, the clinician should be ready to accept a variety of emotions as normal reactions to illness, and to help the patient, also, to accept them. A second implication for the clinician is the need for a considered response to reactions by the patient that are apparently irrational. The response must be based on an appreciation of the psychological mechanisms that account for apparently puzzling responses. Patients who become angry about non-threatening events or who disregard important information are unlikely to be helped by simple repetition of the clinician's view. Hearing distressing information emphasized or repeated is likely to strengthen the psychological defences that are used against it. A better response to a defensive patient would be to help the patient to find a more effective way of coping with the information. Similarly, patients who are inappropriately vigilant will not be helped by restating reassurance. Instead, they need information which can help them to find an alternative and non-threatening way of understanding worrying symptoms or events (Chapter 11).

KEY POINTS

- Physical disease has emotional and cognitive effects.
- Emotional effects are responses to the challenges associated with illness and treatment.
- Why an illness or procedure is challenging may only be apparent when the patient's beliefs about it are understood.

- Challenges of chronic disease include responsibility for medical treatment, continuing obligations to family and society, coping with limitations and pretending to be cheerful.
- Some perplexing reactions by patients, such as disregarding important advice by clinicians, or being angry with them, are attempts to cope with emotional challenges surrounding disease.
- Depression can be fatal in chronic disease.
- Clinicians provide support directly and by facilitating open communication with family and carers.
- Depression often resolves if support and opportunities for effective problem-oriented coping are available.
- Counselling can help to overcome depression that is 'stuck' or that is compromising care.
- Patients make sense of illness in diverse ways. Self-blame is not necessarily harmful.
- Illness changes the way that patients attend and respond to information from their bodies. Cardiac invalidism is one result.

Chapter 8

CHRONIC ILLNESS, DYING AND BEREAVEMENT: STAGES AND CYCLES OF ADAPTATION

KEY CLINICAL ISSUES

- What's wrong with talking about someone 'getting over' a crisis such as bereavement or serious diagnosis?
- Why do patients often not seem to take in what they are told in hospital after diagnosis?
- How is it that seriously ill patients are often as satisfied with life as healthy people?
- How should a clinician respond to a patient who refuses to 'accept' an incurable diagnosis?
- Can people adjust well to bereavement if they do not grieve?

8.1 THE COPING PROCESS

The approach to coping taken in Chapter 7 is sufficient for episodes of acute, time-limited illness and treatment. Although it is a start to understanding the coping response where disease is serious and chronic, it does not go far enough. However, to understand adaptation to such a major challenge, coping must be regarded as a *process* rather than as a one-off response (Chapter 3). Therefore, we need to consider how coping develops and changes over time, as the process of coping changes what it is that the patient is having to cope with and adapt to. This chapter will return to some of the elements of patients' reactions to illness that were introduced in Chapter 7, and it will examine how their significance changes over time.

Many of the effects of illness are common to other challenges that people face. In particular, there are major challenges that occur in health care that resemble chronic illness in one important respect. They are so profound

Box 8.1   Adjustment to crisis: from past to future orientation

Adjustment to serious illness, bereavement or the certainty of death each require a shift from orientation to the past to orientation to a future that is very different from the past. Each orientation means confronting the challenge. By contrast, denial provides a way of withdrawing from it. In the course of adjustment, movement between these three positions can be in any direction, any number of times. For different challenges each position is represented by different behaviours, examples of which are shown here.

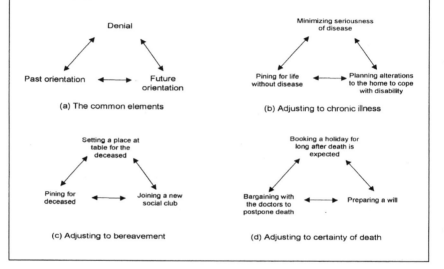

(a) The common elements

(b) Adjusting to chronic illness

(c) Adjusting to bereavement

(d) Adjusting to certainty of death

that those experiencing them cannot return to living in exactly the same way that they did before. That is, people are changed psychologically by the challenge. These include being told that a disease will be fatal and being bereaved. Not surprisingly, adjustment to all these challenges shows similar features (Box 8.1). Adjustment to chronic illness will be considered in detail before examining the similarities with adjustment to dying and bereavement.

8.2 CHRONIC ILLNESS

8.2.1 From Shock to Assimilation

Shontz (1975) provided a useful description of elements of adaptation to chronic disease that distinguishes three stages. The starting point for most patients is **shock**, particularly where the diagnosis was unexpected. At this time, they are bewildered, detached and typically behave automatically without any clear thought or analysis about what is happening. This reaction develops into an **encounter** reaction in which emotional distress and feelings of loss and despair are overwhelming. Denial of the reality or seriousness of the problem characterizes the third phase, of **retreat**. Finally the patient becomes **reoriented** to the reality of the disease and its implications. According to this theory, psychological adjustment is dynamic. This means that the reaction at any time point sets the scene for future reactions. In particular, retreating from the challenge protects the patient from being overwhelmed by the intensity of distress associated with the encounter stage. However, retreat is important for the future, too. It provides the base from which the patient can engage with reality in a gradual, controlled way so as to become reoriented to the changed demands of life.

8.2.2 Stages of Adaptation in Clinical Practice

Although many patients clearly do respond in the sequence that Shontz (1975) described many, equally clearly, do not. Adaptation to a chronic illness rarely occurs in a single step. It occurs repeatedly in response to new losses and challenges (Charmaz, 1995). For some patients, one or other stage is missed. For others, stages are revisited repeatedly. The main value of Shontz's account is therefore not that it establishes a trajectory that every patient must follow—it does not. Instead it highlights two fundamental and opposing processes that underlie adjustment. One is confrontation with the illness and its implications (represented by past orientation and future orientation in Box 8.1). The other is withdrawal (represented by denial in Box 8.1). The apparently very different and rapidly changing clinical pictures that patients can present after diagnosis of a chronic illness result from the balance of these processes.

Stage theories do, though, have practical value for clinicians working with patients and their families. First, they provide a framework for assessing individual patients' adjustment. Secondly, the notion of stages provides a source of reassurance for patients and carers. It can be explained that 'stages' are part of a dynamic process so that, with appropriate support, negative reactions should be expected to give way to other ways of coping.

Thirdly, identifying the stage that a patient is in should be a prerequisite to any intervention—including providing information. Unfortunately, patients tend to receive most information about their condition when shock, intense encounter or retreat prevent their accepting it. For instance, after myocardial infarction, patients receive a great deal of information while they are still in hospital. However, many are in a retreat stage at this time, using avoidance to cope with the challenge. These patients gain least from the information (Shaw et al, 1985).

8.2.3 The Need for Denial

This theory helps to understand some of the observations in previous chapters about the value of denial, which underlies the retreat stage. In Box 8.1, denial facilitates the gradual shift in emphasis from past to future orientation by providing an escape from each. Denial has been studied in particular detail after myocardial infarction. Frank emotional disturbance at this time predicts a poor outcome—in terms of psycho-social functioning, at least (Bennett and Carroll, 1997; Philip, 1988). Therefore, denial can improve outcome by protecting people from emotional disturbance (Hackett and Cassem, 1973; Levine et al, 1987). However, this might be at the expense of poorer adaptation in the longer term (Levine et al, 1987). In breast cancer, too, there is some evidence that patients who react by denial are those who go on to survive for longer (Pettingale et al, 1985). Therefore, denial does not, in itself, indicate a clinical problem. It requires attention when it is so prolonged or so intense that it disrupts clinical management or self-care, or when it disrupts relationships with carers.

Because denial is a way of coping with challenge, it is rare that it can be reduced simply by confronting patients with the facts of their diagnosis. By accentuating the threat, this risks merely strengthening the denial. Instead, it will be important to help by addressing the threat. This will require the clinician to identify the components of the threat for any particular patient and to assess the coping and support resources available (Box 3.7).

8.2.4 Assimilation of Illness

Shontz's (1975) account culminates in the stage of 'reorientation' in which the patient becomes aware of the reality of living with impairment and begins to work out a new way of life. However, there are changes in the way patients see themselves, also. Although it is often used, the term 'confronting' serious illness is misleading. The word suggests an encounter between two parties in which one wins and the other is defeated. The effect of major chronic illness is more complicated than this. Lifespan developmental theory helps in understanding why.

8.2.4.1 Developmental Transitions in Adulthood

Lifespan theory is a body of psychological theory that describes how emotional development takes place in adults. According to the theory, adults progress through stages of emotional development, continuing the development of childhood and adolescence. In adulthood, however, the timing of stages is less dependent on age than on exposure to challenges, including illness. An important stage of adult development revolves around the effects of becoming aware of one's mortality. It is reached by resolving the tension between two forces. One is the despair associated with fear of death and regret at lost opportunities. The other is the need to retain a sense of personal completeness and fulfilment (Erikson et al, 1986; Levinson, 1990). The prize for resolving these tensions is described in slightly different ways in different theories. In general, though, the prize is seen as a personal view of oneself and the world which is richer than the preceding view, which accepts mortality and which values elements of oneself and one's experience that had previously been disregarded.

8.2.4.2 Serious Illness as a Developmental Transition

Diagnosis of serious physical illness, such as cancer, is the kind of event that challenges people's assumptions about life and what is important in it (Weisman and Worden, 1976). As one patient described, 'I think it's [cancer] just brought me down to earth a bit really . . . Life isn't something you can just take for granted' (Byrne et al, 1998). Therefore, diagnosis would be expected to bring forward the kind of developmental transition that occurs naturally with ageing (Salmon et al, 1996a). Indeed, many patients with cancer describe it as, in part, a positive experience and say that life has improved in important ways, typically because its meaning or purpose has been clarified in the face of illness (Salmon et al, 1996a; Cohen and Mount, 1992; Collins et al, 1990; Box 8.2). There is some evidence that elements of assimilation are common in patients with incurable or serious diseases. They attach more value than other people to family and other relationships (Kreitler et al, 1993), and to spiritual matters (O'Connor et al, 1990; Reed, 1987). Health becomes less important to them (O'Boyle et al, 1992), showing the minimization effect described in Chapter 7. It is not only cancer that elicits these changes. A survey of myocardial infarction patients found that more rated their lives as improved than worsened, and most saw some positive changes (Laerum et al, 1987). Half of a group of haemodialysis patients ques-

---

Box 8.2 Negative and positive reactions to cancer

These are some of the feelings that 200 patients with incurable cancers of various kinds described, and the percentages who endorsed each feeling (Salmon et al, 1996). Feelings include fears and resentments (top panel), but also ways in which the illness has added to life or enriched it (bottom panel).

Illness as a source of fear, resentment and indignity

I'm worried I'll be a burden	50%
I expect illness to cause pain in the future	49%
It feels unfair that I have this illness	46%
My illness has upset important plans	43%
I'm embarrassed about illness and treatment	27%
I'm frightened of what dying will be like	22%
I'm a great burden to people	16%

Enrichment of life by illness

Every day there is something I enjoy	87%
I appreciate things more than I did	81%
Minor upsets bother me less now	72%
There are people I feel closer to now	65%
I have a much clearer idea now what is important in life	62%
Something good has come out of my illness	45%
My illness has helped free me from doing things	24%

---

tionned by Krespi et al (1999b) described themselves as having become more sensitive to other people because of their illness. This way of adjusting can be termed 'assimilation' of the illness. The patient does not 'overcome' the disease, but is changed by the encounter.

8.2.4.3 Assimilation as a Stage of Adjustment

Assimilation probably does permit happier adjustment. Chronically ill patients who saw their illness as an opportunity for personal growth were happier than those who coped by blame and avoidance (Felton et al, 1984). This kind of adjustment therefore allows many seriously ill patients to preserve a level of life satisfaction that is as good as that in healthy or less seriously ill people.

The clinician should therefore be ready to facilitate a patient's assimilation (Box 8.3). However, not all patients with serious or incurable disease react by assimilation and there is no basis for arguing that assimilation

Box 8.3   Assimilating a crisis

X had been in intensive care a year ago for 12 weeks following an infection contracted after surgery. Her surgeon and nurses thought she was still depressed and referred her for psychological help. She said that she knew that her medical problems were behind her, and that she did not know why she had not got over them. She said that she could not find the energy to do the things she used to do. Before her illness she used to be very proud of keeping her house clean and tidy but now was too tired. She said that she should have cleaned her carpets and curtains six months ago but had not been able to. (Later, she agreed that she did, in fact, keep her home adequately; it was safe and hygienic, although less tidy than before.) She cried as she talked and repeatedly apologized for this. She said that the illness must have weakened her body and she could not see any prospect of her strength returning.

X's problems of adjustment to her illness are added to by her guilt and anxiety about having these problems. She feels that she 'should not' have them. Discussion is easier once the psychologist explains that: people can take many months, and sometimes a year or two, to get over a major, life-threatening illness; that it is much easier when people have help; and that it is good that she has come for help; it was a brave decision for her because she obviously finds it difficult to talk about these things. With further discussion, the following points emerge.

'Lack of energy' is a metaphor for lack of motivation. X is saying that she no longer *wants* to do some of the things that she used to think important. Since leaving hospital she has changed her views of what is important and fulfilling. Housework no longer seems as important as it did. Things she now values more than she did include time with her husband and friends and in her garden. She has begun to think that she should achieve more in life.

In time, X came to accept that she had not *lost* motivation for life, but had *changed her sources* of motivation. By planning each day some activity that she valued, and being helped to feel positive about these activities, X was able to recover positive feelings about herself. She saw her illness as having given her the opportunity to review her life.

'should' be the final stage of adjustment. Some become more alienated from those around them or disillusioned with life. The factors that explain which path adjustment takes have not been systematically researched. One possible influence will emerge from examining, below, the role of the social network in adjustment.

8.2.5 The Social Context: 'Fighting' Illness to Protect Others

Chapter 7 showed that the social network has a complex role in patients' adjustment to disease, providing both support and additional challenges. Patients feel guilty at the effects of their illness on family and other carers

---

Box 8.4   Fighting for whom?

Fighting and protecting others

Listening to patients with cancer reveals two important attitudes to the illness (Byrne et al, 1999a). One is that 'You've just got to fight it.' The second is concern with the suffering of others who are affected by the patient's illness. Often this is described as more serious than patients' own suffering: 'I couldn't bear what it did to other people. That was the worst part of it.' Patients describe strenuous attempts to protect others: 'I go and see people and friends. Oh, you look great [they say] but I don't tell them that I don't feel great. I don't like to burden them you know, have them worrying about me.'

Fighting to protect others

It is usually assumed that 'fighting' is a way that patients look after their own needs. However, it often seems to be a way to protect others: 'I think with having young children, that's helped me more, you know what I mean, to fight. . . . I've watched my girl and they've been sobbing inside because you're so ill and they have to watch you. And you have to watch them and you think to yourself "I have got to get better because it's not fair for those who have to watch." So you just sort of try to get better for their sake so that they've got no worry, so they're not worrying about you all the time making them upset.'

Therefore fighting comes to mean 'fighting back the tears' so that others do not see the patient's suffering.

---

and try hard to protect these carers from their own suffering and distress. The patient in Box 8.3 apologized repeatedly for crying in front of the clinician.

The concept of fighting spirit was introduced in Chapter 4 because it has become central in theories of coping with cancer. Cancer is notorious for being viewed as a malign invading force that has to be fought (Sontag, 1978), and 'fighting' cancer is part of the ordinary language that surrounds the disease. In fact, the language of fighting is applied to disease quite generally. It is a natural corollary of the 'externalizing' of disease whereby it is regarded as an alien threat, separate from the body (Chapter 5). Close scrutiny of the ways that patients with cancer describe fighting suggests that it is not always motivated by their own personal needs (Box 8.4). Many patients clearly fight in order to protect other people from being distressed by their disease. For them, fighting means *fighting the appearance of emotional distress* rather than fighting the disease. Carers, including clinicians, often conspire with patients to encourage fighting in this sense (Box 8.5). This is probably often a way of protecting the clinician rather than the patient.

Box 8.5   Keeping emotion out of the clinic

Interpersonal processes keep the emotional cost of disease out of the oncology clinic (Byrne et al, 1999a).

Social conventions of greeting preserve the *appearance* that clinicians are interested in the patients' well-being. However, patients view these conventions as prompts to report that they are fine rather than as invitations to disclose distress: 'They [nurses] never talk about the down side of things. They say "How are you?" and you say "Fine" and the doctor says "How are you?" and you say "Yes, alright, you know" but if you say "No I'm not" and burst into tears, you feel so embarrassed then.'

Clinicians also conspire with relatives to minimize emotional expression: 'My wife said the best advice she was given was from a doctor who said "Under no circumstances show him [patient] you are upset. You have to be strong for him."' Another patient said '"I don't want anybody knowing about this' and he [the doctor] said "No, don't worry. Nobody has got to know."'

How might working to protect others influence patients' own adjustment? One possibility is that minimizing patients' emotional expression in this way and foreclosing open communication about their needs interrupts the course of adjustment and prevents progression to assimilation (Byrne et al, 1998). Being released from the need to protect others is an important feature of hospice care, in which open and honest communication is a central principle. Therefore hospice care permits a level of satisfaction with care in terminal illness that is rarely possible in conventional hospital settings (Kane et al, 1984). Rather than urge patients to fight, the clinician who wishes to facilitate the patient's adjustment needs to help the patient and carers to accept that it is safe and important to communicate emotional feelings. The difficulties in openly expressing emotion in such a way in health care settings are considered further in Chapter 10.

8.2.6 Adjusting to Treatment

Just as adjustment to the *negative* impact of *disease* changes over time, the clinician should expect to see complementary patterns of adjustment to the *positive* impact of *treatment*. Cycles of response to the start of haemodialysis, at least, do appear to mirror responses to diagnosis (Reichsman and Levy, 1972). After an immediate improvement in emotional feelings and physical state, a period of disillusion and discouragement reflects appreciation of the limits of what treatment can achieve. Acceptance of these limitations leads to the final stage of adjustment and contentment. Unfortunately, clinicians are often misled by the immediate and transient emotional response to treatment, and believe that patients' depression or anxiety has resolved.

8.3 DYING

8.3.1 The Challenges of Death and Dying

Very young children's accounts of death describe a state which is similar to sleeping and therefore not final. From the age of about five years, a final and concrete view of death emerges although, at first, this is often based on magical or supernatural ideas rather than biological ones. Despite the long-standing view that developmental progression leads inexorably towards a mature 'adult' view of death (Nagy, 1948), the reality of adult views is that they retain all the elements of children's thinking—as do their views of illness (Chapter 6). These are combined into a diversity of ways of understanding death which, in a multicultural country, range from annihilation, through sleeping, to reincarnation or transition to an afterlife. These beliefs concern the state of being dead. Patients also have beliefs about the process of dying. These have sometimes been formed from images of agonizing deaths in the media or from watching the painful deaths of relatives in the past. Some patients' fears of dying are exacerbated by practical concerns for the needs of surviving family—or even pets.

A clinician who wishes to help a patient or a family to cope with the patient's impending death will first need to explore how they appraise the challenge; that is, to understand what they believe and fear about death and dying. However, whatever the details of the challenge, its enormity to most people means that it has much in common with adjusting to chronic illness.

8.3.2 Adjusting to the Certainty of Death

8.3.2.1 Stages in Adjustment

A great many deaths in Western medical care are predicted for weeks or months in advance. Clinicians and other carers therefore need guidance about the emotional changes to expect and how they should help. Understandably, there is little quantitative scientific evidence in this area. Therefore it can be helpful to think of the needs of the dying patient according to an influential scheme described by Kubler-Ross (1970). She outlined five distinct types of response in patients who know that they are dying. The **shock** of discovering that death is inevitable is followed by **denial**. This takes varying degrees and forms, from asserting that medical results are mistaken, through to the feeling of being a spectator of events that are happening to someone else. It is important to distinguish between the situation where a patient has elected for denial and the common situation where carers' failure to accept the inevitability of death has hidden the prognosis from the patient (Prigerson, 1992).

The stage of **anger** centres around the protestation 'Why me?' Anger is, of course, directed at anyone who is available, particularly those who are healthy. Close friends and family typically bear the brunt of it because they are less protected than are others from social obligations upon the patient to be polite. **Bargaining** is a more directed response to the feelings of injustice aroused by the threat of death. It refers to attempts to secure a respite from the certainty of death. The bargaining might be with God or fate, or with clinicians to whom patients often offer anything they can in return for a promise of hope. Alternatively, accepting that death is inevitable, while also feeling that it is random and unjust, leads to **depression**. Finally, resignation, compounded by physical weakness, is the basis of the state of **acceptance**. Acceptance can have a more positive quality, where the patient feels a sense of closure or completeness to life, or that a degree of immortality will be gained through God or through their legacy to their children or others. Kubler-Ross (1970) presented these reactions as stages in a sequence from denial to acceptance, by way of anger, bargaining and depression.

8.3.2.2 Stages in Clinical Practice

The proposed sequence of stages is of less value to the clinician than the descriptions of the stages themselves. There is little scientific support for the sequence, and clinical experience shows that patients can pass through any number of these stages in any sequence or not at all (Box 8.1). A patient can even display features of more than one stage at a time. However, as with Shontz's theory (above), this stage theory is valuable for clinicians working with patients and their families and other carers. It provides a framework for assessment. It also provides a basis for helping carers to understand distressing reactions such as anger or denial in a patient. They can often be explained as natural ways of coping with this most extreme challenge of all. Family can be reassured that a patient's reaction at any time is part of a dynamic process in which it may give way to other reactions. Therefore, the family that wishes to address the implications of death with the patient may need help to wait until the patient is ready. Similarly, they can be reassured that the patient who has resumed denial or anger has not negated all that the family has achieved in discussing practical issues surrounding death when the patient was more accepting.

Kubler-Ross's stages also provide a structure within which to assess the clinical needs of dying patients and their families. Denial, anger or depression do not *necessarily* indicate a clinical problem. They do require attention when they are so prolonged or so intense as to disrupt clinical management, when they disrupt relationships within the family or where the patient is 'stuck' in a way of adjustment that is distressing to the patient or family.

The responses described by Kubler-Ross are ways of coping with challenge. Therefore problems of denial are not managed simply by confronting patients with the facts of prognosis. Instead, it is necessary to help them cope better with the challenge. For this, a clinician will need to identify the components of the challenge for an individual patient. As observed above, it should not be assumed that the principal threat is always the state of death. Fears of dying will typically be more important (Parkes, 1998). Discovering the patient's beliefs about dying and reassuring the patient about modern techniques to manage pain are therefore typically among the clinician's first tasks.

8.4 BEREAVEMENT

8.4.1 The Challenge of Bereavement: 'Appropriate' and 'Inappropriate' Responses

Culturally, there is a strong emphasis on responding 'appropriately' to death of a family member or close friend. The reality is very different (Wright, 1991). When a relative or close friend dies, it is often the worst event ever to have happened to an individual, so reactions to it cannot be shaped by prior experience and are so severe that they are often beyond shaping by cultural convention. Responses to bereavement therefore include many that are regarded by onlookers as 'inappropriate'. As well as feeling distressed and abandoned, survivors may feel guilty for real or imagined failures to protect the deceased from death. Anger can be directed at staff, other relatives or even the deceased. Other 'inappropriate' responses include laughter or trivial comments that reflect psychological defences or conflicting emotions.

8.4.2 Stages of Adjustment

Once again, an account of stages is available (Parkes, 1972), and this provides a way of understanding a set of reactions which might otherwise appear bewildering. These stages, although based on studies of reactions to death of a close person, can be detected after losses of many kinds, including miscarriage, losses of function that occur with progressive diseases, loss of a limb to amputation or of a breast to mastectomy. The proposed stages, unsurprisingly, are similar to those suggested, above, to follow other challenges. The initial reaction to the **shock** of bereavement is **denial and emotional numbness**. Then a state of yearning, or **pining**, is associated with intense images of the deceased and, commonly, with thinking that the deceased is present. Accepting loss brings **despair**, with attendant emotional reactions including depression, resentment or anger. A common reaction to the loss is to blame someone. Feelings of guilt and self-blame, and anger with the deceased, are therefore common. The end point, **reorganization**, involves 'letting go' but also adopting a new sense of meaning in life and, indeed, a new way of life.

8.4.3 Stages in Clinical Practice

The stages constitute rules of thumb and should not be seen as a basis for simplistic assumptions. For instance, although distress and yearning are *common*, there is little evidence that they are *necessary* (Wortman and Silver, 1989). Similarly, although the view that the 'work of grief' is important dates back to Freud (and resembles the emphasis on 'work of worry' in coping with surgical and other stress: Chapter 12), adjustment is not necessarily impaired by suppressing grief (Stroebe and Stroebe, 1991). On the other hand, clinicians see many patients who *wish* to express such feelings about their loss, but are *inhibited* by their beliefs about what is appropriate or what listeners will tolerate. We have already seen, above, that an emphasis on protecting other people might impede adjustment to chronic illness. The same process would be expected in adjustment to dying or bereavement.

These stages, like those in adjustment to disease or the certainty of death, are not an inevitable progression. They indicate two separate internal processes (Box 8.1). One is the struggle between the opposing pressures to cope by denial versus engaging with the reality of the loss. The second process sees a shift in the balance of engagement with the loss from past to future orientation. Because these processes are often finely balanced, external events, moods or thoughts can influence the 'stage' that is adopted. For instance, anniversaries and other events can quickly swing the balance from a future orientation to a focus on the past.

The clinician's task with the bereaved person is therefore normally to facilitate and accept the reactions that are appropriate for that individual. This means ensuring that the bereaved person is not inhibited by the fears that are commonly associated with being open and with expressing feelings—particularly to clinicians. It means also helping the bereaved to accept their own reactions, and to avoid seeing them as signs of 'not coping' or of being 'selfish' or 'shameful'. It may be necessary to explain that the process of grief can take years rather than months.

8.5 CONCLUSION

Serious illness, death and bereavement each confront people with intense challenges because they threaten fundamental assumptions about their lives. It is therefore unsurprising that clinicians studying each have provided similar accounts of the process of coping and adjustment (Box 8.1). Each embodies a struggle between preoccupation with the past and facing the future. In each, also, denial in various forms provides a crucial escape in allowing respite from either task. Each patient or family member will trace his or her own route between these elements of adjustment. The clinician will need to understand and facilitate this individual process rather than impose assumptions about the 'correct' course to follow.

KEY POINTS

- Challenges that are so great that people are changed psychologically by the process of coping with them include diagnosis of chronic illness, bereavement and impending death.
- Ways of adjusting to these challenges reflect the balance of two pressures: withdrawing from the challenge and confronting it.
- In general, confrontation progresses from past to future orientation.
- Denial allows the individual to withdraw and provides a base from which the challenge can gradually be confronted.
- Patients can become 'stuck' in denial or depression that threatens clinical care, relationships or morale.
- Because there are no 'correct' ways of adjusting, the clinician should assess individuals' needs and facilitate their own way of adjusting.
- By protecting family and carers, patients' own adjustment can be distorted. Clinicians often conspire in this.

Part III

TREATMENT

Chapter 9

CLINICIANS' DECISIONS AND PATIENTS' ADHERENCE

KEY CLINICAL ISSUES

- Given the same information, would a computer make the same decision as a clinician?
- Why do clinicians sometimes make the wrong decisions?
- Why do patients often not follow advice that could save their lives?

9.1 AIMS OF CLINICAL COMMUNICATION

Chapter 2 introduced the differing—and sometimes contradictory—views of clinicians' role that society and individual patients hold. These views have led to different expectations for how clinicians should communicate with patients.

The traditional picture of consultation has been that it brings an inexpert patient together with an expert professional. This defines the role of each clearly. The clinician must gather the necessary information, decide an appropriate response and tell the patient exactly what to do. The patient should comply. Because of growing awareness of the limitations of an expert, authority-based model, an alternative view has developed according to which the clinician and patient should be seen as partners. This is examined in Chapter 10. The present chapter examines the sets of expectations on the modern clinician that arise from the traditional view of expert consultation: that clinicians should make expert decisions and that they should ensure patient adherence to these.

9.2 MAKING EXPERT DECISIONS

9.2.1 Decision Making as a Mathematical Process

Few decisions in health care are so obvious that, in the presence of certain indicators, a specific response should inevitably follow. Most decisions have to be made from information which is not cut-and-dried. Nevertheless, ways have been described whereby decisions can be made so logically and rationally that computers can be programmed to make them. These methods have been applied mainly to doctors' diagnoses and treatment decisions. For instance, a diagnosis can be decided by following a sytematic procedure. First, identify all the relevant pieces of information (including symptoms, age, gender and so on), then establish the probabilities that link each piece of information to different diseases and, finally, weigh together the probabilities to discover which disease is most likely (Schwartz and Griffin, 1986). Similarly, a treatment can be decided by weighing the desirability or undesirability of different outcomes against the probabilities that they would happen as a result of each of the possible treatment decisions (Rowe et al, 1998; see Box 9.2).

Where decisions made like this have been compared with those made by clinicians acting intuitively (especially inexperienced ones), the mathematical approach has proved the more accurate (Schwartz and Griffin, 1986; Meehl, 1986). This kind of evidence indicates that clinicians' intuitive decision making does not naturally follow an objective, mathematical process. What are the factors that distort decisions?

9.2.2 Decision Making as Hypothesis Testing

First, many decisions are not made in the single step that occurs in mathematical procedures. Instead, a process typically occurs whereby hypotheses are formed and then tested and evaluated. In complex diagnoses and treatment decisions this hypothetico-deductive process is often explicit. The failure of one decision feeds back into the process and stimulates the testing of alternative decisions. Even within a few minutes of the start of a consultation, the doctor generally has a small number of diagnoses (hypotheses) in mind, including the one that is finally chosen. This hypothetico-deductive process is not intrinsically unreliable. Indeed, it has been the essence of scientific method in natural sciences. However, it opens the clinician's decision making to a number of biases. People tend not to test hypotheses in the way that scientific method requires—by trying to *disprove* them. Instead they selectively seek evidence that *fits* them (Wason and Johnson-Laird, 1972). This means that a clinician who suspects a certain disease would be more likely to look for evidence that is *consistent* with the disease than evidence that might *eliminate* it as an explanation. In this way, a hypothesis that comes to mind early in the process might not be rejected as early as it should.

9.2.3 Short Cuts in Decision Making

The mathematical approach and the hypothetico-deductive model each regard decision making as a rational process. That is, they assume that it is based on reason and logic. This rational view requires a further assumption that necessary resources (particularly time and ability) are available. However, ordinary day-to-day decision making is often severely constrained by practical limitations on knowledge, intellectual ability or time. In practice, therefore, decision making is often aimed, not at making the 'correct' decision, but merely a 'good enough' one (Rowe et al, 1998).

One way in which decision making is simplified in practice is by using **heuristics**. These are rules of thumb which, although often helpful, can mislead. For instance, a common heuristic is 'representativeness'. The kind of error that this can lead to is illustrated in Box 9.1. A piece of evidence is (wrongly) taken to indicate the presence of a disease because it is (correctly) known to be common in people with that disease. The critical knowledge for the clinician in this situation is to know *the probability that pathology is present, given that symptoms have occurred*. However, clinical texts and clinical training tend to begin with pathology and then examine the signs and symptoms that are associated with it. That is, they emphasize the *probability of symptoms, given that the pathology is present* (Eddy, 1982).

Decision making is also simplified by using **stereotypes**. These are ways of viewing categories of individual, such as 'patients who complain', the 'elderly', 'attractive' patients or 'heart-sink' patients. The stereotypes mask patients' individual characteristics and needs but nevertheless shape responses to them (Roter and Hall, 1992).

These biases do not reflect negligence or sloppiness. They meet a need to simplify complex decision-making problems. Therefore, rather than simply expect clinicians to do without these short cuts, alternative ways of simplifying decisions are needed. The increasing use of decision protocols offers one approach (Drife, 1993).

9.2.4 Clinicians' Beliefs and Errors

The different beliefs that patients hold help to explain their different responses to symptoms and treatment (Chapters 5 and 6). Variability in clinicians' beliefs has similar effects. Clinicians do have different beliefs about disease. In the extreme case, doctors differ in their belief as to

---

Box 9.1 Short cuts to decision making

Intuitive decision making does not always reproduce decisions that would be made by objective, mathematical procedures (Eddy and Clanton, 1982).

Imagine you are a specialist who is seeing a patient, Mr X, where the GP has identified a risk of cancer which requires investigation. You know that there is only a 1% (0.01) probability of cancer in someone of this patient's age and sex, and with X's history of smoking etc. You send him for a test, which turns out positive; that is, it indicates that cancer is present. You then check on the accuracy of the test. You find that it correctly identifies 90% of malignant lesions. What is the probability that X has cancer?

Most readers (and most doctors) will estimate around 90%, but this would be wrong. This answer falsely equates the probability of having cancer, given a positive test result p(cancer | positive test) with the probability of having a positive test result, given that cancer is present p(positive test | cancer). The correct answer is that you cannot tell. You need one more piece of information: the probability of the positive test result in men presenting like this, regardless of whether or not they have cancer. Suppose this is 10% (0.1). The probability that the patient does have cancer is given by a formula called Bayes' theorem:

$$p(\text{cancer | positive test result}) = p(\text{cancer}) \times p(\text{positive test result | cancer})/p(\text{positive test result})$$

$$p = 0.01 \times 0.90/0.1 = 0.9$$

There is a 9% chance that X has cancer.

---

whether a disease exists, such as occurs with chronic fatigue (Fitzgibbon et al, 1997). There are variable beliefs about treatment, too. For instance, the inadequacy of some inpatients' analgesic regimes reflects some doctors' and nurses' beliefs that analgesia is dangerous (for example, because of the risk of addiction), or that its purpose is not to abolish pain but to reduce it to a tolerable level (Lander, 1990; Lavies et al, 1992; see below).

There is worrying disagreement in decisions that different doctors make from the same evidence, and even between decisions made by the same doctor but at different times (Schwartz and Griffin, 1986). It is implausible that all this variability can be explained by systematic biases of the sort considered in this chapter. The nature of any human judgement is that a margin of error is attached to it. Nevertheless, overconfidence appears to characterize medical judgements (Schwartz and Griffin, 1986). Confidence is a feature of nurses' assessments, too (Byrne et al, 1999b).

9.2.5 Emotional Influences on Decisions

9.2.5.1 Motivation for Decision Making

Decision making is an 'effortful' task. Therefore, it is not surprising that poor morale impairs it—as it would impair any complex task (Isen et al, 1991). There is also evidence that decision making is less careful, or that care is of poorer quality, for individual patients that are disliked, and for culturally devalued groups such as the elderly (Haug and Ory, 1987) or the poor (Epstein et al, 1985).

9.2.5.2 Emotional Biases

Complex decisions can be broken down into component decisions. 'Decision analysis' of this kind can lead to decisions that diverge from those made intuitively by doctors (Elstein et al, 1986; Box 9.2). Decision analysis is a rational, logical model of decision making. Therefore it assumes that how desirable or undesirable an outcome is (such as the patient being cured or killed) is independent of what causes it (e.g., the doctor or the illness). However, clinicians probably attach more weight to bad outcomes for which they are responsible than to similar outcomes that arise naturally, i.e., from the disease process (Ayton et al, 1997). The premium on avoiding responsibility for bad outcomes is shown by evidence about risky decisions (McNeil et al, 1982). These are heavily influenced by whether the decision is presented as one about the chances of *saving* lives (in which case risky decisions are more likely) or about the risks of *losing* lives (in which case they are less likely). The desire to avoid responsibility for bad outcomes is not, of course, specifically a clinical bias. Clinicians share it with ordinary people (Tversky and Kahneman, 1981).

These findings remind us that decision making in health care is not the purely cognitive activity that we often suppose it is. Decisions about patients' lives and well-being are psychological challenges with emotional costs. Avoiding responsibility for harmful consequences is one way of coping with these costs (Chapter 10). Clinicians' overconfidence (above)

Box 9.2 Decision analysis

Whether and how to provide oestrogen replacement to menopausal women depends on weighing different effects of treatment: *reducing* symptoms; *reducing* risk of fractures; and *increasing* the risk of cancer. The first stage in a decision analysis is to make the different possible outcomes explicit, as in this decision tree (Elstein et al, 1986).

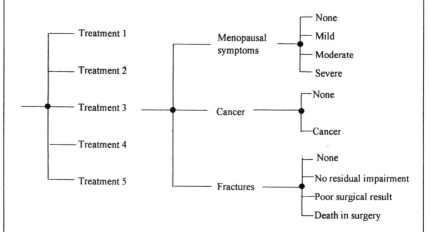

The tree shows five possible treatment decisions, each of which can be expanded, as shown for treatment 3, to show the possible outcomes in each of the three areas. The analysis decides which treatment is best by finding which one has the highest **expected utility**. This value is worked out for each specific treatment by adding together terms representing outcomes of that treatment in each area. These terms are, in turn, produced by multiplying the **importance** of each area by terms representing the **utility** (desirability) of each possible outcome and the **probability** that it will follow each treatment decision. This decision analysis tended to favour active treatment, but the clinicians were more likely to decide not to treat. Perhaps they were deterred by the slight increase in risk of cancer associated with treatment.

---

may also sometimes be a way of coping with having to make difficult decisions that might harm patients.

Clearly, the picture of an expert clinician who dispassionately makes objective decisions about patients is wide of the mark. Overcoming errors and biases in decision making therefore does not just need greater mathematical precision. It requires awareness of the emotional factors that complicate decision making. In the next section, we shall see that patients' decisions to adhere or not to clinicians' recommendations are also subject to emotional influences.

9.3 PATIENTS' ADHERENCE

9.3.1 Obedience, Adherence and Concordance

Having made a treatment decision, a clinician will naturally want to ensure that the patient adheres to it. In clinical literature and textbooks, the importance attached to the 'problem' of patient adherence is evidence of how influential is the view of the doctor as expert and authority figure. It would not seem so natural to talk of adherence or 'non-adherence' to the advice of a solicitor or teacher because these professions are not imbued with the same authority as is medicine. The term 'concordance' would be more appropriate because it would emphasize the equal authority of each party to the interaction. The terms 'compliance' and 'adherence' are often used interchangeably in medical literature. 'Compliance' emphasizes that issues of authority are central. Indeed, 'obedience' could easily be substituted for 'adherence' in the paragraphs that follow. The more conventional term, adherence, will be used in this chapter. However, non-adherence will not be regarded solely as a 'failure' by the patient. It will also be shown to reflect a lack of concordance between patients' and clinicians' beliefs and aims.

9.3.2 The Problem of Non-adherence

Unfortunately for the clinician, patients do not reliably do what they are told. The level of adherence is obviously hard to quantify accurately, partly because it is rarely a simple either/or issue and so the level depends on how stringent a criterion is used. However, whatever criterion is adopted, adherence is generally low. This applies both to instructions for lifestyle change, such as stopping smoking, eating less or taking more exercise, and to instructions for medication regimens which make much less demand on the patient. As a rule of thumb, expect around half of patients to follow instructions, although the actual figure can reach as low as 10% (Ley, 1988, 1997).

Another way of measuring the scale of the problem is by the contribution of non-adherence to poor clinical outcomes. Because patients with chronic disease typically have the main responsibility for managing their condition (Chapter 7), non-adherence can be serious. For instance, non-adherence has been estimated to account for around 50% of deaths of patients with renal failure and for the majority of renal transplant failures in the second year after transplantation (Christensen and Moran, 1998). For many disease conditions, improving adherence to existing treatments could have larger benefits than improving the treatment itself (Haynes et al, 1996).

9.3.3 Causes of Non-adherence

Fortunately, many reasons for non-adherence are fairly clear. Certainly, it cannot simply be blamed on the patient. That is, personality characteristics do not predict who will fail to adhere. Moreover, where patients have a demanding regime with many instructions to follow, such as in insulin-dependent diabetes or renal failure, their adherence to one requirement is no guide to how they will comply with others (e.g., Orme and Binik, 1989). Instead, research has identified many features of the treatment regime and clinicians' behaviour upon which non-adherence does depend (Box 9.3).

Box 9.3 Maximizing adherence

Adherence to clinicians' recommendations depends on patients' understanding, memory and satisfaction. Therefore adherence can be improved by clinicians who address each factor.

Comprehension	Find out what the patient believes about the condition and about how the treatment works
	Ensure the instructions make sense in terms of the patient's beliefs
Memory	Present important information first
	Provide specific, not general, recommendations
	Restrict the information to what the patient can process at the time
	Organize the information: e.g., by importance, time (what to do first, second), or type (benefits of treatment, side effects)
	Repeat important information: if necessary in a follow-up meeting or by providing an audio tape
Satisfaction	Ensure the patient's concerns have been elicited
	Minimize reactance by involving patient in decisions

9.3.3.1 Scale and Complexity of Demand

Non-adherence occurs even with relatively simple tasks, such as taking a course of antibiotics. However, chronic disease imposes such complex demands upon patients that complete adherence can be very difficult. For instance, complex social difficulties surround adherence to dietary or fluid restrictions in haemodialysis patients (Box 7.2). Where patients are cared for by different clinicians, or have access to other clinical advice from books or the Internet, conflicting advice adds to their difficulties.

Patients also differ in the extent that they wish—or can manage—to be involved in complex health care. Adherence to dietary restrictions in renal failure patients illustrates this. Those who adhered best were those for whom their level of preference for being involved in care matched the form of dialysis that they received (see Christensen and Moran, 1998). These were two groups: patients who preferred a high level of involvement and were being treated by continuous ambulatory peritoneal dialysis (in which they managed their own dialysis from day to day); and patients who preferred little involvement and were treated by haemodialysis (in which the dialysis was carried out by clinic staff).

9.3.3.2 Dissatisfaction

Adherence is strongly related to patient satisfaction. Satisfaction is itself a complex topic (Chapter 15). However, it depends particularly on the relationship between the clinician and patient. Therefore adherence, regardless of its implications for health, can be regarded as an indicator of the quality of the clinician–patient relationship. One of the main reasons that patients feel satisfied with a clinician is where the clinician makes them feel that their concerns have been understood (Ley, 1988). This is pursued later in this chapter.

9.3.3.3 Forgetting

An instruction that is not remembered will not be acted upon. Depending, once again, on exactly how stringently it is measured, the amount recalled from medical consultations is variable (30–90%) but averages around 50% (Ley, 1988). Forgetting clinicians' instructions reflects the same processes that influence forgetting in general.

Forgetting occurs for either of two reasons: failure to store the information at all, and failure to store it in such a way that it can be retrieved when needed. Any piece of information that a patient is given has to 'compete' with other information for the information-processing capacity that is needed to store it in memory. This requirement therefore favours material that is **presented first** in a sequence (when there is nothing to compete with it) rather than later. Also, the **less information that is presented**, the higher the probability that any individual item will be remembered.

Once memory is stored, passage of time is relatively unimportant to remembering or forgetting. Material that is remembered shortly after consultation will be stored (in the absence of a neurodegenerative disease) indefinitely. Forgetting then reflects a failure to *retrieve* information. Retrieval is better for material for which **importance is emphasized**, that has **specific implications for the patient** ('e.g., walk for 20 minutes each day' as opposed to 'take plenty of exercise'), and that has been **organized** into coherent categories (e.g., 'what's wrong', 'what tests you need', 'what medicines you need to take', 'what you can do to help yourself'; Ley, 1979, 1988). In essence, information is more readily recalled where it has been stored in memory in a way that resembles a good filing system. That is, the information is well organized and is 'labelled' in a way that reflects its significance.

In many consultations, for instance those which break bad news of a serious disease, it is difficult for the patient to identify which pieces of information are important until later. In this context, providing patients with an **audiotape recording** of the consultation can be helpful (Hogbin and Fallowfield, 1989). This technical approach should not, however, replace more traditional approaches to helping patients in such situations. These include, very simply, **repeating the information** or providing a **follow-up consultation** (Ley, 1988).

9.3.3.4 Patients' Beliefs

Beliefs about illness and the body. Technical and non-technical language alike are ambiguous in clinical consultations because patients and clinicians are apt to use them differently. Clinicians do not understand some lay terms for illness, and patients often do not understand clinicians' terms. Patients' normally limited understanding of medical terms might explain poorer recall of medical information in people with less medical knowledge (Ley, 1988). However, it would be wrong to presume that patients have *less* understanding than clinicians. Chapter 6 showed that patients commonly have a *different* understanding. For example, for many patients the 'stomach' describes the entire abdominal cavity instead of the anatomical structure that clinicians mean by the same term (Boyle, 1970).

Therefore many instances of non-adherence are understandable from the point of view of what the patients believe, despite making no sense to the clinician (Bar-On, 1986). For instance, many patients beginning treatment for hypertension believe that it is an acute disorder. Most of these, perfectly reasonably from their point of view, drop out of treatment. It is those who believe it is a chronic disease who are most likely to adhere (Meyer et al, 1985). There are many examples of non-adherence that can be explained in this way. They include diabetic patients who wrongly believe that their symptoms accurately indicate blood glucose levels (Cox et al, 1993). Similarly, many haemodialysis patients are convinced that the powerful cleansing effect of dialysis will purge the body of disallowed food that has been consumed on the day before (Krespi et al, 1999a).

Beliefs about pain. Many patients believe that the purpose of analgesia is not to abolish pain, but to reduce it to a tolerable level. Behind this lie culturally and psychologically engrained beliefs that pain is a good or formative experience. For instance, in one survey, a third of hospital inpatients agreed that 'pain builds character' (Weiss et al, 1983). Because this kind of belief is so strong, patients continue to receive less analgesia than is necessary, even when they inject their own by using patient-controlled analgesia (PCA; Chumbley et al, 1998; Chapter 11).

Beliefs about treatment. Beliefs about treatment also help to understand non-adherence. For example, **drugs** are widely seen as poisoning or addictive (Horne, 1997; Marchant-Haycox et al, 1998). That is, efficacy and toxicity go together in patients' minds. Therefore, it makes sense to patients to reduce or miss doses, or give themselves 'drug holidays'. Alternatively, patients can be unwilling to change drug regimes out of a superstitious fear of interfering with the *status quo* (Howitt and Armstrong, 1999). Such beliefs are partly cultural and therefore hard for an individual clinician to change in an individual patient. Nevertheless, *specific* beliefs about the drugs that the patient is prescribed are more imortant than beliefs about drugs in *general*, at least for haemodialysis patients (Horne, 1997). This simplifies the clinician's task. Non-adherence to **analgesic regimes**—particularly in hospital inpatients—illustrates the effect of patients' erroneous beliefs. Most surveys show that inpatients request less analgesia than they need to control pain fully, especially after surgery. One reason is their inaccurate beliefs about pain and analgesia (Lander, 1990; Oates et al, 1994). Many believe that analgesia is dangerous (for example, because of the risk of addiction). Clearly, for adequate analgesia patients must be given, not just analgesic drugs, but the information that helps them to accept these drugs (Wilder-Smith and Schuler, 1992).

Patients have much more vivid beliefs, or 'mental representations' (Chapter 6), about some treatments than others. For instance, haemodialysis patients have a simple and clear representation of how **haemodialysis** helps them: by 'cleaning' the blood (Krespi et al, 1999a). Unfortunately, the same patients' belief about how dietary restrictions helped them was much less compelling: 'keeping potassium levels down'. To patients, this is a highly abstract effect and seems a weak basis for adherence. The attempt to improve dietary adherence in these patients might begin by trying to help them construct a vivid mental representation for how adherence will help them.

An interesting form of non-adherence to clinicians' advice is the requests that patients sometimes make for treatment which the clinician thinks inappropriate (Chapter 10). This aspect of non-adherence also often makes sense in terms of the beliefs that patients hold. For instance, seeking antibiotics for a sore throat makes sense in terms of the lay concept of 'germ', which does not distinguish virus from bacterium (Helman, 1978). Even requests for surgery can be understood in this way. Some women's desire for hysterectomy to deal with menstrual problems reflects the power that **surgery**, uniquely, is thought to have, as well as the harm that 'drugs' are thought to cause (Marchant-Haycox et al, 1998). Belief in the special power of surgery might reflect a tradition, shared with many cultures, of treating illness by removing something from the body (Lupton, 1994).

Patients' beliefs about self-help are also important. For instance, patients are normally told to change **diet** and **lifestyle** after myocardial infarction. Whether they do depends on what they believe about these factors (Petrie and Weinman, 1997). Conversely, attributing their disease to factors beyond their control (such as genetics, bad luck or the pressure of life) means that effective self-management is less likely (Bar-On, 1986, 1987). Indeed, the patients who fail to take up rehabilitation after myocardial infarction tend to be those who believe that they cannot control or cure their illness (Petrie et al, 1996).

9.3.3.5 Being Realistic: The Power of Reward versus Beliefs

In general, therefore, adherence is related to the *patient's* view of illness and treatment rather than to the *clinician's* view (Janz and Becker, 1984). A clinician who wishes to maximize adherence should therefore help the patient to understand treatment recommendations in a way that promotes adherence. This, of course, requires the clinician to explore the patient's own understanding and ensure that the recommendations make sense in terms of that. However, it is easy to overstate clinicians' power to change beliefs and the power of beliefs to shape adherence.

This is seen particularly where clinicians' recommendations conflict with powerful motivations. For instance, the immediate (pleasurable) consequences of consuming a disallowed food or drink are powerful motivators to a chronically ill patient on a dietary regime. They are usually more powerful motivators than knowing the delayed (harmful) consequences of consumption and the delayed (beneficial) effects of dietary control. Not surprisingly, therefore, *rewarding adherence* to fluid restrictions in haemodialysis patients (e.g., by lottery tickets or videos) was more effective than trying to *correct beliefs* about the effects of fluid intake (Hegel et al, 1992). Children, in particular, are often motivated by stars on a chart—provided the stars are themselves signs of some other reward, such as parental or carer attention and approval. In practice, the clinician rarely has control over patients' rewards, although patients can sometimes be helped to reward themselves. For instance, they can arrange their lives so that rewarding activities follow a specified level or period of adherence.

9.3.4 Intentional Non-adherence

Non-adherence has been regarded so far in this chapter as patients' *failure*. There are several reasons why non-adherence can be *intentional*; that is, *deliberate*. The clinician who tries to reduce intentional non-adherence simply by the approaches outlined above could well make adherence worse rather than better.

9.3.4.1 Denial

The importance of denial in protecting patients from emotional effects of challenges has been discussed in previous chapters (Chapters 3 and 8). This source of non-adherence cannot be managed simply by repeating instructions and emphasizing their importance. Instead, patients need to be helped to cope with the challenge in other ways (Box 3.7). For example, information can help them to appraise the challenge in a less threatening way and emotional support can mitigate its effects.

9.3.4.2 Reactance

An important cause of disobedience to medical authority is 'reactance' (Brehm and Brehm, 1981). This refers to the psychological state of anger and defiance that results from feeling that one's autonomy has been arbitrarily curtailed. Illness is often seen in this way, i.e. as disempowering (Chapter 6). The feeling of being controlled by disease is compounded by reactance to a clinician who has provided treatment 'orders'. Reactance can be further increased where the clinician is seen as having a surveillance role, such as a health visitor or a practice nurse in a health advice clinic (Bloor and McIntosh, 1990). Resuming excessive alcohol consumption soon after recovering from myocardial infarction can therefore be, not an effect of misunderstanding or forgetting instructions, but a way of defying both the illness and the clinicians and re-establishing a feeling of autonomy (Box 9.4).

Box 9.4 Making sense of non-adherence

A patient's reaction to a clinician's advice does not always make sense to the clinician. It can, however, make sense in terms of what the patient believes.

Mrs X had been diagnosed with breast cancer by a surgeon who said that she needed a mastectomy. X refused and was referred for psychological assessment because the surgeon felt this was an irrational response.

X described feeling that, for too long, key people in her life had told her what to do. Her elder sister and mother do not speak to each other, but always use X to pass messages between them. She describes her husband as controlling, since it has suited him for her not to have much of a life of her own, but to have her at home to look after him and his ageing mother. Being diagnosed with cancer, and being told what to do, as she sees it, by the surgeon has made her realize the way she has allowed her life to be shaped by other people. She feels angry about the cancer and says she is going to deal with it in her own way. She has become vegetarian, is exercising, relaxing, visiting a healer and thinking positively.

X's reaction to the surgeon's recommendation is shaped by her view of life in general. The more that he presses for surgery, the more she will react against him. However, is it ethical for the surgeon to accept her decision at face value? It seems to be a comment on her life rather than a considered decision about her cancer. Before her decision can be trusted, X needs help to address her need for autonomy in the areas of her life where it is important. She also needs to be given the information on which to base a decision, and to be given the opportunity to take control of decision making, for instance by being given time to question the surgeon or specialist nurses.

9.3.4.3 When Patients Think they Know Best

In clinicians' minds, a common view is that the informed and expert clinician is consulted by the inexpert and ignorant patient. This is inconsistent with the way that many patients view the encounter. They see themselves as having authority and expertise that the clinician does not have. In particular, patients' direct **experience of their symptoms** provides a powerful sense of authority over the clinician, who has to use indirect tests to find out about them (Peters et al, 1998; Box 9.5). Knowledge about health and illness is not restricted to professional clinicians. Therefore a second source of patients' feeling of expertise arises through

---

Box 9.5 Patients' authority over their clinicians

Patients do not automatically defer to clinicians' advice. Instead, they can trust their own authority more than clinicians'. These statements by patients about their doctors' attempts to explain their symptoms reveal sources of this sense of authority (Peters et al, 1998).

The infallibility of patients' experience of the body. Perception of bodily symptoms, despite being the result of an interpretative process (Chapter 5), typically feels direct and unambigous: 'I've had ridiculous things said about me. It's as if you don't know your own body. Anything intramuscular is hard to see [on X-rays]. I can feel exactly where it is. If I dig my fingers in it really hurts.' This contrasts with the indirect and ambiguous results of medical tests: 'The X-ray came back as normal, but my impression of that is that I take lousy photos too. They don't show nerves do they?'

The diversity of sources of expert information. Books, magazines and the Internet dispense medical information directly to patients. Often this is more satisfactory to the patient than information provided by the doctor: 'I plodded on wondering why I still felt terrible. Then, in the library, I just picked up this book by chance, a book on ME or whatever. Went back to see Dr B, and said "What about this, do you think this is it?"'

Scrutinizing and testing doctors' advice. Patients scrutinize what they are told and weigh it up against what they already believe: 'Now they think it's a spasm. Well, spasms come and go don't they? Unless it stays in a sort of spasm? I don't think it is.'

---

lay consultation (Chapter 5). A detailed survey of people attending their general practitioner in one English town found that almost all had received advice before attending. The mean number of sources of advice for each patient was 18 (Elliott-Binns, 1973). The picture was similar when the study was repeated 15 years later, except that impersonal sources of information, such as books and television, were more important (Elliott-Binns, 1986). This trend has probably continued, with the recent inclusion also of the Internet (Davison and Pennebaker, 1997). Therefore, patients usually attend a clinician with beliefs about their symptoms which have been highly organized through this process of 'lay consultation'. As a result, the clinician is merely one of many sources of information. Whether the clinician's advice is accepted or rejected by patients depends on how it accords with what they already feel that they know (Hunt et al, 1989; Stimson, 1974).

A third source of patients' authority derives from carefully and thoroughly weighing up evidence and from their **scrutiny of alternative explanations**—including the clinician's (Hunt et al, 1989). This often contrasts with patients' view of clinicians' judgements as hasty or ill-considered (Hunt et al, 1989). In this way, patients can even regard themselves as more open-minded and 'scientific' than their clinicians.

Patients therefore often feel in authority over their clinicians. An example of the kind of non-adherence that can result is the rejection of health visitors' advice by mothers who devalue professional, theoretical knowledge in favour of their own knowledge based on experience (Bloor and McIntosh, 1990). Indeed, some patients who are experienced in managing a chronic illness *are* better informed than clinicians who look after them. Therefore, parents who modify their children's asthma treatment in the light of symptoms and circumstances can achieve better control than by adhering strictly to the medical regimen (Deaton, 1985).

9.3.4.4 When Patients and Clinicians have Different Values

Patients' religious or spiritual beliefs that the clinician does not share can occasionally preclude adhering to certain interventions, such as when Jehovahs Witnesses decline blood transfusions. A more common problem is where patients and clinicians differ in the concern or value they attach to different *consequences* of interventions. For instance, insulin-dependent diabetic patients can fear the immediate consequences of hypoglycaemic episodes more than the delayed consequences of prolonged hyperglycaemia (Hampson, 1997). Medication or other medical procedures can be refused outright by patients because of side effects that understandably concern the patient more than the clinician. In the extreme instance, a patient with a terminal prognosis might value quality of life free from medical intervention more than the chance of living longer. When chronically ill patients kill themselves by withdrawing from treatment, this may reflect a depressive state (Christensen and Moran, 1998; Chapter 7). However, the decision might also be seen as a reflection of the (low) value that they attach to their lives.

KEY POINTS

- The expertness of clinicians' decisions is limited by cognitive and emotional factors.
- Cognitive limitations include:
  — using short cuts, such as patient stereotypes
  — clinicians' own beliefs about illness and treatment.
- Emotional biases in decision making include:
  — morale
  — avoidance of feeling responsible for patients' suffering.
- Patients do not normally adhere to clinical advice.
- Non-adherence arises because of:
  — the scale or complexity of what is required
  — dissatisfaction with care
  — forgetting
  — divergence between patients' and clinicians' beliefs about illness or treatment
  — patients' own authority in deciding not to adhere.
- Adherence to clinicians' recommendations is most likely where:
  — information can be remembered
  — patient and clinician have similar understanding of the problem and treatment
  — patients' 'reactance' is minimized.

Chapter 10

CLINICAL COMMUNICATION: PARTNERSHIP AND OPPOSITION

KEY CLINICAL ISSUES

- Why do clinicians stop patients from telling them their concerns?
- How do clinicians stop patients from telling them their concerns?
- Why do distressed and unhappy patients often tell clinicians that 'everything is fine'?
- Does being sensitive to a patient's concerns guarantee a good consultation?
- How do patients persuade clinicians?

10.1 BEYOND EXPERT CONSULTATION

Because of growing awareness of the limitations of an expert, authority-based model, an alternative view has developed. According to this, the clinician and patient should be seen as partners, albeit ones with different areas of expertise (Tuckett et al, 1985). This view has brought added expectations that clinicians should encourage patients to express themselves fully and should be sensitive to patients' emotional as well as physical needs. A constraint on both the expert and partnership views is the assumption that the aims that the clinician and the patient bring to an encounter always coincide. In practice, universal concordance between clinicians and patients is unrealistic. Therefore this chapter will also examine how clinicians can manage conflict with patients so that decisions reflect patients' needs rather than their requests.

10.2 ESTABLISHING PARTNERSHIPS WITH PATIENTS

Being a partner or collaborator of the patient emphasizes two requirements for communication. The first is, by following normal social conventions that govern interactions between equals, to show respect and interest. The second is to go beyond these normal conventions to more specialized ways of helping patients to express their own areas of expertise; that is, their symptoms, beliefs, concerns and intentions.

10.2.1 Communicating Respect

A meeting of partners, or equals, requires basic social conventions. These include **verbal conventions** such as greeting the patient and introducing oneself, and aspects of **non-verbal communication** such as showing interest by maintaining eye contact and an appropriate posture. Patients adhere and are satisfied where there is good non-verbal communication by the clinician (DiMatteo et al, 1986). Unfortunately, the evidence is that these conventions are often neglected (Davis and Fallowfield, 1991). Verbal greeting is often peremptory, and non-verbal communication is all too easily disrupted by note taking. Of course, it is implausible that so many clinicians lack these basic social skills in everyday life. Instead, they are just not applied in the special conditions of the clinic.

One reason that non-verbal communication is often poor in the clinic is that it tends to express true emotional feelings. In the clinic, therefore, it will often be poor because it displays clinicians' feelings of boredom, irritation or dislike. Clinicians are, of course, only human in preferring well people to sick ones (Hall et al, 1993) and in sharing society's negative attitudes to minority or devalued groups, such as elderly people (Haug and Ory, 1987). Non-verbal communication of such feelings explains many instances of patient dissatisfaction with clinicians. Recall that satisfied patients are more likely to adhere to clinicians' recommendations. Therefore non-verbal communication of negative emotions can explain why patients' adherence to treatment recommendations is poorer where the doctor has low job satisfaction (DiMatteo et al, 1993).

10.2.2 Facilitating Patients' Disclosure

Chapter 6 showed that patients have firm beliefs and intentions that the clinician needs to know. Earlier in this chapter we saw that understanding and working with patients' beliefs was important if the clinician is to achieve patient adherence. Therefore, although patients are often hesitant about expressing their needs and beliefs, clinicians are responsible for overcoming this. There is evidence that the extent of therapeutic improve-

---

Box 10.1 Disclosure versus distancing

Clinicians have many ways to facilitate patients' disclosure of sensitive or emotional material. They also have as many ways to 'distance' patients and *prevent* disclosure.

How to encourage disclosure	How to distance a patient
Allow patient time to find the words to express feelings	Fill silences in conversation
Empathize with the patient	Control emotional expression; e.g., say 'There's no need to cry'
Use open questions	Use closed questions
Ask questions about psychosocial issues as well as physical problems	Ask questions only about physical problems
Seek clarification of patients' psychosocial comments or emotional gestures or tone	Ignore patients' psychosocial comments or emotional gestures or tone
Summarize to the patient what you think the patient has told you	Reassure the patient
Offer educated guesses as to what the patient might be feeling or wanting to say	Offer advice to the patient

---

ment depends on how fully patients feel that they have been able to discuss their problems with the clinician (Bass et al, 1986). Clinicians have several techniques at their disposal to facilitate disclosure (Maguire et al, 1996b; Box 10.1).

Unfortunately, the proportion of relevant information that clinicians elicit is often low (Davis and Fallowfield, 1991). There are several reasons. They include clinicians' **failure to check** or clarify their understanding of what the patient has said, and **premature focus** on the first problem that the patient presents, even at the expense of missing the main problem. In addition, clinicians tend specifically to **focus discussion on physical symptoms and treatments** and restrict patients' opportunity to bring psychosocial material into the consultation (Campion et al, 1992; Heaven and Maguire, 1997). That is, the communication techniques that are used are more often ones that emotionally distance patients (Maguire, 1985; Box 10.1).

Setting patients at ease and eliciting information therefore requires careful use of verbal and non-verbal strategies during consultation. However, preparing patients *before* consultation can also help. For example, just encouraging and guiding them to ask questions and to tell the doctor what they think is important can encourage a more active role (Robinson and Whitfield, 1985) and even improve health outcomes (Greenfield et al, 1985).

10.2.3 The Challenge of Patients' Suffering

Establishing a relationship based on partnership means being more sensitive and open to the patient. This means being more sensitive and open to the patient's suffering. However, clinicians differ in how much they achieve this. Breaking bad news reveals these differences starkly. Clinicians who attend to their patients' emotional needs break news of serious illness very differently from clinicians who do not (Maguire, 1998; Box 10.2). Sometimes, insensitivity is because the clinician simply does not know what to say. The problem can therefore be remedied by teaching better communication skills (see below). However, there are other reasons that require a different solution.

Other people's suffering is normally very unwelcome. Becoming a clinician does not stop this being the case. Specific factors add to the challenge that patients' suffering presents to clinicians. One is often the **inability to relieve suffering**. There is also clinicians' **awareness of causing suffering**—such as by breaking bad news. A patient's suffering can evoke the clinician's **fears of mortality** or vulnerability. Similarly, a patient's death can evoke **feelings about significant figures** in the clinicians' life, such as parents (Lyth, 1988). Chapter 3 described some of the psychological processes that protect people against severe challenge—and protect patients from challenges associated with illness. Because clinicians are people, also, they use similar processes to protect themselves from challenges associated with suffering patients. We shall see that their sensitivity to patients' suffering is reduced in consequence.

10.2.3.1 Coping with the Challenge: Professional Defence and Burn-Out

Hospital nurses are particularly exposed to their patients' suffering because of the continuity of care that they provide. Therefore research into how clinicians cope with patients' suffering has focused on nurses. Surveys confirm that patients' pain, suffering and death are upsetting

---

Box 10.2 Breaking bad news

Breaking news of serious disease, such as cancer, exposes clinicians to patients' emotional distress. In these dialogues, surgeons gave diagnoses of cancer in different ways. Surgeon 1 discouraged the patient's emotional expression by avoiding the word cancer, controlling the dialogue, emphasizing treatment, being positive and providing a large amount of information. Surgeon 2 allowed the patient to express her concerns and fears, which allowed the surgeon to provide a degree of reassurance.

Surgeon 1   'We've got all the results here and I'm afraid the bad news is that you do have a growth, but the good news is that it's only a small tumour and we'll be able to sort it out for you. We've got it in time. You'll need an operation, I'm afraid. But there's basically two kinds of operation we can do. We can do a mastectomy, which means taking the breast off, or we can do a lumpectomy, which means we just take out the tumour itself. If you had the mastectomy we can give you a reconstruction afterwards so you'll be back to your proper shape. Now, I know it's a lot to take in. Would you like to tell me what you would prefer now, or would you like to speak to one of the nurses about it? She can answer your questions.'

Patient   'Uh, no, I don't know. You said I could speak to someone?'

Surgeon   'Yes. That's right. The nurses. They're very helpful.'

Patient   'Yes, I suppose, thank you. Can I speak to them now?'

Surgeon 2   'You had some tests when you came to the hospital last week, didn't you? Do you have any feelings about what might be causing your problems?'

Patient   'Not really. Well, I suppose I have been worried. Anyone does with something like this, that it might be, you know, cancer or something.'

Surgeon   'I'm sorry I have to tell you that you do have cancer.'

Patient   'Oh, I don't think I can cope with this. I don't think I'm ready for it.'

Surgeon   'Before I go on, will you tell me why you think you won't cope? What's the worst thing about what I've told you?'

Patient   'It's just that my mother, you know, she got the same thing and it killed her. It was horrible.'

Surgeon   'When was that?'

Patient	'Oh, it was 15 years ago. But it still feels like it was last year.'
Surgeon	'I'm glad you told me that, because it means that I can explain how things have changed since your mother was ill. We're much better at treating breast cancer now. Would you like me to tell you about what we've found, and about the ways that we can treat it?'

(Bailey and Clarke, 1989). The surveys do not suggest that these challenges are any more important than more mundane issues like low staffing or bad management. However, the challenge of patients' suffering is probably understated by survey procedures because these rely on respondents' conscious awareness. Many of the ways of coping described below keep the challenge out of conscious awareness.

Organizational defences. By observing nurses at work, Lyth (1988) developed a theory of stress and coping in nursing, focusing largely on *unconscious* defensive methods of palliative coping (Chapter 3). She argued that nursing organization and practice have developed in ways that defend nurses against their patients' suffering. For instance, there are several ways to depersonalize patients (Box 10.3). These include the use of the body part, medical condition, surgical procedure or bed number to refer to a patient ('the hip in bay number 2'). Care is routinized (e.g., four-hourly rounds) rather than responding to the individual needs of each patient.

Psychological defences. Children's suffering is understandably more upsetting, or challenging, than adults'. Therefore, Byrne et al (1999b) examined the ways that paediatric nurses coped with the pain and distress of their child patients after major surgery. Two ways that these nurses described their children were striking. Some descriptions **minimized the validity of the children's complaints** of pain. Others presented the children in ways that signified that they **did not deserve help** (Box 10.4). That is, beliefs about the children and their behaviour were used as defences against the threats arising from the children's suffering. From the account of stress in Chapter 3, this should not be surprising.

Hospital nurses' duties were previously structured around *tasks* (e.g., one nurse being responsible for bathing and another for toileting). This provided a convenient way of depersonalizing the patient and routinizing care. The emphasis now is on organizing care around *patients* (each nurse being responsible for all care of certain patients). It should be expected that, as *organizational* arrangements which help nurses to cope

---

Box 10.3 How to depersonalize a patient

These are observations of paediatric nurses looking after children after major orthopaedic surgery. They illustrate some of the ways that clinicians can depersonalize patients (Byrne et al, 1999b).

1. *Speak about the patient in her presence in the third person*

Nurse 1 'Shall we move her now?'
Nurse 2 'Yes.'
Nurse 1 [to child after starting to move the bed] 'We are going to move you onto the big ward. Do you want to go onto the big ward?'

2. *Ask the patient's views, but then discount them*

Nurse 1 'Do you want to have your catheter out now or later?'
Child 'What do you mean? No, no, do it later. Mum, what are they going to do?'
Nurse 2 'It's better if we take it out now to get your bladder working again properly.'
Child [as procedure begins] 'Please, no, not now.'

3. *Block the patient's attempts to negotiate*

Nurse 'Shall we turn you?'
Child 'Please come back in a few minutes, and then you can.'
Nurse 'That won't make any difference. Come on, let's turn you over.'
Child 'Please don't touch my scar. Please, please, why can't you come back in two minutes when the morphine [self-administration using patient-controlled analgesia] has worked.'

4. *Routinize care*

Child 'I want to be turned, it hurts on this side. Please turn me over.'
Nurse 'No, Sam, it isn't two o'clock yet. It's important that we turn you every two hours.'

---

with patients' suffering are set aside (such as task-based nursing), *psychological* mechanisms like those described above would come into play more.

Although this research has focused on nurses, the behaviour of all professions with patient contact can probably be understood in this way. We saw above that doctors who clearly possess exquisite social skills

---

Box 10.4   Nurses' emotion-focused coping with the challenge of
patients' suffering

Paediatric nurses, interviewed about their patients' suffering after major
orthopaedic surgery, described many reasons why that suffering should
not be regarded as real. In this way, the threat that it presented to the
nurses could be reduced (Byrne et al, 1999b).

Distress was attributed, not to pain, but **parents' anxiety:** 'Her
parents [being] very anxious is related on to [the child], making her
very anxious as well,' or **the child's own anxiety**, being 'more
afraid of the pain than being in pain'. Other children were thought to
be **wilful or dissimulating** in complaining and 'won't eat anything'
or 'won't do anything for herself'. Another was 'just moan moan moan,
that's all she does'. Yet another 'deserved an Oscar for her performance'. In other children, complaints were said to reflect the **child's
nature or personality**. They were 'wingey', 'wimpy' or 'ratty', or
just 'the sort of child that is miserable'. 'Teenagers are a pain anyway.'

---

outside the surgery can behave coldly and impersonally with patients.
This, too, might partly be a way of defending against their patients'
suffering.

Burn-out. The sensitivity of even the most committed newly qualified clinician can be worn down through repeated exposure to patients.
This is the mechanism behind the syndrome of burn-out in caring
professions (Maslach, 1982). **Depersonalization** of patients is a key feature
of burn-out. However, the syndrome entails costs for the clinician, too.
These include feelings of **failure to meet one's expectations** for
what should be achieved at work and feelings of **emotional exhaustion**
(Box 10.5). Burn-out does not reflect clinicians' personality characteristics. That is, there is no 'type' of person who is most likely to
burn out. Instead, burn-out results from features of the job. The most
important risk factors for burn-out are **long duration of patient
contact** and **high intensity of contact**. It is particularly likely where
the challenges of patient care are compounded in three ways. One is where
the clinician has **little control** over work. The second is where there is
ambiguity over what exactly is expected of the clinician and how well the
clinician is delivering it. The third factor that promotes burn-out is the
absence of emotional support for the clinician.

Box 10.5 Burn-out

Burnout, although a problem of clinicians, affects their patients, too. These examples of items from the Maslach Burnout Inventory (Maslach et al, 1996) illustrate three different facets of the syndrome.

Emotional exhaustion
I feel emotionally drained from my work.
I feel used up at the end of the day.

Depersonalization
I've become more callous toward people since I took this job.
I worry that this job is hardening me emotionally.

Failure to meet one's expectations
I don't deal effectively with the problems of my patients.
I don't feel I'm positively influencing other people's lives through my work.

10.2.3.2 Patients' Collaboration in Protecting Clinicians

Patients do not generally complain about the ways in which clinicians defend themselves from the patients' suffering. Indeed, they collaborate. Even patients with cancer are selective in disclosing *physical* symptoms to hospice nurses rather than their fears and emotional difficulties (Heaven and Maguire, 1997). Ironically, the more anxious and depressed patients are even less likely to disclose their emotional feelings. The cheerful bonhomie of the oncology clinic is typically fed by patients and clinicians alike—although it clearly contrasts with the gravity of what is at stake for the patients. As one patient observed about her visits to an oncology clinic: 'We sit there with forced smiles on our faces, pretending to be strong, like the bloody Dunkirk spirit.' What is happening in this kind of situation is that patients are joining in protecting their clinician (and each other). Therefore patients who cry in front of the oncologist, nurse—or even counsellor or psychologist—typically apologize as if breaking a rule.

These findings are from outpatient settings. It might be suspected that patients would feel less need to protect staff in an inpatient ward. After all, the role of the ward staff is specifically to look after the patients' needs. This suspicion would be incorrect. Inpatients are also very reluctant to let clinicians know their needs (Chapter 12). To understand why inpatients work particularly hard to protect clinicians, we need to appreciate the way that they define their role as to meet clinicians' needs (e.g., not to be

---

Box 10.6   Giving permission to disclose distress

Patients typically collaborate with clinicians to protect them from the patients' distress. However, it is possible for clinicians to signal to patients that they do not need to be protected.

X had undergone treatment for cancer and had attended the oncology clinic to see the doctor several times during the year since she was diagnosed. The opening interaction between them normally went something like this:

Surgeon   'How are you doing?'
Patient   'Fine, thanks.'
Surgeon   'Good. Everything's OK, is it?'

The consultation then addressed the surgical or medical problem of the moment.

A specialist nurse sat in with a consultation one day and thought that the patient's claim to feel 'fine' sounded too hasty to be taken at face value. She arranged a series of meetings with her. This was the opening interaction at their second meeting.

Nurse   'How have you been feeling this last week?'
Patient   'OK. Fine. Just getting on with things really.'
Nurse   'OK, now tell me how you've *really* been feeling.'
Patient   'Lousy, really. I've been feeling out of my head all week.'

---

delayed; not to be burdened with the patient's distress) rather than their own. This is pursued in Chapter 12. For the present, it is important to appreciate that, when clinicians try to exclude emotional material from consultations by conveying cheerfulness, importance or time pressure, this chimes with patients' readiness to protect them. The interaction is expedited, but at the cost that important issues are not voiced. It takes very little for a clinician to signal to a patient that protection is not needed. The effect on what the patient is ready to disclose can be considerable (Box 10.6).

10.2.4 The Challenge of Patients' Sexuality

Patients' suffering is not the only trigger for psychological defences. Other emotional challenges arise in clinical care. In particular, intimate procedures have to be carried out without evoking patients' or clinicians' sexuality. This clearly requires depersonalization of the patient. The matter-of-fact attitude with which a male doctor performs a gynaecological examination, or with which a female nurse catheterizes a male patient, helps to achieve this. For instance, the clinician might warn the patient of imminent penetration of the vagina or penis by saying that he/she is just going to 'pop' something 'inside'. This helps to protect both parties from seeing the encounter as either erotic or humiliating (Lupton, 1994). In this instance, of course, the patient is *protected* by the clinician's defensive coping.

10.2.5 Improving Clinicians' Sensitivity to Patients

10.2.5.1 Communication Skills Training

A psychological analysis can *explain* limitations of clinicians' behaviour. It does not *justify* them. Indeed, it is important to use this analysis to find ways of overcoming those limitations. One popular approach is to teach communication skills. This rests on the assumption that clinicians' communication with patients is limited because of lack of skill. Basic interviewing techniques can be improved in the the same ways that other kinds of skill can be learned (Maguire, 1990). The key ingredients of skills training are therefore **demonstration, practice** and **feedback**. More difficult communication, such as dealing with emotional patients or breaking bad news, is not so easily trained. Where training in these areas is successful in the short term, improvements in clinicians' behaviour often decline subsequently (Maguire et al, 1996a). Moreover, skills can improve without any effect on patients (Heaven and Maguire, 1996). Also, becoming more effective at eliciting patients' concerns does not necessarily mean becoming more able to cope with them. Sometimes, trained clinicians even make *more* use of distancing strategies (Maguire et al, 1996a)!

10.2.5.2 Managing the Emotional Challenge

Communicating in challenging situations cannot just be addressed as a *cognitive* problem, i.e., a lack of knowledge or skill. This chapter shows that a broader approach is needed that deals with the *emotional* factors that limit sensitivity to patients. The simple model of stress and coping (Chapter 3) indicates three approaches: reduce the degree of challenge that is appraised; provide more emotional support; or help clinicians to find better ways of coping.

Reducing and reappraising the challenge. How to reduce the challenge depends on what the challenge is. For some clinicians, it is associated with a failure to address their own fears about **vulnerability and mortality**.

Although these issues are rarely acknowledged in physical health care, they can be addressed where clinicians accept the need to think about their own part in the doctor–patient relationship (Balint, 1957). There are also the feelings of **helplessness** and **failure** that result from feeling unable to respond to patients' suffering. Skills training (including communication skills) can help in finding responses. Often, however, clinicians need help to appreciate that the feeling of personal failure is mistaken. Responses that are, in fact, entirely appropriate are often wrongly seen as a failure. Common examples are not being able to stop a patient from crying, or not being able to fill a silence during consultation. Support and effective supervision can be the vehicles for reappraisal: seeing that experiences are shared helps to see that they are not personal failures. In other situations, feelings of helplessness or failure reflect constraints imposed by the organization—for example, the lack of privacy for patients when bad news is being broken, or the absence of support staff who can stay with a distressed patient in a busy clinic.

Support. Where threat cannot be reduced, it can be managed in ways that are preferable to the defensive methods described above. Availability of support is restricted by the common belief amongst clinicians that 'admitting' to emotional reactions is unprofessional. Of course, burdening a *patient* with one's own emotional feelings clearly is unprofessional. However, to disclose them to another *clinician* could mean setting into motion the wheels of mutual support (Parkes et al, 1997). Therefore, nurses who feel supported by their colleagues are better able to explore their patients' concerns and feelings (Wilkinson, 1991). Probably, many programmes that are regarded as training communication skills are successful in the short term because of the mutual support that they facilitate.

Problem-focused coping. Several opportunities for problem-focused coping have already been suggested here. They include organizational rearrangements to allow more time or privacy in a clinic, as well as attending training programmes to improve skills.

10.3 MANAGING OPPOSITION AND CONFLICT

10.3.1 Sources of Conflict

Disagreement is implicit in some instances of 'disobedience'—or nonadherence—to clinicians' instructions (Chapter 9). However, non-adherence rarely leads to overt conflict. Except where the courts become involved, patients' authority over their own bodies is final. It can be exercised by simply not taking prescribed medication, or not attending a consultation.

Box 10.7 Conflicts between clinicians and patients

Conflicts occur when a patient seeks a resource that the clinician does not wish to give the patient. The following conflicts occurred in different settings over different resources (surgery, drugs, emotional support). Nevertheless, there are similarities in the things that patients said to engage the clinician.

X asked his GP to refer him to the hospital because of his painful back. The GP knows that the patient was examined by a surgeon a year ago and no problem was found. She thinks that the patient is depressed and that he needs psychological help rather than surgery. She thinks that the risks and costs of surgery far outweigh any likely benefit. However, X tells the GP that the pain is getting worse and that nobody else can know how painful his back is. He does not think he 'can go on much longer'.

Y, who has lung cancer, is deteriorating rapidly. He is visited at home by a community nurse and explains to her that he has nothing left to live for and wants her to help him end his life quickly by giving him more morphine than he should have. He says that no one who is not in his situation can possibly understand what it is like, that all the treatment he has had has just prolonged the misery and that he will find a worse way of killing himself if she does not help.

Z is 20 years old, haemophiliac and HIV-positive. He lives alone with little social life and no friends. He has fortnightly visits from a specialist nurse. He has started to telephone her office every few days asking for advice, and recently telephoned to say that he desperately needed to see her. When she arrived he said he had noticed a pain in his leg that had now gone. She tells him that he is relying on her rather than building an independent life. He becomes distressed and says that he does not think he can cope if she is not there to provide help when he needs it. Before she goes, he asks her how many paracetamols would be fatal.

Instead, conflict is more likely to arise where the patient seeks something that the clinician is unwilling or unable to give. Clinicians, especially doctors, are gate-keepers for valued resources. These do not just include treatment. Attention from the clinician, forming an alliance with the clinician and being licensed to adopt the sick role are also valued (Chapter 6). Therefore, what patients seek is bound to conflict sometimes with what clinicians wish to provide (Box 10.7). Perhaps what the patient seeks would be harmful or costly to the patient. Perhaps it would be costly or unethical for the clinician or would deprive needier patients of resources. Although this kind of conflict is part of clinicians' day-to-day experience, this is not reflected in research and technical writing. 'Conflict' rarely appears in the index of a book on health psychology or on communicating with patients. There is little attention, either, to one of the elements which make for conflict: the power that a patient can exert in consultation. This reflects a continuing tendency to see patients as passive and helpless in the face of clinicians' power.

Studying conflict is simplified where patients seek physical treatment from doctors but where there is no evidence of the physical pathology that would normally indicate treatment. Sometimes, doctors will think that these symptoms are part of the normal range of physical experience and should be tolerated by the patient (Chapter 5). Alternatively the symptoms might seem to reflect emotional or social problems which should be treated in other ways (Chapter 13). Recent work has begun to reveal ways in which conflict is conducted in this kind of situation (Box 10.8; Marchant-Haycox and Salmon, 1997), and these are outlined below.

10.3.2 The Patient's Influence

When a patient presents an objective symptom such as a skin rash or a swelling, the clinician can see, prod or poke the symptom. There may be other signs of pathology that can be assayed, X-rayed or scanned. The situation is very different when patients present subjective physical symptoms, such as tiredness or pain, without any detectable pathology. Only the patient can feel the symptom. Only the patient can assess it and describe it. The symptom can be neither scrutinized nor questioned by the clinician. This is the basis of the power that a patient has over a clinician when presenting subjective symptoms (Shorter, 1992; Box 10.8). The patient's **privileged knowledge** extends to the suffering that those symptoms cause. Patients often express how severe their symptoms are by **describing psychosocial effects** instead of more 'objective' properties such as intensity or duration. Having established the scale of their suffering, the patient's task is then is to establish which party has **responsibility** for it. Merely presenting symptoms in the context of the clinic implies that they are the clinician's responsibility, but patients can make this transfer of responsibility more explicit. One particularly powerful way is by emphasizing that clinicians have failed or harmed the patient in the past. **Catastrophization** and citing **external authority** have the potential to increase the patient's influence (Box 10.8).

Box 10.8   How to influence a doctor

Patients can exert considerable influence over clinicians' decisions, but this influence is rarely stated explicitly. Here are examples of how patients can influence doctors to take responsibility for their suffering and provide treatment, even in the absence of any physical pathology that would indicate treatment (Salmon and May, 1995; Marchant-Haycox and Salmon, 1997; Peters et al, 1998).

Emphasize privileged knowledge of the symptoms: 'You can't know what it's like.'

Disclose psychosocial effects of the symptoms: This response was to a gynaecologist who asked how bad a patient's menstrual symptoms were: 'I'm not sleeping sometimes through it [pain]. And the friend who I go out with, we are not having a proper relationship because half the time it's too painful.'

Establish that the clinician is responsible: Clinicians' responsibility can be emphasized by describing their culpability. Criticisms such as 'What I had before did absolutely nothing for me. It's actually worse than it was before' sometimes refer to previous attempts at treatment, but also to procedures that were exploratory: 'This came on me when they put a tube inside. Since then, when I go to the toilet, it squirts everywhere.'

Catastrophize: Non-specific statements that 'I don't think I can go on', can be supported by specific predictions: 'I'm frightened what I'll do to the children.'

Cite external authority: Other doctors are commonly cited in support of the patient's view of the diagnosis or the treatment that is needed. Relatives or friends attest to the level of need: 'My daughter actually says to me, if you don't get it [surgery] done soon, she'll wheel me to the theatre and do it herself.'

10.3.3 The Doctor's Response

The ways in which some doctors respond to these presentations demonstrate the difficulties that can arise where clinician and patient have very different understandings of the patient's problem. One strategy whereby doctors attempt to counter patients' claims is by emphasizing the area over which *they* have **privileged knowledge** through their special instruments, tests and knowledge; that is, the world inside the patient's body

(Marchant-Haycox and Salmon, 1997). In popular imagery, such as television programmes set in hospitals, the doctor is usually the character with the stethoscope. This emblem emphasizes doctors' special access to the inside of patients' bodies—an area beyond the scrutiny of the bodies' owners (Lupton, 1994). A characteristic response of gynaecologists reporting normal test results to women presenting menstrual symptoms is to refer to having 'looked around inside' and having confirmed that 'everything was normal' (Marchant-Haycox and Salmon, 1997). The patient cannot dispute the conclusion, but is still left with the need to explain the symptoms. This can lead to consultations which each party tries to resolve by drawing the consultation into the domain in which they, alone, are expert. The patient focuses the dialogue on the unpleasantness of the symptoms and the psychosocial distress that they cause. The doctor focuses on the normality of the body.

10.3.4 Resolving Conflict

This analysis confirms what clinicians already know: patients can have considerable power over them. More than this, it provides an objective basis from which to understand 'patient pressure'. Until now, this has been recognized from clinicians' subjective feelings rather than patients' behaviour (Armstrong et al, 1991; Chapter 6). Specifically, the analysis identifies strategies whereby patients can exercise influence and to which clinicians must be able to respond. It also shows the limitations of two common types of response.

First, conflict cannot necessarily be resolved by the clinician simply being more sensitive to the patient's psychosocial agenda. Psychosocial complaints can be presented by a patient so as to secure, not the *psychosocial* help that the patient might need, but *physical* intervention (Salmon and May, 1995). Secondly, clinicians will not solve the problem by asserting their own authority, for instance by telling the patient that he/she is wrong or by trying to 'win' the conflict by emphasizing their special knowledge. This risks reactance against the clinician (Chapter 9). Reactance would merely entrench the patient's position. Where a patient has a specific treatment in mind, any implication that this will be denied can obviously escalate the conflict. The invitation to 'try something else first' can be interpreted in this way. This invitation also establishes a clear way for the patient to gain the desired treatment: to fail to improve with the alternative. In some instances, the clinician will be able to collaborate with such a patient on a more subtle basis (Box 10.9). However, on occasion, the clinician will be unable to avoid overt conflict except by acquiescing to a patient's demands.

Box 10.9   Collaborating with the demanding patient

X is 38 years old and has strenuously demanded a mastectomy because of breast pain. There is no pathology, although there is a history of emotional problems and of negative attitudes to her sexuality. There is also a history of previous surgery in the absence of pathology. The surgeon is reluctant to carry out a mutilating procedure that is unlikely to help. Consider two possible ways of responding.

1. He tells her that he does not think this will help and that he thinks there are emotional problems which lie behind this and that she should see someone about these. He refers her and tells her that he will see her again and consider operating if the counsellor cannot help.
2. He tells her that, although there is nothing going on in her breast that he needs to remove, many people have pain in parts of the body, even where there is nothing seriously wrong that needs to be put right. He tells her that it is just as bad as pain that is caused by a wound or injury. But because there is no damage causing this sort of pain, it is much more difficult to treat. He explains the phenomenon of 'phantom' pain, whereby pain is still felt in an amputated part of the body, once that part has been removed. In his experience, he explains, people only get the benefit of surgery in instances like this if they have prepared for it. This means learning to cope with the pain as well as possible before the operation, and sorting out any other problems in her life beforehand. Then all her energies can go into recovering from the operation. He will ask her to see a colleague who has helped people in this position before. Once they have completed their work together, he will see her again.

Option 1 wins delay, but at the cost of the patient's greater insistence on surgery. The counsellor will fail because of the patient's reactance and because failing to be helped is the criterion for receiving surgery. Option 2 may not succeed either, but it offers the chance of a collaborative relationship on a broadened agenda (Chapter 13).

Referring to the clinician and patient as opponents reflects the way that many interactions are, in practice, conducted. In reality, of course, the clinician and patient *are* on the same 'side'—the patient's. The challenge for the clinician is to find a basis for forming an alliance with the patient against the symptoms (Chapter 6). A basis for forming an alliance specifically when there is no pathology to treat is described in Chapter 13.

10.4 CONCLUSION

Communication is at the heart of this book. Psychological influences on health care occur through communication, particularly between clinicians and patients. However, it is clear that the quality of psychological care is not ensured simply by an emphasis on 'good communication'. The demands on communication are too complex, and often contradictory. The demands that this and the preceding chapter have described reflect the three roles that the modern clinician needs to be able to adopt: expert, partner and opponent. Each has its limitations, and none provides a complete framework for a consultation. The clinician therefore has to adopt different roles with the same patient and in the same interaction. Being aware of these different roles, and of the demands and effects of each, should allow the clinician to find a better balance between them than simply leaving this to chance.

KEY POINTS

- To partner the patient, the clinician must communicate respect and facilitate disclosure.
- Respect requires basic social conventions of interaction between equals.
- Clinicians have communication techniques to facilitate patients' disclosure.
- Clinicians also have techniques to inhibit patients' disclosure.
- Clinicians use these techniques to protect themselves from patients' suffering.
- Patients collaborate in protecting clinicians from their own suffering.
- Disagreement between patient and clinician is normally resolved without overt conflict.
- Patients can influence clinicians to secure responses that the clinician does not wish to provide.
- Where conflict has arisen, conventional clinical responses often exacerbate it.

Chapter 11

PATIENT EMPOWERMENT: INFORMATION, CHOICE AND CONTROL

KEY CLINICAL ISSUES

- Does informed consent deal with patients' information needs?
- What is the difference between information and explanation?
- Should patients be given choice and control over treatment whenever possible?
- What is the difference between control and involvement?
- Whose interests are served when patients are encouraged to take responsibility for their care?

11.1 CULTURAL FASHIONS AND SCIENTIFIC RESEARCH

Patient care is influenced, not just by scientific developments, but by political and cultural factors (Chapter 2). For instance, seeing patients as 'partners' in care has emphasized the importance of providing patients with information about illness and treatment. More recently, the growth of the consumer model of care has led to an emphasis on providing patients with the opportunity for choice and involvement in their care. However, these issues have not just been the province of politicians and planners. They have been areas of research, too. The resulting scientific evidence does not always support the assumptions that are made about what patients seek by way of information or control, or about how they react when it is offered.

11.2 INFORMATION AND EXPLANATION

11.2.1 Patients' Appraisal Needs

Clinicians are familiar with the idea that patients have physical health care needs, and even emotional needs. Less freely acknowledged are patients' cognitive, or appraisal, needs. That is, they need to understand what is happening to them. Meeting these needs is important for several reasons.

11.2.1.1 To Inform Patients' Treatment Decisions

In general, surveys indicate that patients want to be informed in detail about their condition and treatment, even including slight risks associated with each (Ley, 1988). This converges with the importance of informed consent. However, the procedures of informed consent have mainly been established to meet clinicians' needs, ensuring that they are protected from medico-legal challenges. Patients' needs have been neglected. For instance, it is common for consent to be requested once patients are already commited to a procedure. As an example, consider the usual timing of informed consent for surgery. Patients are normally asked for their consent once they have already been admitted for surgery. At this stage, most have made practical arrangements to have the children looked after or to take time off work. They are emotionally committed, too, having perhaps spent much time talking with friends and family about the procedure. Furthermore, the information is often given in ways that are not understandable to the patient. In particular, because such information is given as a standard procedure, there is often no opportunity for the clinician to clarify an individual patient's understanding and to tailor the information accordingly. Where the information cannot easily be remembered, and where no written information is given for the patient to keep, patients cannot review their decisions afterwards in an informed way. Therefore informed consent is routinely compromised by many of the same factors that prevent effective communication in normal clinical practice (Chapter 9). Truly informed consent requires greater attention to meeting patients' need to understand their treatment.

In chronic illness in particular, patients also need information so that they can manage their own condition effectively. This includes technical information about measuring physiological parameters, such as in insulin-dependent diabetes, but it also includes information about how to respond to symptoms and sensations such as during cardiac rehabilitation (Box 11.4).

Nevertheless, patients' own views indicate that information is not sought primarily in order to make decisions about treatment. That is, many more patients seek and value information than wish to have an active role in making decisions about their treatment (Coulter, 1997; Richards et al, 1995). Also, patients who seek most information tend to be those who prefer clinicians to make decisions for them (Miller et al, 1988). We shall go on to examine other reasons why information is important to patients.

11.2.1.2 The Need to Understand

An important source of appraisal needs is simply patients' need to 'make sense' of symptoms and illnesses. This has been a common thread through previous chapters and does not need to be described again. Going to the doctor with a symptom is the end result of a process of thinking about the symptom and what it might mean and discussing it with other people. It is important to remember that the process continues after consultation, whatever the severity of the problem (Chapter 6). For instance, patients make sense of being given an antibiotic for a sore throat by concluding that some germs must be present which need to be killed by drugs. Many patients who have been diagnosed with cancer conclude that this must be a punishment for previous misdeeds.

11.2.1.3 The Need to Reduce Anxiety

The desire for a great deal of information, for instance before surgery, is often a sign of anxiety or a predictor of anxiety later (Mahler and Kulik, 1991). Being anxious does not just mean that patients may have threatening beliefs about what is happening to them. There are also changes to the way that information is being processed. Patients attend selectively to signs of danger and tend to recall memories that are frightening (Williams et al, 1997; Chapter 7). These processes help to ensure that an anxious patient's view of a clinical procedure is often very different from the clinician's.

Anxiety in patients undergoing treatment or investigation is conveniently divided into two kinds. **Outcome** anxiety refers to fears of what the results will be. **Procedural** anxiety arises from fears about the procedure itself. Whereas outcome anxiety is often unavoidable, procedural anxiety should usually be regarded as evidence of a failure of clinical care. In each of the procedures in Box 7.3, the patient made a threatening appraisal of a danger which was unreal or exaggerated. The clinician's task is, first, to identify what the patient believes, then to help the patient correct that belief. Many patients suspect that their fears are incorrect and are too embarrassed to disclose them readily. Disclosure will therefore depend on the clinician being able to reassure the patient that intense and groundless fears are normal.

11.2.2 Meeting Appraisal Needs by Information

11.2.2.1 Information about Patients' Experience

Information is obviously central in meeting these cognitive needs. For ease and convenience, information is sometimes given in a package to large numbers of patients. This kind of information is therefore not tailored to individual patients' needs. Anxiety in *advance* of procedures can often be dealt with in this way (e.g., Marteau et al, 1996). However, careful preparation can also reduce the anxiety that arises *during* procedures. A study of patients undergoing a routine procedure, a barium enema, illustrates the power of this approach. Distress normally increases as the procedure continues. However, this increase was prevented by explaining to patients beforehand what would happen and, in particular, the sensations that would be experienced (Wilson-Barnett, 1978).

For information to be most effective, it should concern patients' own *experience*: i.e., what will happen to the patient and what it will feel like and what he/she can do about it. Information about the *clinicians'* perspective on the procedure, such as how it works or what equipment is called, is unlikely to be so helpful. Information about sensations that patients will experience is therefore particularly important (Suls and Wan, 1989). It is not hard to understand how this kind of information might help patients. Knowing that sensations that are experienced are normal effects of the procedure could prevent the threatening appraisals that patients showed in Box 7.3. Similarly, information about what patients can do to cope is also able to reduce distress as well as stimulate appropriate problem-focused coping such as practising physiotherapy exercises before hospital admission for hip replacement (Butler et al, 1996) or cooperating with passage of an endoscopy tube (Johnson and Leventhal, 1974).

11.2.2.2 Information about Risk

The need for informed consent focuses a specific problem of communication: how to respond to patients' need for information about risks, such as side effects (Ley, 1988). Patients, like clinicians, make different decisions depending on whether risks are presented in terms of bad or good outcomes (Chapter 9). That means, stating the chances of survival after a treatment is more likely to lead to consent than stating the chances of the alternative outcome: dying. This exposes the more general problem that patients are not used to weighing chances of important events statistically. Therefore even minor differences in the ways that information is given or that questions are asked lead to very different decisions or answers. Medico-legal requirements mean that statistical information may be necessary. However, gamblers aside, patients do not normally think in terms of probabilities or odds. Therefore their need for information about risk can often be addressed by comparing the probability of clinical outcomes with other chance events, such as winning a lottery, contracting another disease or having a traffic accident.

11.2.2.3 Variability in Effects of Information

Scientific evidence about effects of information has been mixed, so generalization is very difficult. Although normally helpful, information sometimes *increases* distress and even increases pain and disability (Parker et al, 1984). Effects of information also vary between procedures and between individuals, and according to the amount of information that is given.

Differences between procedures. Information about major surgery is less likely to improve outcome than is information about minor invasive procedures (see Salmon, 1994). Indeed, when patients undergoing major and minor surgery have been compared, information reduced distress only in the minor group (Lindeman and Stetzer, 1973). Information can even *increase* distress before major surgery without any postoperative benefit (Langer et al, 1975). One problem is that information is intrinsically more distressing for major procedures.

Variability between patients. As well as having different effects in different procedures, information has different effects in different patients. Those who are already extremely **frightened** are most likely to be reassured by information (Sime, 1976). People can also be distinguished according to whether they tend to use information to help cope with stress in normal life. The terms 'monitors' and 'blunters' have been devised to distinguish two types of people: those who cope by gathering information about challenges versus those who cope by avoiding information (Miller et al, 1988). A **monitor** would be expected to cope with, for example, waiting for elective surgery by finding out as much as possible about it. Perhaps friends would be sought out who have had the same operation. Magazine articles would be scoured and relevant television programmes would be keenly watched. The **blunter**, by contrast, would try to put it out of mind and avoid any relevant information. Providing information to every patient would therefore be incompatible with blunters' normal coping styles. There is, indeed, evidence that it is the monitors who are most helped by packages of information provision. In minor surgery, for example, the patients who are helped by detailed information are those who prefer to have it (Auerbach et al, 1983; Martelli et al, 1987).

Blunters, on the other hand, have been made more anxious by being given information that they neither need nor seek (Miller and Mangan, 1983). It is easy to see how information can increase distress in practice. Being told, for example, that a negative outcome is very *unlikely* will cause some patients to worry that it is *possible*. Information about the value of following treatment recommendations will make some patients anxious about what will happen should they not be able to follow them exactly.

Effects of differing amounts of information. Information is not like a drug. There is no simple dose–response relationship between the amount given and the extent to which distress is reduced. Indeed, a small amount of information can be more effective than a large amount (Marteau et al, 1996).

11.2.2.4 Patients' Understanding of Information

Children. Because of their restricted ability to conceptualize illness and treatment and the dangers that arise from them (Chapter 5) children might be more resilient than adults faced with similar procedures (Schmidt, 1998). Therefore, giving detailed information to children might often be unnecessary. Where information is to be given to a child, it is clearly important to use language that can be understood and to provide information that is compatible with the child's level of understanding. Language limitations are obvious. One seven-year-old child became very upset on the evening before he was due to undergo a tonsillectomy. He had been told that the doctor would 'put you to sleep'. A few weeks previously a vet had given him a similar message about his pet dog.

Cognitive development limits children's understanding, not only of illness and symptoms (Chapter 6), but also of treatment. One child of 10 years revealed her way of understanding her impending orthopaedic surgery by drawing a picture of her leg in which a large safety pin protruded from it. Her concrete way of thinking had been applied to the information that her leg was to be 'pinned'.

Adults. Problems of language and understanding are not, of course, restricted to children. Language abilities are usually overestimated by clinicians, who routinely provide information in ways that are only intelligible to people with similar intelligence and education to themselves (Box 11.1).

Previous chapters have shown that adult patients and clinicians often have very different ways of understanding symptoms and procedures (Chapters 5 and 6). Therefore, information that makes perfect sense to the clinician can be meaningless or even misleading to the patient

---

Box 11.1 Seeking patients' permission for research

Ethics committees are to protect patients' interests when they are asked to take part in research. The consent form is central to this. Patients sign it to show that they understand and agree to what is being asked of them. The following passage is from a consent form that is recommended by one ethics committee.

> I understand that my participation is voluntary and that I am free to withdraw at any time without my medical care or legal rights being affected. I understand that sections of my medical notes may be looked at by responsible individuals from the University of X or from regulatory authorities where it is relevant to my taking part in research. I give permission for these individuals to have access to my records.

The passage has long sentences and long words. Therefore, its readibility score, calculated by the Flesch formula (see Ley, 1988) is very low: 39.1. This is the level of an academic text and means that only around half the population would be able to understand it. The passage is easily rewritten. The following translation has a readability level of 88.4, the level of a comic. At least 95% of the population would understand it. Whose interests is this ethics committee protecting?

> I am clear about the following points. I do not have to take part. I will only take part if I want to. I can leave this study at any time. If I do, it will not affect my treatment in any way. Researchers from X University might see my medical records. This will only happen if they think it will help them with the research. I will let them do this.

(Box 11.2). The clinician who wishes to provide information must decide whether this should be conveyed in terms of clinicians' or patients' ways of thinking. For example, to encourage physical exercise (see Box 13.1), explaining that it 'conditions' the body will often be more valuable than specifying its physiological effects. Similarly, the clinician's view that a patient is free from pathology can be unacceptable to some patients unless their need to understand their symptoms is addressed(Box 13.4).

11.2.2.5 Giving Information in Practice

The evidence shows great variability in effects of information and in the desire for it. Therefore, how is the clinician to manage information needs in practice? Questionnaires do exist to distinguish patients who prefer to

Box 11.2   The language of information provision

This patient's treatment for breast cancer included surgery and radiotherapy. A few months later she was interviewed by a researcher. Her comments expose the gulf that can exist between how the clinician provides information and what the patient experiences.

> After surgery, I got a lot of swelling [under the arm] which by watching TV and talking to the other patients I know what it was now. I was not prepared for that although I was told in hospital 'If you have your lymph glands done you do get some fluid' but you see that didn't mean a thing.

To the clinician, this lady had been accurately informed as to what to expect. This information was, however, in terms which made sense only to the clinician. To find information that could help to make sense of her symptoms, the patient had to turn to sources that spoke her language.

---

have information from those who prefer not to (Krantz et al, 1980). These are valuable research tools. However, it is unrealistic to expect clinicians routinely to subject patients to a questionnaire before deciding whether or not to give them detailed information about an impending procedure. Indeed, too much concern with formal ways to identify which patients need information, and then with setting up formal programmes to provide information, is probably misguided. Patients identify their own information needs very readily, but these typically remain unmet. Among other reasons, patients avoid 'burdening' staff with their concerns (Peerbhoy et al, 1998; Box 11.3). In many clinical settings, it would be a major change in practice for clinicians simply to ask patients what they would like to know, to make it easy for patients to tell them, and then to answer patients' questions in ways that they can understand! This would require clinicians' attention to the ways described in Chapter 10 whereby patients and clinicians *avoid* talking about distressing topics.

Therefore it is probably unnecessary for the clinician to be concerned about the details of the research literature about information provision. Equally, it is important to be unpersuaded by the political and cultural emphasis on the necessity to provide detailed information. It is much more realistic for patients to be asked what they are concerned about and what information they would like. It seems likely that patients would accurately identify themselves as in need of information or not. Their answers to such simple questions might well distinguish the monitors from the blunters. Unfortunately, there is little research evidence about

---

Box 11.3   Barriers to questioning clinicians

Comments by inpatients shortly after surgery revealed barriers that deterred them from questioning clinicians (Peerbhoy et al, 1998).

One patient's comment that 'I'm not one for pushing forward and asking questions' implied the need for a degree of assertion that she could not muster. Others felt intimidated: 'I had Dr X here, all the students and everyone, and I had all set out what I was going to say. I did have little questions to ask, personal ones and that, but I forgot and then he went.'

Other comments revealed fear that overt questioning would be disapproved of. One patient would 'sort of chat to people and gain information without being pointedly asking for it'. Similarly, another would ask questions 'as long as it doesn't put them [clinicians] to any trouble or anything'.

---

whether basing information provision on this choice improves outcomes by comparison with providing or withholding it across the board. Probably the necessary studies have not been done because clinical researchers tend to assume that the clinician should always decide what is best for the patient!

11.2.3 Meeting Appraisal Needs by Explanation

11.2.3.1 Explanation in Clinician–Patient Interaction

Clearly, information can add to the challenge that patients are under unless they are helped to use it constructively. The point here is that patients' cognitive needs are not primarily for 'information'. Instead, they are for 'explanation'. To *explain* aspects of illness or care, clinicians must engage with patients in an active process of making sense of information that they have. Explanation will often, of course, involve giving patients additional information; but it also includes helping them to make use of this information and to make links between different pieces of information. The crucial requirement is that explanation is firmly based, not on the *clinician's* way of thinking, but on how the *patient* thinks (Box 11.4).

Patients are highly 'scientific' in thinking about their symptoms (Chapter

Box 11.4   Explanation: meeting a patient's appraisal needs

X became increasingly housebound, depressed and pessimistic about the future after leaving hospital following a myocardial infarction. A specialist nurse assessed her and concluded that her beliefs about her condition were probably central in her problems. Therefore X needed to understand her condition better. Elements of the nurse's work with her are illustrated here. They are similar to the approach described in detail in Chapter 13 for patients who need help to understand symptoms where there is no serious pathology.

Patient's presentation	Nurse's response
X thought that exertion could kill her. She could not go further than her front gate without feeling that her heart was being strained	*Identifying the belief and providing explanation.* Questioning revealed a 'mental representation' of myocardial infarction according to which any exertion is risky. X thought that infarction was the result of a weakness in a blood vessel of the heart which could be burst open by increased blood pressure—such as exercise would cause. The nurse drew a picture of the heart and its blood supply, showing arterial narrowing. She used this to show how the heart attack could occur, checking X's understanding at every stage. She gave the diagram to the patient to take home and offered to answer any of her questions about it at their next meeting
X was not reassured, because she felt pains when she walked to the shop and thought they must be a 'warning'	*Challenging the belief.* The nurse asked X about her pain in detail and helped her to see that it was different from the pain that she remembered at the time of her heart attack. She then explained that there are many reasons that people feel pains after a heart attack. Sometimes it's because of overbreathing or chest muscles tensing. Anxiety can make both of these worse. Sometimes the pains don't have any obvious cause at all and they may just be the body sounding a 'warning' because its alarm system has become too sensitive. Then a treadmill test was carried out, once the procedure had been explained to X. She knew that she would be wired to machines that could measure the activity of the heart and show whether it was behaving normally. Soon after beginning at a low workload she signalled that she was feeling the

Continued

Patient's presentation	Nurse's response
	pains that worried her. She was shown that her heart was performing normally
X was still frightened that she might do too much	*Changing the patient's agenda by redefining the problem.* The nurse helped X to see that her main problem was getting her confidence back. She agreed with X that she was sensible to take things gradually. They agreed that X would begin by walking to the local shops with her husband. Benches and other resting places were pinpointed so that she could rest until she felt able to go on. X would keep a diary of what happened and bring it to the next meeting in two weeks' time

6). They attach great weight to empirical evidence (especially their own symptoms). They use their existing knowledge to understand symptoms and, within the limitations of this knowledge, they critically evaluate what the clinician says. This means that changing patients' beliefs is not always achieved by a simple 'expert' statement from the clinician. An alternative approach—cognitive therapy—is outlined in Chapter 13. Although that account focuses on patients without physical pathology, the principles are generally applicable. One of the principles is that the best way of changing patients' beliefs is by helping them to 'discover' for themselves.

This principle, called 'collaborative empiricism', is particularly important where patients have strong fears and beliefs about how they should respond to their symptoms (Box 5.2). For example, a common problem after myocardial infarction is 'cardiac invalidism' (Chapter 7). The patient, and perhaps the spouse, wrongly believe that any exertion by the patient is dangerous. Challenging this belief requires the clinician to identify its detailed basis and provide convincing contrary evidence. The most convincing evidence of all for the patient who doubts that he can exert himself safely is, of course, when he does so (Chapter 13, Box 11.4).

11.2.3.2 Explanation by Modelling

In some situations it is necessary to have a cost-effective procedure for giving information that does not depend entirely on individual clinicians talking with individual patients. 'Modelling' seems to be particularly effective in circumventing many of the difficulties arising from language, patients' beliefs and differing levels of cognitive development. In modelling, observers learn by watching another individual. Modelling by using video-filmed patients has been applied most successfully with children. For example, watching a film of a boy gradually overcome his anxiety during hospital admission reduced anxiety in 4- to 11-year-old children before and after surgery (Melamed and Siegel, 1975).

Modelling is applicable in adults, also. An example is a study in which preoperative information improved recovery from coronary artery bypass graft surgery (including reduced levels of postoperative hypertension; Anderson, 1987). To attribute this benefit simply to the information would be to miss the importance of the way that the information was conveyed. Patients were shown filmed interviews with recovered patients. The film presumably guided patients to process the information in a non-threatening way so that, whatever their own concerns and information preferences, they came to anticipate their own safe recovery. A supportive relationship can be an effective vehicle for modelling in real life rather than on film. For instance, having a postoperative room-mate while awaiting cardiac surgery accelerated postoperative recovery by comparison with having a preoperative room-mate (Kulik and Mahler, 1987). Perhaps the postoperative room-mates helped the preoperative patients to anticipate their own successful outcome (however, there are similar benefits of a non-surgical room-mate, suggesting that what may be important is support from fellow patients who are not themselves very anxious; Kulik et al, 1993).

11.3 PATIENT PARTICIPATION: CHOICE, CONTROL AND INVOLVEMENT

11.3.1 Benefits of Choice and Control

Research into effects of offering choice and control has been more limited in medical and surgical care than research into effects of offering information. However, the effects have been intensively studied in non-clinical research. Two effects have been well established that are potentially very important in clinical settings.

11.3.1.1 Commitment and Adherence

Social psychology research has shown that commitment is increased by the act of making a choice. For instance, support for a political party, liking of a particular kind of food or a belief in the superior qualities of a specific make of motor car are all increased by making the relevant choice;

i.e., by freely voting for the party, selecting the food from a wide variety in a supermarket or buying that make of car. The potential for applying this principle to clinical situations was illustrated by an early experiment. This compared the effectiveness of placebo (i.e., pharmacologically inert) sleeping tablets given in two different ways in hospital inpatients (Totman, 1976). One group of patients was asked to choose one from two types of tablet (each designed to look different although equally inert) after trying each. This group benefited more (i.e., fell asleep sooner) than patients in the second group. Patients in this group had been given one or the other tablet without being able to choose. One patient who had been given the choice even volunteered that the sleeping tablet was the best ever experienced! It seemed that, having chosen one type of tablet, patients believed this tablet to be more powerful and this enhanced its effect.

This example is trivial. Its clinical importance does not lie in helping patients to sleep on a hospital ward. Nevertheless, the study does have a profound clinical message. It shows that a real, objective choice is not necessary for psychological benefits. Even the *perception* of having a choice is sufficient. This is supported by many other social psychology experiments on how to change people's attitudes. In general, the greatest commitment to a decision is achieved when individuals are led to adopt the behaviour that the researcher intends, but in such a way that they feel that *they* have made the choice. That is, commitment is greatest when the persuasion is least obvious.

It is easy to see how these findings should be applied to clinical situations. The message is especially important where adherence is at issue (Chapter 9). Whereas emphasis on the *clinician's authority* leads to reactance, emphasizing *patients' participation* in a decision maximizes commitment— and therefore adherence (Box 11.5). Similarly, ensuring that patients, rather than clinicians, take responsibility for treatment regimens enhances adherence (Lowe et al, 1995).

11.3.1.2 Reducing the Stress Response

Non-clinical research has shown a second set of benefits of choice and control. These concern emotional and physiological aspects of the stress response (Chapter 3). In general, exercising control over the challenge that provokes subjective distress or a hormonal response can reduce the response. The effects are particularly clear on the adrenocortical limb of the physiological stress response. Once again, it is the *perception* of control that matters: even where choice or control does not materially reduce a challenge, the perception of exercising a degree of choice or control is enough to reduce the physiological effects (Steptoe, 1983).

Box 11.5   Helping a patient to choose treatment

Box 9.4 described a patient who had reacted against what she felt to be an order from her surgeon to have surgery for breast cancer. She had been told that she 'had to have the operation' or else the cancer would probably spread and she would not be alive in five years' time. How else might she have been presented with the recommendation?

'Your cancer is the sort that usually does not respond to radiotherapy or chemotherapy alone. What we know is that having the mastectomy means that we'd expect you to be alive after five years and then we'd expect you to live your normal lifespan. Without the operation, people with your clinical picture don't do well and over half are not alive in five years. Tell me what else you would like me to tell you so that you can decide what's right for you. Or perhaps you'd like to talk it over with one of the specialist nurses.'

11.3.2 Choice and Control in Clinical Practice

The evidence that exists about effects of choice and control in clinical practice tends to show findings that would be expected from the non-clinical evidence. That is, in general, choice and control have been associated with better outcomes.

11.3.2.1 Feeling in Control over Chronic Illness

In chronic illness, the complex demands of clinical care fall upon patients as much as—and often more than—clinicians (Chapter 7). This means that patients' control over their illness is crucial for effective management. Once again, however, the patients' *perception* of the control that they have is also important in its own right. There is some evidence that patients who feel that they have a degree of control over the course of their chronic disease are better adjusted to it and better able to manage it (Affleck et al, 1987). Helping to increase patients' feelings of control is not a mysterious clinical task. It is a very practical matter of ensuring that patients feel that they are able to influence the challenges that confront them. It can therefore be achieved in the course of routine care (Box 11.6).

11.3.2.2 Choosing or Controlling Treatment

There are a few situations in health care in which patients are explicitly invited to make choices. That is, patients are offered genuine alternatives

Box 11.6 Enhancing patients' feelings of control

Feeling in control over events is important for managing chronic disease and for successful recovery from myocardial infarction. Routine care provides many opportunities for clinicians to enhance or reduce patients' feelings of control. These examples are for a patient recovering from myocardial infarction, but they would apply to any patients whose recovery depends on their active participation in rehabilitation.

Control over who/what	How to enhance control	How to reduce control
Clinicians	Physiotherapist negotiates with the patient to shape the exercise programme	Physiotherapist tells patient which exercises to carry out
	Physiotherapist asks for the patient's view of how the exercises are feeling	Physiotherapist praises the patient
	Doctor tells the patient she will visit later to answer his questions, and suggests that he might like to make a list of them first	Doctor visits without telling the patient when or why
	Nurse asks about the patient's experience, explaining that this might help her to improve care for patients in future	Nurse does not ask for patient's views
Rehabilitation	Encourage mental rehearsal of rehabilitation exercises; explain that this is a technique that sportsmen and women use to improve performance	Give patient nothing to occupy his/her mind
	Ask patient to keep a diary of exercises, noting how difficult they feel so that further exercises can be planned	Patient's exercises are recorded by nurses. Patient told what exercises to do and when
	Ensure patient understands *how* rehabilitation, relaxation and stress management can help his/her heart recover from myocardial infarction	Emphasize to the patient *that* exercise etc. are important for rehabilitation

Control over who/what	How to enhance control	How to reduce control
Physical and emotional state	Provide a relaxation training programme; ensure graded and progressive approach to provide feelings of skill mastery. Explain that this will be the first step in learning about stress management later on	Do not ask the patient to learn new skills
	Provide patient with a notebook; ask him/her to note down any worries or questions day by day; nurse visits regularly to review the notes and address concerns	Reassure patient that everything is going well

for responding to a clinical problem. In many centres, women with breast cancer are, depending on the characteristics of the tumour, invited to choose their form of treatment. They can choose mastectomy, in which the breast is removed, or lumpectomy, in which the tumour is excised and the breast spared. In this situation, there is some evidence that choice does improve psychological adjustment around the time of surgery and postoperatively, whichever choice is made (Morris and Royle, 1988).

Realistically, of course, choice is impractical in most treatment decisions. Patients do not have the expertise. However, there are ways in which patients can take control of aspects of their treatment. In acute hospital care, an example of this is now routine after major surgery: 'patient-controlled analgesia' (PCA). Using this technique, patients who are in pain press a button to trigger a machine to inject a pre-set amount of morphine through a cannula implanted into one of their veins. Surveys have confirmed that patients are normally more satisfied when analgesia is given in this way than when it is administered in the usual way by nurses (Ballantyne et al, 1993).

11.3.2.3 Self-Control

Realistically, however, the opportunity for patients to exercise significant control over technical aspects of their care is limited. Therefore, some research has focused on patients' capacity to exercise control over *internal*, mental events. Purely mental procedures include teaching and encourag-

---

Box 11.7   Cognitive coping imagery

Coping and involvement can help protect against stress, including surgery. However, realistically it is often hard to find ways that patients can be involved with some treatments. Instead, they can be encouraged to take control over their own thoughts and fears. These extracts are from an audiotape that guided patients to visualize challenges associated with forthcoming surgery (Manyande et al, 1995). They followed a period of relaxation training designed to produce a relaxed and accepting state of mind. Patients who listened to the tape found it easier to cope with pain and were physiologically less stressed by surgery.

. . . While remaining as relaxed as possible, imagine each of the situations that I describe, as vividly as possible. Imagine it is the day of your operation. You've had nothing to eat or drink. You feel hungry and thirsty and you know that you can't eat or drink. Your mind is occupied by the thought that you can *easily* manage without food or drink for the day. You feel *positive* about what you're going through. You know you can easily cope . . .

. . . Now it's the day after your operation. You're ready to get out of bed with a little help and even to eat light food. You may feel weak, and pain from the wound. But you know you can overcome these feelings. After a few steps on your own you realize it's not as difficult as you'd imagined. You eat with a big appetite and you know that soon you will be ready to go home, where you will finish recovering from your operation . . .

. . . By imagining yourself coping well you will help yourself to cope well. You will be better prepared, more able to cope. You will recover more quickly. Your mind is a powerful thing, and its ability to prepare your body for what you will be going through is much greater than is commonly realized. Always see yourself actively coping with the situation you experience, regardless of how unpleasant it might normally be . . .

---

ing patients to recognize signs of their distress, to identify the fears that distress them and then to use relaxation or self-talk to counter their distress. This kind of approach has helped patients through diverse procedures, including cardiac catheterization (Kendall et al, 1979) and inpatient surgery (Langer et al, 1975; Box 11.7).

The extent to which patients can exercise control over physiological processes is more controversial. Relaxation techniques, at least, can be used to achieve both emotional and physiological benefits, especially where physiological disease processes are exacerbated by stress responses. Benefits of relaxation are therefore seen in a variety of conditions such as hypertension (Patel, 1997), asthma (Smyth et al, 1999) or in reducing nausea and anxiety in cancer chemotherapy (Burish and Jenkins, 1992). However, other procedures are probably best seen as conveying the *perception* of self-control over physiological processes. For instance, patients can mentally rehearse rehabilitation exercises before they are ready to try them in real life, in the same way that sportsmen and women prepare themselves for the real thing (Box 11.6). Similarly, some patients with cancer 'visualize' their body fighting the disease in the hope that this will help the fight.

11.3.2.4 Differences between Patients

Common sense suggests that people differ in the level of involvement or control that they want—just as they differ in the amount of information that they want (Chapter 9). There is some evidence to support this (Baron and Logan, 1993). Paradoxically monitors, who seek more information about medical problems than do blunters, seem to prefer to leave decision making to their clinicians (Miller et al, 1988). More educated patients tend to prefer more participation in decision making (Coulter, 1997). Reflecting the relatively recent cultural importance of autonomy (Chapter 2), it is likely that older patients seek less control than younger ones (Coulter, 1997; Lorber, 1975). A questionnaire to measure these differences between individuals has been described (Krantz et al, 1980). In practice, it is easier just to ask the patient.

11.3.3 Caveats about Patient Control

11.3.3.1 Burdens of Control

Control is often regarded in psychological literature as uncomplicated and wholly positive in its effects. In practice, however, control in clinical settings is complex and has negative effects, too, as does information (see above).

In chronic illness, there is evidence of the potential burden associated with having control **where the patient's condition is poor**. Patients with renal failure can receive haemodialysis in hospital, which affords them relatively little control over the procedure, or at home, where they are responsible for attaching themselves to the dialysis machine. Alternatively they undergo continuous ambulatory peritoneal dialysis (CAPD: in which the patient is entirely responsible for changing bags of dialysate, attached to a catheter that enters the abdominal cavity, in the course of normal daily activities). Where disease is most severe, the group that is at greatest risk of depression is the CAPD patients; that is, the patients with the greatest burden of self-management (Eitel et al, 1995). This might be a warning that, although control is fine when things are going well, it can feel a burden when they are not.

Part of the burden of control is the sheer **complexity** of managing complex conditions and juggling the various competing needs. This is obviously particularly difficult in chronic disease (Chapter 7, Box 7.2). In acute care, patients' experiences of patient-controlled analgesia (PCA) illustrate similar dilemmas (Chumbley et al, 1998). *Clinicians* tend to think that patients can easily manage their pain with this technique because of the direct control that it provides over analgesia. Asking *patients* reveals a different picture. Many find it very difficult. It takes some trial and error to work out how to use it. They have to juggle their wish to reduce pain against their (accurate) fears of side effects from using PCA, particularly nausea, and their (inaccurate) fears of overdosing or becoming addicted.

Another burden is the **responsibility** that goes with having control. Patients are very ready to blame themselves for their disease (Chapter 7) and feeling responsible for treatment will exacerbate self-blame, particularly where the disease is not successfully managed. Providing patients with choice over acute care therefore entails serious psychological risks. For instance, although short-term effects of choice over treatment for breast cancer seem to be positive, it is not clear how long these benefits last. In particu-lar, it is important to know what happens if and when disease recurs. A woman who has a recurrence of cancer in a breast that she chose to retain in favour of lumpectomy might be burdened with feelings of responsibility for the 'wrong' decision.

11.3.3.2 Professional Defence

One problem with 'giving control' to patients is therefore that, whether or not patients can or do exert real control, they are given a degree of *responsibility*. Responsibility tends to stick with patients once it is given. This can be illustrated by the way that clinicians failed to take back responsibility for managing one patient's pain when her PCA machine malfunctioned so that it gave no analgesia (Box 11.8).

Speculatively, it seems that the emphasis on patients' control in health care is not entirely motivated by patients' needs. Instead, it might reflect clinicians' continued need to protect themselves from feeling responsible

---

Box 11.8   Who is responsible for managing patients' pain?

With patient-controlled analgesia, patients use an electronic machine to inject analgesia into a vein when they wish. When these patients' machine malfunctioned, it exposed the way that this technique had moved responsibility for analgesia from the clinicians to the patient (Taylor et al, 1996b):

Patient 1   'Nurses felt they couldn't do anything. They said it was working when it wasn't . . . People didn't believe me that the pump wasn't working. No one seemed to be able to help.'

Patient 2   'They kept saying to press the button but I couldn't feel it working. I was in terrible pain the first night . . . I wasn't taken seriously when I said I was in pain. I said the machine wasn't working and they should give me something different and the nurses just told me the machine was working and told me to keep pressing.'

---

for patients' suffering (Hall and Salmon, 1997). Again, detailed descriptions of patients' experiences of PCA are consistent with this (Taylor et al, 1996a, 1996b). It is usually assumed that the reason patients are satisfied with PCA is because they value the feeling of control that it affords them. In practice, control seems not to be an issue for them (Box 11.9). Instead, they are positive about PCA because it releases them from having to depend on nurses for their pain relief. This freedom is valued, in turn, because it is often difficult to get attention from nurses when it is needed and because, besides, patients want to avoid disclosing their suffering to the nurses (Chapter 10).

11.3.4 Involvement

11.3.4.1 The Paradox in Patients' Attitudes to Control

Some of the findings described above contradict the common assumption that patients always value being in control. Surveys of patients' attitudes to breast cancer treatment show very clearly that healthy clinicians or academics are likely to misunderstand what patients want in relation to control (Beaver et al, 1996; Degner and Sloan, 1992). Women *without* breast cancer thought that they would want to take the active role in treatment decisions were they to develop the disease. However, patients who

---

Box 11.9   Patient-controlled analgesia

Patient-controlled analgesia is widely regarded as one of the best examples of providing patients with control over aspects of their care. Patients are positive about PCA and it is usually assumed that this is because of the control it gives them. However, when Taylor et al (1996) asked patients about their experience of PCA, they found that control was not important: 'When you're in pain, you don't care whether you're in control.'

Instead, patients gave three reasons for being positive about PCA. Each was because it freed them from needing to control nurses:

It avoids 'bothering' the nurses: 'It's great that I didn't have to bother nurses. I wouldn't dream of bothering other people.'

It avoids the problems of nursing care: 'When you call, sometimes no one comes. If you have to have a nurse to attend you sometimes you never get the attention, but this is very good. You do it yourself.'

It saves embarrassment: 'You feel embarrassed to call the nurse each time. This way, no one knows you're in pain.'

---

already had the disease preferred a passive or collaborative role. They wanted the surgeon to take the initiative in management decisions. This is consistent with other evidence that patients with cancer want their doctors to take responsibility for making decisions. There is also evidence that hospital inpatients reject the opportunity to feel in control (Chapter 12). In primary care, too, there is evidence that patients tend to prefer a more directive approach from the general practitioner (Savage and Armstrong, 1990).

Nevertheless, when asked, patients say they welcome opportunities to exercise control and freely take on the language of having control. Patients receiving PCA, for example, respond very positively to questions about how much control they feel they have—even though their other answers show that their control is very limited (Chumbley et al, 1998). These findings set up a paradox. Being *offered* choice and control, and describing oneself as having control, are valued by patients, even though *exercising* control is not so valued and is often not possible.

Another study of breast cancer patients points to a way of resolving the paradox (Fallowfield et al, 1990). Patients treated by surgeons who believed in offering choice of treatment were less unhappy than those seen by more directive surgeons. However, this result held even for patients to whom the non-directive surgeons had not, in fact, been able to offer choice. Whether the patient was specifically offered a choice was therefore not the critical factor. Instead, offering choice appeared to be a marker of some other aspect of surgeons' style which helped to minimize their patients' suffering.

11.3.4.2 The Value of Involvement

Resolving the paradox is not, in principle, difficult. In general, the clinician should recognize that patients wish to be *involved* in decisions, but without taking the *responsibility* for them (Thompson et al, 1988). There is often scope for helping patients to feel a degree of involvement, whether or not choice or control is practicable (Box 11.10). First, involvement means listening to these patient's concerns and preferences, and ensuring that the patient understands that these have been taken into account in management decisions. Secondly, it means providing the patient with opportunites to help with clinical care.

There are significant benefits of involvement, over and above those that information giving alone provides. For instance, giving information in advance about how a gastroscopy would feel reduced distress during the procedure (Johnson and Leventhal, 1974). However, the procedure itself was facilitated if this message had been combined with guidance about how the patient could help. This guidance helped the patient to be involved by controlling breathing and swallowing as the gastroscopy tube was passed. Similarly, prior information from childbirth classes helped to 'desensitize' women and so reduce their anxiety on arrival at the labour

---

Box 11.10 A failure of involvement

This 53-year-old lady is describing physiotherapy exercises during the few days after knee replacement.

They [physiotherapists] get the job done. And when they think that they can't get any more results from that joint, then they don't push it any further, then, when they think they've got the maximum out of the joint.

She depersonalizes 'the joint' and describes it as entirely under the control of the physiotherapists. Might rehabilitation be expedited were she to feel more involvement?

suite. However, pain *during* labour was decreased most by teaching patients ways to be involved: monitoring contractions so as to guide breathing and relaxation (Leventhal et al, 1989).

Feeling involved is a state that can only be recognized by the patient. Therefore, it is important that patients are offered ways of being involved that make sense to them. A major concern for hospital patients is to 'fit in' with staff (Chapter 12). In a recent study, surgical patients were invited to take control over as much of their care as possible (Peerbhoy et al, 1998). The patients interpreted this as 'cooperating' with clinicians and doing as much as they could to 'help' them. One patient stated this role very clearly: 'It's up to you [patient] to help them [staff].' Therefore, while they rejected the invitation to take 'control', they were open to feeling 'involved'.

11.4 BEYOND COGNITIVE AND PARTICIPATION NEEDS: DIGNITY AND SAFETY

The concepts of explanation and involvement come closer to what patients seek than the more limited ideas of information and control. However, the paradoxes and problems that research on information and control has identified point to more fundamental patient needs that are rarely acknowledged in clinical or research literature.

11.4.1 Dignity and Control

Consider how the offer of choice and control arise in normal, everyday life, outside the clinic. In some situations, it is an invitation to make a real decision. That means that the outcome cannot be predicted, such as when asked to choose a meal in a restaurant. In other cases, however, the offer is merely a social convention. Visualize the situation where you wish to use something belonging to a friend: a book, for example. You ask him before you take it. However, you do not *have* to ask because you are in his house and you know where it is on the shelves. Moreover, you know that your friend will not deny permission. He could not do so without threatening the friendship. Besides, you often borrow things from each other and they are always returned. Therefore, in asking whether you can borrow this book you are not inviting a real choice. Instead, you make this request so as to recognize your friend's feelings of autonomy and dignity (Slugoski, 1995). These feelings would be challenged were you simply to take what you seek.

Autonomy and dignity are even more important where the individual's body, rather than property, is at stake. One surgical patient, invited to exercise control over her care, responded: 'You're treated with the height of respect and kindness and that's all you want really' (Peerbhoy et al, 1998). Viewing control and involvement in this way can help to explain the paradox that patients value being invited to feel in control, even where objective control is very limited or is not wanted.

According to this view, the language of control and choice should be central to the way that clinicians conduct their routine encounters with patients, from seeking consent for a throat examination or blood pressure measurement to deciding on major surgery. Unfortunately, it is still considered normal by many clinicians to carry out a procedure on a patient's body without first going through the ritual of choice and permission that they would never omit when merely seeking to use a friend's property. Moreover, even where the language of control is used by clinicians so as to respect the patient's autonomy and dignity, their subsequent actions often undermine their words (Box 10.3).

11.4.2 Dignity, Support and Information

There are many clues that what patients find most helpful about information provision is not the information that is provided. First, benefits appear not to be related to the amount of information transmitted or remembered (Andrew, 1970; Marteau et al, 1996). Furthermore surgical patients, at least, seem to value information as 'useful' even when no other effect on recovery can be detected (Ridgeway and Mathews, 1982). Also, there is no evidence of a dose–response relationship linking amount of information to amount of benefit. Finally, information is not always valued according to whether it helps in making decisions. Its functions often seem to be more to do with the patient's need to feel respected or safe (Box 11.11).

Although written information can be effective (Ley, 1988), information is *more* effective when provided face to face by a clinician rather than in a leaflet (Leigh et al, 1977). Therefore it is likely that, as with the provision of control or involvement, information provision is a vehicle for other beneficial processes that arise through the social interaction. Emotional support is one such process (Chapter 3). That is, receiving information directly from a clinician indicates that the patient is valued by the clinician and that the patient's concerns are respected and understood. The value of support is seen very clearly in patients undergoing surgery (Chapter 12).

Box 11.11   Uses of information

Peerbhoy et al (1998) talked with surgical patients about their attitudes to asking questions and getting information. No patient described using information to help make decisions. They valued it for other reasons.

To help make sense of what is happening: 'The more I ask, the more I get to know, is helping me better, to get to know the problem.'

To feel safe: 'I just checked why there were different dosages. So I got the answer. That was all I wanted.'

To feel respected: 'They should answer your questions to the extent of respecting you as an individual, not as a lump of meat.'

There is an even more subtle process going on, however. To think about what this might be, consider once again the scenario, above, where you wished to borrow your friend's book. The chances are that you would not simply say that you want to borrow it. You would provide some information about why you want it and what you were going to do with it. That information could well be immediately forgotten by the friend. Its content is not important. Its function is to legitimize the request (Langer and Abelson, 1972). This, too, can be seen as a way of respecting the friend's feelings of autonomy and ownership. These could be threatened were you to ask for his property merely on a whim. One of the patients in Box 11.11 made it clear that, for her, being given information in response to her questions was a way that her feelings of dignity could be preserved. Therefore providing information in routine clinical practice that justifies and explains what a clinician will do is another way of ensuring that the patient's feelings of dignity and self-worth are preserved.

11.4.3 Safety

Concepts of information provision, choice, involvement and support have become highly influential in the psychology of health care. The present chapter adds involvement, dignity and autonomy to the list. Nevertheless, this lengthening list should not blind us to other concepts that might be even more important. In particular, *danger* is implicit in most clinical settings. Feeling *safe* in the face of this danger is likely to be most patients' priority. Extensive research has shown that animals are highly motivated by signals which promise respite from unpleasant, threatening events ('safety signals'). Unfortunately, safety is not so well researched in people.

Nevertheless, a recent study of PCA has indicated that patients' feelings of safety are important (Chumbley et al, 1999). Patients' positive feelings about PCA depended on how *safe* they felt. Contrary to the usual assumption, how much they felt in *control* was unimportant—except inasmuch as it was one factor that contributed to feeling safe.

The fundamental importance of the concepts reviewed in this chapter, including support, information giving, control, involvement and autonomy might well be that they help patients to feel safe. Valuing clinicians for the 'alliance' they form with the patient against disease (Chapter 6) also perhaps reflects the need to feel safe in the face of danger. Patients are unlikely to feel safe in a setting where clinicians seem not to care about them or understand them, and where they fail to show that they respect the patient's autonomy.

11.5 CONCLUSION

Reasons for providing patients with information and opportunities for control or involvement are summarized in Box 11.12. For ethical and

Box 11.12 Information and involvement: the 'needs iceberg'

Providing patients with information and the opportunity to be involved in decisions meets different needs. The most obvious is the medico-legal requirement for informed consent. However, there are many other psychological needs which are met in this way.

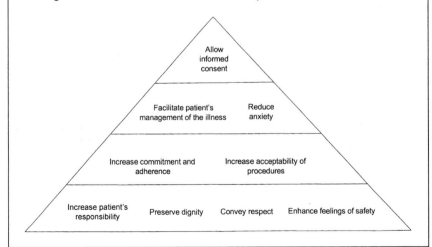

medico-legal reasons, patients need basic information so that their consent to treatment can be sought. There are other needs to be met by information, also. Both information and control are often prerequisites of effective care, for instance for the patient with a chronic disease that needs careful self-management, or for the patient at risk of an acute problem who needs to watch for signs that require urgent investigation. Beyond this, providing opportunity for control or involvement has important psychological functions. It improves the acceptability of a procedure or treatment and increases commitment and effectiveness. However, it must be remembered that patients differ in the degree to which they seek information and control, and the sensitive clinician will identify the level of each that an individual patient seeks. Also, information and control can be ways of shifting responsibility to the patient. This will often be an important part of clinical care, for example in helping dependent patients of the kind described in Chapter 13. In other instances, however, it might be less justified because it meets clinicians' rather than patients' needs.

Beyond these needs, it is important to be aware of other psychological needs that are served by providing information and involvement. Patients can be helped in this way to feel that they are respected as individuals and that they are safe in the care of clinicians who are sensitive to their needs and concerns.

KEY POINTS

- Patients' cognitive needs are met by information and explanation.
- Information has both beneficial and harmful effects.
- Explanation means that patients are helped to make sense of information.
- Needs for participation can be met by arranging for patients to make choices, feel in control or feel involved.
- Choice and control over treatment can increase commitment to treatment and can reduce stress responses.
- Choice or control over treatment can also burden patients with complex tasks and with responsibility for treatment failures.
- Patients value being involved, but often interpret this as helping staff.
- Being offered information, choice and control conveys respect for patients' dignity and autonomy.
- Psychological aspects of management can help to meet patients' overriding need to feel safe in a dangerous environment.

Chapter 12

HOSPITALIZATION AND SURGERY

KEY CLINICAL ISSUES

- What are the psychological challenges that face inpatients?
- Why are most inpatients so obliging?
- What makes a patient a 'bad' patient?
- Are nurses good providers of emotional support to their patients?
- Should parents stay in hospital to support their children?
- What is convalescence for after surgery?
- Is reassurance a good way to calm patients down before surgery?

Being ill and consulting clinicians in primary care or outpatient clinics is part of ordinary life for many people. Being admitted to hospital is a very different experience. Typically, inpatients are in an unfamiliar and threatening environment and are exposed to procedures that are potentially dangerous, embarrassing or undignified. They have little opportunity to influence the ward routine and are separated from familiar people. The physical and psychological traumas of surgery accentuate these challenges. Being a medical or surgical inpatient therefore focuses intensely many of the issues introduced in previous chapters. There are also additional psychological problems associated with being in an alien environment controlled by other people and with being removed from normal everyday life. This chapter will first identify some of the psychological needs that are associated specifically with being an inpatient. From this perspective, it will go on to examine psychological management approaches that have been described specifically for medical, and particularly surgical, inpatients.

12.1 CHALLENGES FOR THE INPATIENT

Systematic surveys of hospital patients identify a wide variety of concerns. In an influential survey, medical and surgical patients in the

---

Box 12.1   Challenges of hospitalization

Admission to hospital exposes inpatients to a variety of challenges, many of which are not directly related to illness and treatment. These were among challenges that emerged from surveying hospital inpatients in the USA (Volicer et al, 1977).

Problems of home life	Losing income because of illness Missing special family occasions
Worries about serious illness	Knowing I have to have an operation Thinking I might have cancer
Unfamiliarity of surroundings	Strangers sleeping in the same room Unusual smells
Indignity	Having to be helped with a bedpan Being fed through tubes
Loss of control	Not having my call light answered Not being able to get newspapers or TV when I want
Lack of support	Having a room mate who is too ill to talk to me Staff being in too much of a hurry

---

USA were asked to rate a large number of events for their stressfulness (Volicer et al, 1977; Box 12.1). Some events, such as having insufficient insurance to pay the hospital, are relatively specific to the health care system in which the patients were studied. Most, however, are generally applicable. Many threats were not directly related to the hospital at all. They concerned, instead, **family, home or employment**. Whether there will still be a job to go back to, whether the children—or the business—are being well looked after and whether the cat will leave home are all fears that patients voice—when given the opportunity. Fears of **serious illness**, and of problems arising from **treatment**, were obviously important, too.

Most challenges were not so tangible. They reflected the psychological variables that have been introduced in previous chapters. Many events were threatening because they were **unfamiliar**; others because they were **undignified** or embarrassing. Several challenges refer to the loss of **autonomy** and **isolation** from sources of social support. Some important challenges for inpatients are only hinted at in this list. Other surveys have found that patients were concerned about **whether staff liked them** (Johnston, 1982).

Surveys like this, where interviewers decide the questions in advance, have the benefit that standardization of questions allows patients' responses to be counted. However, less structured interviews can reveal ways of thinking that the interviewers could not have anticipated. Interviews of this kind with inpatients have shown the importance that patients attach to 'fitting in' with what they think is expected of them (Peerbhoy et al, 1998; Waterworth and Luker, 1990). This does not seem to have declined in importance over the last quarter century (Tagliacozzo and Mauksch, 1972).

Where patients are children, additional challenges arise from the ways that they appraise clinical procedures that they experience or anticipate. For instance, concrete thinking leads some children to see painful procedures as punishment. Similarly, children can assume that what happens to other children in their ward indicates what will happen to them. When one child undergoes a painful procedure, or even dies, others might expect the same fate.

Two of these sets of challenges—loss of autonomy and isolation from support—are particularly significant. First, they are known to be important characteristics of institutional care of all kinds (Jones and Fowles, 1984). Secondly, although distressing in their own right, their effects are even more damaging because they reduce patients' resilience to challenges in general (Chapter 3). Therefore these two features of the inpatient experience will be considered in detail.

12.2 THE LOSS OF AUTONOMY

Surgical and medical inpatients' feelings of autonomy are inevitably restricted by the medical problems that caused admission, by the requirements of nursing, medical or surgical procedures and by the routine that a complex organization such as a hospital requires. However, additional restrictions arise from attitudes of patients and clinicians. Research on clinicians has focused on nurses. In the absence of evidence to the contrary, there is no reason why the lessons of this research should not be applied also to other clinicians.

12.2.1 Clinicians' Expectations: 'Good' and 'Bad' Patients

The distinction between 'good' and 'problem' (or 'bad') inpatients was introduced a quarter century ago (Lorber, 1975). Good patients were those with relatively straightforward medical problems and who accepted their treatment stoically. Problem patients were those who complained or were emotional or dependent on nurses. This group included patients who were seriously ill, but also many in whom the level of complaints and dependence were not seen by staff as justified by their physical condition. 'Bad' patients are probably disliked because their problems or behaviour make it difficult for clinicians to see themselves as effectively caring for them and treating them (Kelly and May, 1982). Unsurprisingly, when good and problem patients were interviewed, they turned out to have different beliefs about how they should behave. Good patients were more likely to believe that they should be passive and accepting; 'bad' patients were more likely to seek an informed and involved role (Lorber, 1975).

Recent research has shown that 'good' and 'bad' patients are still distinguished by clinicians along the lines that Lorber (1975) described. In one survey, patients were regarded by their nurses as 'popular' if they were in little pain and were not anxious (Salmon and Manyande, 1996). By contrast, those who were in most pain or were thought to be coping with it least well were described negatively, as 'demanding' or 'dependent'. The importance that nurses attach to patients *not* showing pain and distress has been borne out in detailed observation of the interactions of nurses and patients. For instance, it has long been known that patients' requests for analgesia sometimes receive the response that 'You shouldn't be having so much pain now' (Cohen, 1980). Box 12.2 describes similar observations in paediatric nursing (Byrne et al, 1999).

12.2.2 Patients' Expectations of Passivity

It would be simplistic to attribute patient passivity just to clinicians' attitudes. Patients also bring to the hospital firmly engrained expectations that staff will take control. That is, they view staff as having authority over them. In fact, interviews with surgical patients have revealed several different types of authority that clinicians are felt to have (Peerbhoy et al, 1998; Box 12.3). Most important is the authority that goes with the clinicians' 'ownership' of the ward (Tagliacozzo and Mauksch, 1972). That is, patients view the hospital ward as a kind of foreign country. As with any foreign country, there are rules or conventions which, although largely unwritten, are important and have to be obeyed. These rules are seen as looking after the interests of the clinicians who own the territory in which patients are temporarily resident. In this way the hospital, which exists to look after the needs of the patients, is seen by patients as an environment in which they have to look after the needs of the staff! Appreciating that patients tend to view the hospital ward in this way helps to

---

Box 12.2   The importance of being a 'good' patient

Paediatric nurses were interviewed about their children's postoperative pain and distress and were observed managing it (Byrne et al, 1999b). Nurses' attitudes depended on whether or not patients displayed suffering to them.

Patients who did not display suffering. Nurses were positive about patients whom they thought were free from pain: 'She's doing brilliantly well. She's no pain at all now' or who were not asking for pain relief: 'She's really good. She isn't even asking for painkillers.' Occasionally, a nurse was explicit that it was the absence of a *display* of pain that was important: 'She's great. She doesn't say when she's in pain.'

Patients who displayed suffering. Displays of suffering were often described as if they were inappropriate or as if they broke a rule: 'She shouldn't be in this much pain.' Occasionally, this meant confrontational interactions, as with this patient who complained that he did not feel able to eat:

Nurse   'You must [eat]. Look, I've told you who is the boss around here. It's me. OK?'
Patient   'I don't feel like it.'
Nurse   'Now you have got to eat it or I'll sit on your stomach, and I'll snitch on you to Mr D. [surgeon]. You know what will happen then. You won't be able to go home for ages.'

---

explain why they are often so reluctant to 'disturb' nurses by disclosing pain or requesting analgesia.

Of course, expectations about how to behave in hospital are learned long before admission. They are influenced by encounters with clinicians in primary care and at outpatient clinics as well as from the media. Once admitted to hospital, however, patients' expectations clearly connect with staff attitudes in a mutually reinforcing way.

12.2.3 Which Patient Role to Adopt? Costs and Benefits

12.2.3.1 Being a 'Bad' Patient

Underlying the distinction between 'good' and 'bad' patients is the issue of control (Chapter 11). 'Good' patients are the ones who allow clinicians to keep control. 'Bad' patients are those who control the clinicians. Being

---

Box 12.3 The authority of hospital staff

Interviews with surgical patients reveal different bases for the authority which they feel clinicians have over them (Peerbhoy et al, 1998).

Divine authority. Clinicians were commonly described as 'angels' or as allied with God: 'Just put yourself in their hands and God's hands.'

Expert authority. This is the authority that arises because 'They [clinicians] know what's best.' It follows that: 'You should just go along with what they're doing for you because they know more about what they're doing for you than you do.'

Territorial authority. This refers to the feeling of being in a foreign territory that is owned by clinicians and where there are rules about how to behave: 'When you come into a strange place, you know, you don't know whether you're doing the right thing or whether you're putting people out.' It follows that the patient's role is: 'It's up to you to help them' and to avoid being 'a nuisance': 'I wouldn't ask him [surgeon] that [duration of surgery] because I think he's got enough to cope with.'

---

a 'bad' patient should, therefore, lead to better care by ensuring that the patients' needs are met. However, there are serious costs also. In Lorber's (1975) work, being a 'bad' patient had several potentially negative consequences: staff sometimes showed their annoyance by ignoring these patients, medicating them or even discharging them prematurely.

Patients can find ways of exercising some control over clinicians, short of becoming a 'bad' patient. 'Reactance' (Chapter 9) occurs where patients find ways of exercising counter-control in the face of rules or constraints that seem arbitrary to them. Many instances of reactance are petty, such as smoking in the ward toilets or male patients propositioning female nurses. Other instances are potentially more serious, such as non-adherence or discharging oneself prematurely.

12.2.3.2 Being a 'Good' Patient

Thirty or so years ago, at least, inpatients who were happiest tended to be those who preferred clinicians' authoritarian approach (DeWolfe et al, 1966). Therefore adopting the role of the 'good' patient might make it easier for people to adjust to being inpatients. However, this role also has serious problems. The term 'learned helplessness' has been used to refer to an individual's generalized belief that he/she cannot control events that happen to them (Seligman, 1975). It is thought to underlie the passivity which follows experience of uncontrollable events, even when exposed to new events that *can* be controlled. The hospital ward provides just the kind of environment that would be expected to induce helplessness (Taylor, 1979). What happens to patients depends on clinicians and the hospital routine, so patients soon learn that they have little influence. There is some evidence that helplessness does develop during the course of a hospital stay (Raps et al, 1982). That is, patients become passive and demotivated. In this way, learning the role of the passive, 'good' patient could interfere with recovery by reducing motivation for self-care and rehabilitation.

12.2.3.3 A New Role of 'Good' Patient

Inpatients' psychological needs will not be met by helping them to choose either of the two roles that are being contrasted here. Instead, the roles need to be changed so that patients seen as 'good' patients are those who are as motivated and as active as they wish in their recovery and rehabilitation, who identify their care needs and who ensure that clinicians meet these needs. For this to happen, both clinicians' and patients' expectations need to change.

12.3 ISOLATION AND SUPPORT

Social support is important in protecting people from physiological and emotional stress responses when they are exposed to challenges (Chapter 3). Therefore support is particularly important in protecting inpatients from the stress associated with the challenges described above. However, in hospital, patients are separated from normal support networks.

12.3.1 Support from Clinicians

Feeling supported by clinicians seems to protect hospital patients against both emotional and physiological stress responses. For instance, reduced depression (Rosenberg et al, 1988) and reduced immunosuppression in inpatients (Linn et al, 1988; Levy et al, 1990) and better adjustment after surgery (Auerbach et al, 1984) have all been associated with feeling supported by clinicians and others. Reflecting their continuous contact with the inpatient, nurses have been the main focus of research into inpatient support.

The primary requirement for an individual to be supported is to feel that others understand and respect his/her concerns (Chapter 3). However, evidence continues to accumulate to show that nurses are inaccurate at identifying patients' concerns or worries (Davies and Peters, 1989; Herbert and Salmon, 1994; Johnston, 1982). In particular, nurses underestimate their patients' pain or ability to cope with it (Salmon and Manyande, 1996). This is not just inaccuracy. This and previous chapters (Chapter 10) have identified emotional factors—on the part of both patients and clinicians—that prevent clinicians from understanding patients' needs. In particular, patients do not disclose their needs to clinicians, and psychological and organizational mechanisms protect clinicians from being fully aware of their patients' suffering.

12.3.2 Support from Patients and Visitors

Although patients' worries are not accurately detected by clinicians, the hospital environment contains one group of people who are more sensitive. These are the other patients (Johnston, 1982). Most mutual support between patients is carried on informally, without the involvement or even knowledge of staff.

Support from family and visitors can also be important. For instance, having more visits from spouses was linked to faster recovery from cardiac surgery (Kulik and Mahler, 1989). However, generalization is unhelpful, and each patient's support has to be assessed individually. Chapter 3 showed that close relationships have harmful as well as beneficial effects on health. Moreover, the direction of support is often the reverse of what might be expected. That is, the patient who is ill has to support the distressed family member! Patients often describe 'putting on a brave face' to protect their visitors from being distressed by their condition.

12.3.3 Parents' Support for Children

12.3.3.1 The Need for Parents' Support

The importance of parents' support for their children depends on the stage that a child's emotional development has reached. From about one year old, children begin to show distress when separated from parents, particularly in unfamiliar environments such as a hospital ward or clinic. Older, but pre-school age, children have normally learned to tolerate brief separation. However, their tolerance can be severely tested by challenges, such as hospitalization, that involve repeated or prolonged separation. In such circumstances, children can revert to separation behaviours that had been abandoned, such as tantrums or bed-wetting (Ramsey, 1982). Even after the child has returned home, behaviour sometimes regresses so that the child who had previously learned to cope with mother going into a different room now insists on following her. Being aware that a child is displaying 'normal' reactions to separation can help clinicians and parents to accept behaviour which might otherwise be interpreted as inappropriate for the child's age. In particular, it can help to avoid the risk that a child is regarded by clinicians as 'disturbed' or 'over-dependent'. Awareness of what is 'normal' might have protected one nurse from commenting that a 14-year-old boy 'won't even let his mum go home. I mean, the age of him' (Byrne et al, 1999b).

Separation from parents used to be a routine consequence of prolonged hospitalization. At one time, it was even thought to be better for young children than repeatedly subjecting them to the trauma of separation (Bowlby, 1973). The scale of this trauma was indicated by a characteristic reaction to separation in hospital. An initial 'protest' of crying and searching was followed by withdrawal and reduced activity, regarded as a state of 'despair'. In a final stage of 'detachment', the child appeared to have recovered but, on the parents' return, seemed to be uninterested in them or even to reject them. The current emphasis in inpatient care of children is to prevent the protest and withdrawal reactions from occurring. Therefore, parents now often remain with their children in hospital.

12.3.3.2 Substituting for Parents' Support

However, the evidence does not support pressure on parents to stay with their children any more than they wish. In hospitals today the benefits of continued close contact with parents are probably much less than in the spartan environments where the early research was conducted (Schmidt, 1998). Moreover, the presence of attentive and non-threatening staff can prevent disturbing effects of separation (Branstetter, 1969). Therefore harmful emotional effects are now probably very limited. Indeed, there are probably positive effects for many children because of the change in environment and because of the new social opportunities that the hospital ward affords (Schmidt, 1998).

Box 12.4 A failure of collaboration between parent and nurse

The opportunity for a collaborative relationship is lost where parents and nurses have very different views about the child. The following interchange illustrates one parent's failure to establish with a nurse a common understanding of her child's problems (Byrne et al, 1999b).

Interviewer	'How is Anne today?'
Mother	[to nurse] 'Well, er, she's doing OK, isn't she?'
Nurse	'Oh no, no, she isn't coping well at all, she was hysterical this morning . . . she's really not doing well.'
Mother	'I think she is quite tired really. She'll be much better after a sleep.'
Nurse	'Yes, she'll probably be alright, but then today when I tried to wash her she was just screaming and going manic.'
Mother	'I think she gets frightened.'
Mother	[to interviewer after nurse leaves] 'I was quite surprised that the nurse should say she's not coping well. I mean, well, considering her age and what she has been through, I would say she is coping really well.'

12.3.3.3 Parents' Role and Needs

Parents' presence in specific situations, such as undergoing anaesthesia (Glazebrook et al, 1994), is probably more important. However, it would be naive to assume that their presence is always helpful. Parents who are very distressed can make their children more anxious (Bush et al, 1986). Parents' attempts to explain procedures to children can also make them more distressed (Jacobsen et al, 1990). Parents who are distressed need support from clinicians. Unfortunately, relationships between nurses and parents are often problematic. Where children are seriously ill, parents' views are influenced by their need to see their children as stronger and more cheerful than they are (Grootenhuis et al, 1998), and parents' special relationship with their children can make nurses resentful (Byrne et al, 1999b). Parents' common reports of feeling at odds with nurses indicate that the opportunity for a collaborative relationship is often missed (Box 12.4).

12.4 THE NEEDS OF SURGICAL CONVALESCENCE

In general, the psychological needs of surgical patients are shared with other inpatients. However, one set of problems is unique to surgery: subjective physical malaise and immobilization are common in postoperative convalescence. The term 'postoperative fatigue' has been used to describe this phenomenon. Fatigue is potentially harmful for recovery. It weakens motivation for rehabilitation and exposes the patient to muscle loss and other harmful effects of immobilization. The extent of *psychological* need associated with convalescence depends on whether and how psychological factors influence its course, or whether it is entirely a physiological phenomenon.

12.4.1 Is Convalescence Physiological?

Surgery, like other major challenges, evokes the stress responses described in Chapter 3. Hormonal and metabolic disturbance lasts for many days after major surgery and reflects the severity of surgery rather than specific details of the type of surgery. It has been assumed that postoperative fatigue reflects this and related responses (Christensen and Kehlet, 1993). Indeed, on this assumption, anaesthetic techniques are used to inhibit the physiological stress response. Nevertheless, there is very little evidence to support the assumption that the stress response influences convalescence. Indeed, extensive research has failed to find any convincing physical cause of postoperative fatigue (Salmon and Hall, 1997).

12.4.2 Is Convalescence Psychological?

12.4.2.1 Emotional Factors in Postoperative Fatigue

The extent of psychological challenge that surgery constitutes is shown by the intense anxiety that typically surrounds it from before admission until after discharge home (Johnston, 1998). Patients are also liable to be depressed or angry, although these responses have been studied in less detail than anxiety (Salmon, 1994). The emotional response is independent of the physiological response (Salmon et al, 1988).

Psychologists are used to understanding fatigue in other clinical settings as an aspect of emotional disturbance, particularly depression. It turns out that postoperative fatigue is also correlated with anxiety and depression (Aarons et al, 1996; Christensen et al, 1986; Pick et al, 1994). Moreover, patients who were *fatigued after* surgery tended to be those who were *unhappy before* surgery (Aarons et al, 1996). Therefore postoperative fatigue appears to be, at least in part, an instance of a phenomenon introduced in Chapter 5: the physical presentation of emotional disturbance. Chapter 13 shows that such presentations confuse clinicians and patients alike and lead to prolonged and unnecessary dependence on medical services. In the same way, postoperative convalescence might be prolonged unnecessarily.

The role of emotional mechanisms in convalescence remains somewhat speculative and more evidence is needed. Emotional state *pre*operatively seems not to have a profound influence on surgical recovery (Salmon, 1994). However, more detailed study of *post*operative emotional state is needed. Moreover, most previous research has focused on anxiety, whereas depression might prove more important in postoperative fatigue.

12.4.2.2 Expectations of Fatigue

Patients and clinicians *expect* that major surgery leads to prolonged malaise or fatigue and that this will, in turn, necessitate a long convalescence. Expectations are powerful influences on patients' responses to medical and surgical procedures. The placebo effect demonstrates their strength (Chapter 5). Optimistic patients have been found to recover more quickly from cardiac surgery (Scheier et al, 1989)—perhaps because they *expect* to do better. Therefore, universal expectations of prolonged convalescence might help to explain why convalescence *is* normally prolonged after major surgery. Animals are presumably free from the influence of culturally based expectations about their convalescence. Therefore it is interesting that they return to normal activity much more quickly after major surgery than do people. Culturally rooted expectations may help to make prolonged convalescence a peculiarly human phenomenon (Salmon and Hall, 1997).

In general, postoperative stay has gradually and steadily shortened during the past half-century. Changes in surgical techniques or clinical care do not account for the shortening (Coulter and McPherson, 1987). Instead, this change probably reflects the gradual change in expectations in response to financial pressures on health services. The slow pace of the change attests to the strength of these expectations.

One way of testing the clinical importance of psychological factors in postoperative convalescence is to find whether the course of convalescence is changed by psychological means. This is considered below.

12.5 MEETING INPATIENTS' PSYCHOLOGICAL NEEDS

In summary, therefore, inpatients are faced by severe challenges. Two of these are particularly significant because they compromise patients' ability to respond to challenges in general. These are the loss of autonomy and of support. Finally, surgical convalescence presents a potential area of psychological need, also. Against this background, the final part of the chapter will consider approaches to psychological management which have been developed with particular reference to inpatient care.

12.5.1 Calming Patients Down before Surgery

12.5.1.1 The Appeal of Reassurance and Relaxation

The diversity of inpatients' concerns complicates the task of clinicians who wish to help them. Individual patients' needs have to be identified, then appropriate explanation has to be provided together with support and perhaps help in tailoring coping responses to the patients' needs and capacities. A simpler approach that could be applied to all patients would be very welcome by many clinicians. Although clinical procedures are frightening for the patient, they are normally regarded as routine and safe by clinicians. Therefore clinicians rely heavily on reassurance to manage patients' psychological needs. Another approach to 'calming' patients, or 'stopping them from worrying', is to provide relaxation training, and this has been adopted in some inpatient settings. Therefore it is necessary to look carefully at whether these do provide a safe, inexpert way of addressing patients' psychological needs.

Despite its routine nature, very little systematic research has examined the effects of trying to calm patients down in these ways. Probably this is because it is widely regarded as wholly innocuous or as a humanitarian rather than scientific matter. Nevertheless, there have now been a few studies in surgical patients and these indicate a need for caution.

12.5.1.2 Effects of Reassurance and Relaxation

Reassurance by nurses was the subject of one uncontrolled comparison of recovery of patients undergoing inner ear surgery in two hospital wards. In one ward, the nurses routinely gathered patients together preoperatively to reassure them about forthcoming events; in the other, preoperative psychological preparation was absent (Salmon et al, 1986). Reassured patients were, as expected, less anxious preoperatively. However, one hormonal index (urinary cortisol excretion) indicated that they reacted to surgery with a *greater* stress response. Preoperative relaxation training has similar effects. There is some evidence that it reduces anxiety preoperatively (Manyande et al, 1992) and that relaxed patients can be easier to anaesthesize (Abbott and Abbott, 1995; Markland and Hardy, 1993). There are also several reports that patients who have learned to relax improve more quickly in mood, pain and clinical indices (Johnston and Vogele, 1993). However, relaxation training has led to *increased* hormonal stress responses to surgery (Wilson, 1981; Manyande et al, 1992).

The contradictory nature of this evidence is unsatisfactory. Consider, first, the evidence of the hormonal responses. It is doubtful that this has any clinical significance because, despite the usual assumption, these responses seem not to be important to convalescence (see above). Nevertheless, the hormonal responses are theoretically interesting. Although often assumed to reflect purely physical challenges of surgery, particularly incision, they are components of a psychological stress response (Chapter 3). Therefore it should not be surprising that they are sensitive to psychological aspects of surgery. Their apparent increase by reassurance and relaxation therefore provide a warning that patients who are calmed down in these ways might go on to find the challenge of surgery more stressful.

Neither is the evidence for the *benefits* of reassurance or relaxation compelling. The most common indices used—analgesic intake, hospital stay and even self-reports of distress—are poor indicators of patients' needs. They are just as likely to indicate patients' willingness to complain. On this basis, reassurance and relaxation might simply make patients even less ready to complain than they normally are. A recent study of preoperative relaxation replicated the familiar finding that relaxation training reduced analgesic intake once patients had returned to the surgical ward. By contrast, however, relaxation *increased* the analgesia received immediately after surgery while the patients were still in the recovery room of the operating theatre (Manyande and Salmon, 1998). The analgesia that is given at this time is probably a better indicator of patients' pain than is analgesia on the surgical ward. Patients' complaints in the operating theatre are unlikely to be as inhibited as on the surgical ward, and theatre staff are geared to expect pain and to administer analgesia readily. Similarly, an alternative preoperative relaxing procedure, acupuncture, increased the intensity of pain reported during and immediately after surgery to remove impacted third molars (wisdom teeth; Ekblom et al, 1991). Therefore this pattern of results indicates that simple approaches to calming down patients who are worried about an impending challenge might *increase* the subjective and physiological stressfulness of the challenge. Of course, it is not only clinicians who resort to reassurance. Evidence in children undergoing medical procedures suggests that mothers' reassurance can interfere with their children's adjustment to the procedures (Bush et al, 1986).

12.5.1.3 Explaining the Effects: The 'Work of Worry'

This pattern of findings can be explained by a theory which was developed a half-century ago specifically to understand psychological influences on surgery. The background to the theory was the view, emanating from Freud (Chapter 2), that an individual could reduce the negative emotional impact of a stressor *after* it had occurred by mentally 'working through' it. This view is seen in the present-day belief in the value of counselling after psychological trauma. Janis (1958) argued that the principle could be more powerfully applied to 'working through' a stressor *before* it occurred and he suggested that the stressfulness of surgery could be reduced in this way. He coined the term 'work of worry' to describe this process of mental preparation whereby patients could, he thought, prepare themselves for the challenge of surgery and thereby reduce its negative impact and expedite their recovery.

'Worry' meant, to Janis, not a passive state of emotional distress, but a process of actively thinking about forthcoming challenges in such a way that the threat associated with them is reduced. Preoperative relaxation and reassurance would therefore be expected to interfere with this natural preparatory process. Because of this, the impact of surgery would be greater. The clinical relevance of this interpretation is not clear. *If* the interpretation proves to be correct, and *if* the responses to surgery that are affected by mental preparation are important in recovery, then 'calming patients down' *might* impair recovery from surgery. Until their clinical importance is clearer, this pattern of results and theory contains a warning for clinicians to question an aspect of their behaviour with patients that is often automatic. Their readiness to reassure patients does not necessarily reflect patients' needs. It might, instead, reflect *clinicians'* own needs—to be protected from patients' distress (Chapter 10). Simplistic attempts to suppress patients' anxiety might amount to medicalization of a way that patients naturally cope with impending challenge.

This theory of the 'work of worry' was developed specifically for surgery. However, if it is correct, the phenomenon that it describes would be expected to apply more generally. Chapter 4 described another instance in which 'calmer' patients have a worse outcome. Amongst patients with certain kinds of cancer, prognosis is better in those who are emotionally expressive, even to the extent of being seen by clinicians as disturbed or demanding. A study of surgery (mastectomy) for breast cancer connects these two areas of research. Women who were overtly distressed around the time of surgery survived without recurrence for longer than those who were ostensibly calm (Dean and Surtees, 1989). Perhaps the women who were calm were suppressing a natural process of mental preparation—or had been encouraged by clinicians and family to calm themselves (Chapter 14).

12.5.1.4 The Need for Alternative Responses to Patients' Distress

This is not to argue that clinicians should tolerate anxiety in their patients. Apart from the humanitarian need to reduce it, anxiety interferes with clinical care. There is even some evidence that anxious patients are harder to anaesthetize (Williams et al, 1975). Therefore hospital clinicians should aim to relieve anxiety. However, the evidence presented here indicates that the 'short cut' of simply trying to 'stop patients worrying' should be regarded with great caution. Instead, there is no substitute for the approach described elsewhere in this book (see Chapter 11). The clinician must identify what each patient appraises as challenges, and then provide the necessary information and explanation. Chapter 11 described approaches to providing explanation, for instance by modelling on video-tape or in real life. The aim is that the patient can arrive at less threatening ways of appraising those challenges or be equipped with ways of coping with them. Box 7.1 described one patient's appraisals of the challenges surrounding minor surgery. Attempts to reassure this patient would inevitably fail without first allowing the patient to disclose what worries her. Box 12.5 illustrates how hasty reassurance can even increase a patient's distress.

Research into effects of psychological management of surgical patients' state has emphasized the preoperative period. This reflects theoretical interest in the preparatory effects of preoperative worry. Nevertheless, the effects of preoperative emotional state on later recovery are not clear enough to justify the special concern with this period. The analysis of convalescence, above, suggests that psychological (and perhaps even pharmacological) interventions to relieve depression and anxiety could usefully be targeted postoperatively. Systematic research on this possibility is awaited.

12.5.2 Improving Support

12.5.2.1 Distinguishing Support from Reassurance

Emotional support is, of course, very different from reassurance (Chapter 3). Box 12.5 shows that attempts at reassurance can even be *un*support-ive. That is, telling patients that what they are worrying about is not at all dangerous is interpreted by the patients as failure to understand and

Box 12.5 A failure to reassure

A clinician's attempt to provide reassuring information can sometimes expose a gulf between the patient's and clinician's understanding of a patient's problems. The patient is more likely to feel isolated than supported. This 52-year-old lady is describing her experience of her surgeon's attempts to reassure her before mastectomy for breast cancer.

Patient	'The surgeon just said that everything would be alright. They had got it in time and I'd live longer than he would. He said the reconstruction would make me back to normal and I would hardly see the difference.'
Interviewer	'Did that help?'
Patient	'Not really. I was really worried at the time and maybe that was what I wanted to hear. But at the back of my mind, I was still worried. Later on, after I came out of hospital, I kept thinking about what he said.'
Interviewer	'What were you thinking?'
Patient	'Well, it can't be that cut-and-dried, can it? I mean, you hear of people that have been given the "all-clear", then it comes back again. It made me think, I know it seems silly, but I wondered if he was taking it seriously enough, if he'd checked me out properly. He said that breast cancer was just like any other disease now, they knew how to treat it. But I've seen articles about it since I was done. People die from it, don't they? It might be just another disease to him, but it's not to me. And the reconstruction. Well, it's not back to normal. It might *look* OK to him, but it doesn't to me, and it doesn't *feel* right. I think it doesn't feel right to my boyfriend either. Or maybe he's just worried about damaging it. We've being having a difficult time before I was ill and I'm worried this will be the last straw. Maybe the doctor doesn't expect me to have a boyfriend at my age.
Interviewer	'What would you like the doctor to have said instead?'
Patient	'I wanted him to let me tell him what I was worried about. My mother died from bowel cancer. The hospital didn't tell her. She didn't know how bad she was. She had an operation, too. It was awful, terrible. I had this other lump, you know, five years ago, on my back. They said it wasn't cancer, but now I'm wondering if it's connected with this.

Continued

> I tried to ask about it but he just said that was nothing to worry about. But that doesn't stop me worrying, does it? It just makes me feel awkward about bringing it up. And I wanted him to know that it does still matter to me how I look, even at my age. I know it sounds silly, but I think maybe they'd take more care if they knew.'
>
> Interviewer 'Have you asked about these things at outpatient visits since you came out of hospital?'
>
> Patient 'I tried asking, but I feel silly. They just say I'm worried about nothing. Then I can't find the words and I'm out the door before I know what's happening.'

accept their concerns. This provides yet another illustration of what can go wrong when patient and clinician work with different understandings of the same problem (Box 11.2).

To improve the ability of nurses and other hospital staff to provide the support that patients need is not a simple task. Chapter 10 identified two sets of psychological factors that help to distance clinicians from patients. Clinicians lack specific listening skills; and skills that they do have are suppressed because of a perceived need to distance themselves from patients. Addressing each of these can release clinicians' support for patients. However, additional approaches become possible in inpatient care.

12.5.2.2 Making Support Routine

Routine is important in institutional care of all kinds. Therefore, one way to improve support is to make supportive interactions routine parts of clinicians' work. Studies in surgical wards by anaesthetists and nurses have shown that this is possible. In one of the first studies of this kind, patients were visited by an anaesthetist preoperatively for a conversation which included non-specific counselling and support. These patients had a lower analgesic requirement postoperatively and were discharged sooner (Egbert et al, 1964). Unfortunately, these outcome measures are ambiguous (see above); conceivably, preparation might simply make patients more appreciative of staff and less likely to complain so that they received less analgesia and were discharged sooner! However, more recent studies have confirmed the value of the anaesthetist's visit in reducing postoperative anxiety. Preparing patients for surgery face to face in this way is more reassuring than simply presenting similar information in a booklet (Leigh et al, 1977).

12.5.2.3 Ensuring Continuity of Relationships

Feeling supported requires a confiding relationship. This, in turn, requires continuity of care. Therefore continuity of care from individual clinicians can ease patients' transition from a coronary care unit to a general medical ward (Klein et al, 1968). Other discontinuities of care can be managed in a similar way. In one study, patients were accompanied to the operating theatre by a familiar ward nurse who was also present upon recovery. The provision of support in this way affected one important clinical outcome: it reduced the incidence of postoperative vomiting (Dumas and Leonard, 1963).

12.5.2.4 Facilitating Patients' Mutual Support

It was observed, above, that being an inpatient normally means being in the company of many other individuals who share the same challenges and experiences. Fellow patients seem to be more accurate at identifying patients' concerns than are nurses. Therefore clinicians can improve their patients' support by facilitating the mutual support between them. Once again, studies in surgical patients show that clinical outcomes can be improved where a nurse merely convenes a meeting of patients pre-operatively and facilitates their support of each other (Schmitt and Wooldridge, 1973).

12.5.3 Increasing Patients' Control and Involvement

12.5.3.1 Enhancing Involvement in Clinical Interactions

It would be wrong to assume that, because patients *expect* a very passive role, this is what they *want*. Moreover, the dangers associated with this role mean that it is not what patients usually *need*. Therefore clinicians often need to find ways of increasing patients' feelings of control or involvement (Box 11.6). The approaches described in Chapter 11 are available for inpatients as well as other patients and enormous potential remains for exploiting these opportunities as they arise in the course of routine care (Box 11.10).

12.5.3.2 Routinized Approaches to Enhancing Involvement

There are, of course, special considerations for inpatients. At first sight, the loss of autonomy that is inherent in being an inpatient makes the clinician's problem more difficult. However, the clinicians' control over the routine of the hospital ward provides the vehicle for attempts to influence patients' attitudes. There is considerable evidence from surgical patients that routinizing this aspect of patient care can be effective. Of course, attempts to encourage hospital patients to take a more active role are constrained by what patients find acceptable. Attempts to increase patients' feelings of control over their treatment or medical or nursing care are likely to be rejected by many patients (Peerbhoy et al, 1998). Interventions aimed at increasing 'involvement' (Chapter 11) or enhancing control of the patient's own physical and mental state are most likely to succeed.

Many reported studies have used specialist psychologically trained researchers who engage patients in mental procedures which help them gain control over their own thoughts and fears. For instance, they help patients to identify their concerns and then to engage in relaxation or self-talk to cope with them (Langer et al, 1975). This approach can be seen as facilitating the 'work of worry' (above). Arguably, though, psychological care should not depend on the availability of a specialist clinician. Other approaches that can be applied in routinized ways by clinicians who are routinely available include simple physical exercises or mental procedures that require minimal teaching. For instance, exercises that are often taught by physiotherapists for mobility or breathing control might well be important for their psychological effects in providing involvement. Simple mental exercises can be taught that help patients feel more in control of their own physical or emotional reactions. These can use imagery whereby patients are guided to visualize themselves coping effectively with forthcoming challenges (Box 11.7) or to rehearse mentally movements or exercises that will later be practised for real.

From the theory presented in Chapter 3, helping patients to feel in control or involved should reduce cortisol responses to surgical stress, as it does in other forms of stress. This has, indeed, been found in two studies. In one, patients learned behavioural exercises (breathing and muscular control; Boore, 1978). In another, the coping treatment was purely mental (Box 11.7; Manyande et al, 1995). Whether these hormonal effects are clinically important is doubtful (see above) but they show, once again, that psychological and physiological processes are closely connected in physical health care.

12.5.4 Changing Expectations

There has been little systematic attempt to change expectations of recovery in inpatients. Therefore the role that expectations might have in shaping surgical convalescence (above) remains untested. There have been claims that surgical recovery can be improved by audiotaped suggestions of speedy recovery, played to patients while anaesthetized. These reports mostly depend on ambiguous indices of recovery (self-reports or analgesic requirements) and they have not been consistently confirmed (see Salmon, 1994). Besides, the extent to which patients can be influenced by messages like this while they are unconscious and anaesthetized is highly controversial.

Some of the psychological procedures that are aimed at increasing patients' feelings of control and involvement could be regarded also as changing expectations. However, the power of any psychological intervention that attempts to change individual patients' expectations is severely restricted because more conservative expectations are fed continually by other clinicians and patients and by the ward environment as a whole. Change at the ward or hospital level is probably needed before changed expectations can be reliably transmitted to patients. This possibility has yet to be tested by research. Nevertheless, a recent report is encouraging. It described how a postoperative regimen of pain relief, exercise and rehabilitation following laparoscopic major colonic surgery under regional anaesthesia dramatically shortened convalescence (Bardram et al, 1995). Some patients were discharged after only two days. Instituting such a regimen would have been a powerful influence on patients' and clinicians' expectations. This influence might well have been the critical ingredient. The investigators apparently did not consider this possibility—reflecting clinicians' continuing neglect of the importance of psychological factors that are integral parts of physical treatments, whether intended or not.

12.6 CONCLUSION

12.6.1 Clarifying the Aims of Psychological Management

It is important to be realistic about what the psychological management of medical and surgical inpatients should be designed to achieve and how it should be evaluated. The present evidence is not sufficient to justify using psychological management to change *clinical* outcomes. Instead, psychological management should be aimed primarily at meeting patients' *psychological* needs. These include feelings of disempowerment, loneliness, depression and fatigue. It is unfortunate that psychological management has often been evaluated by spurious or misleading clinical criteria. For instance, extensive research has demonstrated that preoperative psychological preparation can reduce analgesic intake in surgical patients (see Salmon, 1994). The evidence that patients normally receive insufficient analgesia (Smith, 1991) suggests that psychological management should be aimed at the psychological factors discussed in Chapters 9 and 10 so as to *increase* the use of analgesia! Similarly, the same research has shown that psychological care can shorten the length of stay after surgery. Whether an earlier discharge is in patients' interests is not examined in these studies. If it *is* a desirable outcome, there are probably easier ways to achieve this, as health managers have shown in recent years.

There is, however, enough evidence to show that psychological management *can* have physiological effects. Until the clinical significance of these effects is clearer, researchers and clinicians should be open to the *possibility* that psychological management might impair or improve clinical outcomes. Evaluation should therefore include clinical outcomes as well as psychological variables.

12.6.2 Who should Deliver Psychological Management?

This chapter has argued that clinicians' control over the environment of inpatients provides significant opportunities for managing their psychological needs, for example by routinizing procedures which convey support or involvement. It is important to reiterate the warning in Chapter 11 against assuming that psychological needs have to be met by special techniques. They are probably best addressed as part of the routine clinical care. A good example of how this can be achieved in practice is a report of how pain after surgery was steadily reduced by successive changes in routine nursing and anaesthetic management, including changes in the information that was given to patients and the ways in which patients' needs were assessed (Gould et al, 1992). Interestingly, once these changes had been carried out, introducing a special technique (patient-controlled analgesia; Chapter 11) had no additional effect.

KEY POINTS

- Inpatients' concerns extend beyond illness and treatment to include unfamiliarity of surroundings, worries about home life, embarrassment and whether clinicians like them.
- Inpatient care challenges patients' autonomy.
- Patients whom nurses regard as distressed or in pain, or who assert their needs, risk being seen as 'bad' patients.
- Inpatient care isolates patients from supportive networks.

- Support from clinicians is normally limited and support from family and visitors is variable. Fellow patients provide valuable support.
- Parents are important sources of support for children, but need not be pressured to be continuously available. Attentive clinicians and a rich hospital environment mitigate effects of separation.
- Possible psychological influences on fatigue during surgical convalescence include emotional disturbance and expectations of prolonged convalescence.
- Using reassurance or relaxation to calm patients before surgery might interfere with mental preparation for it.
- Psychological management before surgery can influence emotional state—and perhaps clinical outcome.
- It is not yet clear whether surgical recovery might be improved by changing patients' and clinicians' expectations, or by improving emotional state postoperatively.
- Procedures to improve support or to increase patients' feelings of involvement can be made routine in inpatient care.
- Patients' psychological needs should primarily be met, not by special techniques, but in the course of routine clinical care.

Chapter 13

PSYCHOLOGICAL TREATMENT OF UNEXPLAINED PHYSICAL SYMPTOMS

KEY CLINICAL ISSUES

- Why is it wrong to say that someone is tired because they have chronic fatigue syndrome?
- What is somatization and which clinicians need to know about it?
- Why are patients with unexplained symptoms so often negative about clinicians?
- How can clinicians engage with patients who are disillusioned with medical care?
- How can clinicians help patients to appreciate that their needs are more psychological than physical?
- What is cognitive therapy?

13.1 THE PROBLEM OF UNEXPLAINED SYMPTOMS

13.1.1 The Concept of Somatization

A large amount of primary care and hospital treatment arises from consultations where no physical pathology can been found. It is fair to assume that, in most of these cases, none exists. The phenomenon of seeking physical treatment in the absence of physical pathology is often described as 'somatization'. The term is sometimes narrowed to refer to physical symptoms that are presented, not just in the *absence* of physical pathology, but in the *presence* of emotional problems. However, Chapter 5 showed that physical symptoms in the absence of physical pathology do not necessarily signify emotional problems. Therefore the term somatization will be used here in the broader sense.

The organization of health care systems embodies dualism (Chapter 2). That is, it fairly rigidly separates physical and psychological health care.

Somatization challenges this dualism. Patients' *physical* symptoms lead them into the physical health care system. This, however, is usually ill equipped to meet their needs, which are more likely to be *psychological* and range from just being reassured to receiving psychotherapy. It follows that many patients who fall into this group are poorly served.

The psychological needs of somatizing patients are not, in principle, very different from those of other patients with whom this book is concerned. They have symptoms that they need to understand and they are frightened about them. Many somatizing patients are as disabled, handicapped and dependent as patients with chronic diseases caused by serious physical pathology (Stanley et al, 1999). It is only the absence of a biomedical condition that distinguishes the patients from others. This simplifies their psychological management considerably. Indeed, there are now very well-understood principles and procedures for helping somatizing patients. The management of somatizing patients will be considered in detail in this chapter for two reasons. First, we shall see that they are an important clinical problem throughout physical health care. Secondly, because the absence of physical pathology simplifies psychological management, important aspects of a psychological approach to patients in general can be delineated very clearly in this group.

13.1.2 Functional Diagnoses

In clinical practice, the existence of a somatization problem is often obscured by 'functional' labels or diagnoses, such as irritable bowel syndrome, fibromyalgia or chronic fatigue (Chapter 5, Box 5.5). Chronic pain patients also belong in this group where their pain, whether dating from acute injury or having no apparent cause, is unaccounted for by *present* pathology. There is a widespread impression among patients and clinicians alike that these labels 'explain' the condition in the way that conventional medical diagnoses do. Unfortunately, interpreting functional diagnoses in this way is circular because they are purely descriptive labels. For instance, saying that someone has abdominal pain because they have irritable bowel syndrome amounts to saying that they have abdominal pain because they often have abdominal pain! As one patient with irritable bowel syndrome appreciated: 'IBS is what they call it when they don't know what it is (Peters et al, 1998).' In practice, many somatizing patients have multiple syndromes at the same time or over a period of time (Stanley et al, 1999), so these diagnostic labels are not even very useful in distinguishing between distinct groups of patients. Medical diagnoses are, however, often valued by patients as a way of demonstrating the legitimacy of their problems (Henningsen and Priebe, 1999).

Both clinicians and informed patients are, of course, aware of the evidence that arises from time to time of physiological *correlates* of functional disorders. What is wrong is to assume that these represent *pathology* and *cause* the disorders. For instance, there is some evidence that 'tension headache' is associated with scalp muscle contraction. However, this is just as likely to be a *response* to the headache as the *cause* (Hopkins, 1992).

13.1.3 The Scale of the Problem

Medical and surgical wards contain many of these patients (Fink, 1992). For instance, amongst inpatients admitted with acute abdominal pain, the functional diagnosis of non-specific abdominal pain (Barker and Mayou, 1992) is more common than appendicitis. A significant minority even of those who go on to appendectomy turn out to have histologically normal appendices (Fink, 1992). In hospital outpatient clinics, the proportion of patients who have no physical pathology is considerable. Many estimates fall in the range of 30–70% (Bass, 1990). Estimates are more difficult in primary care where definitive investigations are usually not carried out. Nevertheless, around a fifth of patients attending with new episodes of physical illness have symptoms which fit even the narrow definition of somatization; that is, they are more likely to be attributable to emotional disorder than physical causes (Bass, 1990).

Many patients with unexplained symptoms are reassured by negative results of investigation and do not return. However, some go on to receive symptomatic treatment. This treatment accounts for a substantial proportion of Western societies' consumption of health care. There are also financial, social and iatrogenic costs to the patient of procedures which are often ineffective. Patients who persistently present somatizing symptoms therefore constitute the main clinical problem in this area. Even this subset of somatizing patients is a sizeable group. In the UK, general practitioners estimate that clinically significant physical symptoms of at least three months duration, without physical disease, account for nearly a fifth of consultations (Peveler et al, 1997). This group accounts for many 'frequent attenders' at primary care (Baez et al, 1998) and patients whom clinicians find difficult to help (Sharpe et al, 1994). At the extreme of the group are those who have become known as 'heart-sink' patients because of the feelings of helplessness engendered in clinicians by their persistent complaints (Butler and Evans, 1999).

Somatizing patients therefore include some of the highest users of health care and some of the most impaired and dependent patients that clinicians have to care for.

In the USA, health care costs of persistent somatization in primary care have been reduced by instituting programmes of regular consultation with the family doctor in which the patients are discouraged from consulting other doctors (Smith et al, 1995). This is one approach to *containing* the problem. However, successful *treatment* of somatization depends on addressing the beliefs and needs which drive patients' consultation. This means engaging with the patient, helping the patient to focus on psychological needs that can be met, and then meeting those needs. These elements of psychological management are considered in turn below.

13.2 ENGAGING THE PATIENT

13.2.1 Challenges to Engagement

13.2.1.1 Patient Disenchantment

Clearly, these patients do not fit the traditional biomedical model, according to which the patient brings a symptom that the expert clinician assesses, diagnoses and treats (Chapter 2). Neither do they fit the consumer model, in which the doctor's task is to satisfy patients by meeting their requests. Where symptoms persist, any clinician seeing the patient is usually merely one in a long sequence of clinicians who have failed to help. Therefore, patients are not only **anxious** about what the symptoms mean. They are **frustrated** with clinicians who have not 'done their job' by explaining or treating them. **Anger** and resentment are also present where patients feel that they have not been taken seriously or that their symptoms have been dismissed as unreal (Chapter 5). A clinician therefore often has to consult with the patient in the shadow of previous accumulated failures (Peters et al, 1998). Added to these barriers is the feeling of **rejection** where the patient suspects that the referral that led to the consultation is an attempt to offload the problem (it often is). Where referral is to a psychologist, psychiatrist or counsellor, the patient can see this as further evidence that the symptoms are being dismissed as unreal (they often are). At the extreme, these reactions provoke reactance (Chapter 9) and a determination to prove the clinician wrong. Engaging productively with such a patient is a formidable task.

13.2.1.2 History of Investigation, Reassurance and Treatment

Obviously, symptoms must be investigated to exclude treatable pathology and to reassure both clinician and patient. Investigation or referral often occurs, however, because the clinician feels the need to 'do something'. Sometimes they are intended to reassure. Investigation and reassurance are invariably regarded as helpful, or at least totally innocuous. Both parties are satisfied—in the short term. The patient is satisfied by the clinician because anxieties are eased. The clinician is satisfied by seeing the patient go away satisfied. The problem is that this cycle of mutual satisfaction tends to escalate (Box 5.3). The patient becomes more dependent on reassurance. The clinician has to deliver larger or more frequent 'doses'.

Where the patient is convinced of a physical problem, reassurance often confirms that the clinician 'doesn't understand'. Therefore, for the patients who are the focus of this chapter, being reassured is likely only temporarily to ease their concerns. It may even exacerbate them, and it will often have become one of the factors that maintains their problems (Warwick and Salkovskis, 1985).

Symptomatic treatment can also be destructive (Box 5.3). Patients' belief that something is physically wrong is reinforced: 'They wouldn't be treating me unless there was something wrong.' Patients' dependency on external solutions is increased. Treatment that fails can increase patients' anxiety that something very serious is wrong which even the doctor does not understand.

13.2.1.3 The Patient's Authority over the Clinician

A mistake that many clinicians make is to assume that the patient sees the clinician as the expert (Chapter 9). Chapter 9 showed several ways in which patients can see themselves as much more expert than their clinicians, especially in the absence of pathology (Box 9.5): their belief in their infallible knowledge of the symptoms; their access to various sources of medical information; and their careful scrutiny of evidence and alternative explanations—including clinicians'. Where there is a history of unsatisfactory investigation and treatment, doctors' perceived incompetence adds to patients' sense of authority (Peters et al, 1998).

13.2.2 Forming an Alliance

A striking finding from interviews with patients who have persistent unexplained symptoms is that doctors are not necessarily valued or deprecated according to whether they succeed or fail to diagnose or treat the patient's symptoms. As one patient commented: 'I appreciate all the doctor's done. Not helped mind, but tries everything, blood levels and tests. He's a good doctor' (Peters et al, 1998). Chapter 6 showed that patients commonly view symptoms as expressing a malign and menacing entity, separate from themselves. Patients therefore value a clinician who simply establishes an alliance with them against this entity (Chapter 6). Of course, doctors typically forge an alliance with this kind of patient by offering repeated investigation and referral. Other strategies provide a more constructive basis for alliance (Goldberg et al, 1989; Salmon et al, 1999). Two that are particularly important are described below. Their application in a specific treatment programme is illustrated in Box 13.1.

13.2.2.1 *Establishing Therapeutic Optimism for Realistic Treatment Goals*

Physical medical treatment can often be provided satisfactorily to a patient who does not actively cooperate. By contrast, psychological treatment requires the active cooperation, and therefore motivation, of the patient. Because of this, the clinician's optimism at the outset of treatment is important, particularly since many of these patients have become resigned to failure of health care to address their problems. Optimism should be directed realistically. Often, freedom from symptoms is an unrealistic goal. It can also be a highly threatening one to patients whose symptoms have become central to their identity and way of life. Instead, more realistic targets for optimism will often be to reduce disability, to improve coping with the symptoms (and with clinicians' inability to treat them), and to reducing dependence on health care.

13.2.2.2 *Being Sensitive to Patients' Individual Needs*

The deceptively simple injunction to listen to the patient is, in reality, complex. It is not just a matter of using appropriate verbal strategies (including open-ended questions and reflection) and non-verbal techniques (Chapter 10). It is the purposes for which these techniques are employed that matters. Listening has a number of functions in this context (Box 13.2). The obvious one is to gather information. However, a second is to ensure that patients feel that their individual problems are heard and the reality of their own symptoms and suffering is accepted.

Box 13.1 Engaging patients in physical exercise

Physical exercise training has many psychological and physical benefits. Crook et al (1998) used it to mobilize patients who, although impaired by physical symptoms, had not been helped by previous symptomatic treatment. It was not enough simply to invite patients to take part. Successful engagement depended on a physiotherapist establishing optimism for realistic goals, showing sensitivity to the patient's individual problems, and helping the patient to understand how exercise could help. Here are some responses to one patient with fibromyalgia.

Patient's complaint	Physiotherapist's response
'Everything before has failed.'	*Encourage therapeutic optimism*: Explain that this new treatment has helped many other patients; it's different from what has been tried before because it involves working with the patient to find the right level of exercise for each patient
'I can't walk more than a few yards. How can I exercise?'	*Set realistic treatment goals*: Establish achievable targets so that success is experienced from the start; increase targets in phase with confidence and capacity
'This might be OK for other people, but it's not for me.'	*Show sensitivity to patient's individuality*: Identify specific fears about exercise; ask in detail about the experience of it
'I don't see how this is going to help me. Whenever I try I get worse.'	*Provide explanation*: Explain that exercise helps condition the body, so that it can better repair itself and cope with the strains that life imposes. Explain that, for someone with fibromyalgia, a short walk is as challenging to the muscles as a marathon is to an athlete. So some discomfort is a sign that the muscles are being stretched and used

---

13.3 CHANGING THE PATIENT'S AGENDA

In some patients, symptoms indicate emotional problems which require help (Chapter 5). In others, anxiety or depression are secondary to symptoms or are products of iatrogenesis whereby dependency has grown through ever-increasing involvement with medical care. None of these problems can be addressed as long as the consultation is just about providing physical treatment for the patient's physical symptoms.

Box 13.2   Interviewing and listening

Listening to patients talk about their symptoms is a prerequisite to helping them, even when symptoms do not indicate physical pathology. Asking and listening about different areas has different functions.

Area	Function
Symptoms and the distress and suffering they cause	Shows that clinician accepts that symptoms are real and distressing
Beliefs and worries about symptoms	Identifies erroneous beliefs that need to be modified
How symptoms affect the patient's behaviour with family, friends and other clinicians	Indicates how the social network might help to maintain symptoms
Effect of symptoms on the patient's life and what life would be like without symptoms	Indicates degree to which patient relies on symptoms for social and other rewards; indicates motivation and opportunity for change
Descriptions of emotional feelings or events	Indicates patient's ability to express emotion other than in the language of physical symptoms

---

Therefore the clinician must help the patient to broaden the basis for the consultation (Goldberg et al, 1989).

13.3.1 Normalizing Symptoms

Clinicians often succeed in reassuring patients by simply telling them that they are 'normal', or that there is 'nothing wrong'. The problem with this is that the patient is left without any explanation for the symptoms and the clinician–patient relationship can become strained. Because of the influence of dualism (Chapter 2), the patient may well be angry at the implication that the symptoms must be unreal or imaginary. The patients who are the focus of this chapter have not been satisfied by being told that they have no pathology. They need explanation that reconciles the existence of symptoms with the absence of pathology. This is not difficult. In the area of statistics, we are familiar with the idea that extremes can be 'normal', although not usual (Box 13.3). This is only one of

---

Box 13.3   What does it mean to 'be normal'?

Patients and clinicians often work with a 'black-and-white' view of the difference between 'normal' and 'abnormal'. This view means that patients can think something is wrong (because they have symptoms) when the clinician believes they are normal (because there is no pathology). A more realistic model of normality is a graded one based on the statistical 'normal distribution'. According to this, symptoms vary in the normal population even in the absence of pathology.

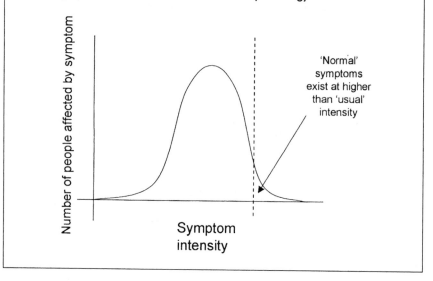

---

many ways in which symptoms can be reconciled with the absence of pathology (Box 13.4).

13.3.2 Recognizing Psychological Needs

The same techniques that can allow patients in medical and surgical clinics to disclose concerns or emotional problems are important here (Chapter 10, Box 10.1). However, somatizing patients often appear unable or unwilling to set aside the language of purely somatic problems. Therefore, it is important for the clinician to remember that somatic language is commonly used in a metaphorical way to describe emotional feelings (Chapters 2 and 5). For instance, the irritable bowel patient who describes

---

Box 13.4   Explaining that a symptom is 'normal'

Many patients are reassured and satisfied by being told that 'nothing is wrong'. Many are not satisfied because they then have no way of understanding their symptoms. They suspect that the clinician thinks the symptoms are imaginary, or that the clinician has not taken them seriously and missed something important. These three doctors are each explaining to patients with menstrual problems that they are 'normal'. Two out of the three do this in a way that reconciles the absence of pathology with the patient's experience of symptoms (Marchant-Haycox and Salmon, 1997).

1. There's nothing wrong inside. We've had a look and your womb is perfectly normal.
2. The womb is like a finely tuned machine. Which means that the problem with your periods is one of the sort of finer control of the way your womb is working. And we know that there is a very fine hormonal control on how your womb is working and how heavy your periods are and unfortunately sometimes it tends to give up and that's when your periods tend to get too heavy.
3. I think that the pain you have is worse than most women's, even though there isn't any disease in your womb that we need to treat. Most people get pains in some part of their body. For some people it's their back, others get headaches. Usually they're just part of normal life and don't mean that anything is wrong. For most people the pains are not too bad and they can just put up with them. But people vary a lot. For every 100 people that have pain that isn't too bad, there will be one or two who are affected quite badly. There are a few people who don't get any pains like this at all. Being at either extreme like this doesn't mean there's anything wrong with your body. What we can try to do, though, is find a way of making the pain smaller or making it easier to bear.

---

his bowels as 'in turmoil', or 'ready to burst', or himself as 'full of shit', might be disclosing some feelings about himself (Guthrie, 1992). If the clinician simply observes that 'you feel in turmoil' or that 'you feel that something awful is going to happen if you don't keep control over yourself', the patient can sometimes be helped to say more about these feelings.

13.3.3 Providing a Psychological Explanation

In reality, many patients are not ready to broaden the agenda by allowing psychological factors to be identified. They might believe that doing so means accepting that the symptoms are unreal. For clinicians to provide an acceptable explanation that incorporates psychological factors is therefore crucial (Box 13.5). However, providing explanation is rarely straightforward and somatizing patients present several pitfalls.

13.3.3.1 Explanations that Legitimate and Exculpate

Useful clues about providing explanation have emerged from comparing explanations that somatizing patients accept from their doctors with those that they reject (Salmon et al, 1999; Box 13.5).Typically, explanations that are accepted meet two requirements. First, they accept the reality of the symptoms by providing a plausible, **tangible mechanism** to explain them. Whereas psychological diagnoses are felt by many patients to deny the symptoms, biological mechanisms are thought to legitimize them. Secondly, accepted explanations invoke mechanisms for which the patient cannot reasonably be expected to be responsible. Therefore, they **free the patient from blame** or responsibility for having caused the symptoms.

The explanation in Box 13.5 can legitimize a patient's suffering and exculpate the patient for it. However, it achieves this by invoking mechanisms over which the patient has no influence. Therefore, not only does it protect the patient from feeling culpable for having the symptoms, but, unfortunately, it denies the patient any responsibility for managing them. Indeed, it invites the expectation that the doctor will be able to take responsibility—probably by using drugs. Since, by definition, these patients are not greatly helped by symptomatic treatment, such an explanation sets the scene for later difficulties.

13.3.3.2 Explanations that Empower

Box 13.5 also illustrates an explanation that is more likely to be successful. It provides the patient with responsibility for *managing* the symptoms, but without implying responsibility for *causing* them. It uses the idea of tension to broaden the patient's agenda to include psychological factors.

Many patients already believe or suspect that stress has contributed to their symptoms when they consult their doctor (Chapter 6). 'Stress'

Box 13.5   Rejected and accepted explanations

Listening to patients describe doctors' attempts' to explain their symptoms helps to identify the features that determine whether an explanation is accepted or rejected (Salmon et al, 1999).

Rejected explanations

These are usually seen as denying the reality of symptoms, typically where negative test results indicate that 'nothing is wrong': 'They don't know, but they can't tell you that. So they say it's nothing.' This also happens where symptoms have been attributed to anxiety or depression: 'She [GP] says it's anxiety and depression . . . It's not bloody psychological. . . . She thinks it's all in the mind.' Worse still, explanations can be seen as 'blaming' the patient: 'The doctor doesn't think anything is wrong. He keeps saying I'm just unfit. Isn't that stupid?'

Accepted explanations

In the following explanation, the doctor had found a way to make a diagnosis of depression acceptable to the patient. The explanation's success depends on having provided a tangible reason which freed the patient from blame while reassuring the patient that no more threatening disease process was at work: 'I have clinical depression. It's not the normal depression, it is in fact the clinical type. The doctor explained it to me quite well actually. It's between the neurones, in these synapses something goes awry. And that happens in clinical depression; an imbalance, exactly.'

Another explanation also provided the patient with the opportunity for taking some control over the symptom, but again without implying responsibility for having caused it: 'He [GP] explained about tensing myself up so the neck kept hurting.'

---

exculpates patients by connecting with long-standing and widespread cultural beliefs whereby illness is blamed on other people and the demands they make (Helman, 1994; Chapter 6). The value of stress as an explanation goes beyond this, however. It provides patients with the opportunity to examine, and exercise some influence over, the circumstances which cause or maintain their difficulties. For instance, the patient who accepts that his chest pain becomes worse when arguing with his wife can begin to examine ways of improving his relationship with her (Chapter 3).

13.4 COGNITIVE THERAPY: MEETING PATIENTS' NEEDS TO UNDERSTAND

13.4.1 Background to Cognitive Therapy

13.4.1.1 Applications of Cognitive Therapy

Many patients can be helped and their health care costs can be reduced when general practitioners use the techniques described above (Morriss et al, 1998, 1999). However, patients who are firmly convinced of a physical cause of their symptoms need something more (Morriss et al, 1999). The variability and fluidity of somatizing patients' presentation in primary care make systematic research difficult. By contrast, patients attending hospital clinics have, by definition, usually accepted a specific diagnosis and their symptoms are usually focused on a single organ or functional syndrome. This has allowed the evaluation of intensive programmes of treatment, called 'cognitive therapy', which build on the general approach described above. The principles are applicable very generally. Effectiveness has already been demonstrated for several clinical groups in outpatient clinics, including chronic fatigue (Sharpe et al, 1996), irritable bowel syndrome (vanDulmen et al, 1996) and patients with mixed unexplained symptoms (Speckens et al, 1995). A similar approach is used in programmes for managing chronic pain, too (Compas et al, 1998; Turk et al, 1983). Usually programmes of cognitive therapy have been separated from the routine clinical service and have been delivered by psychologically trained clinicians. However, the principles of cognitive therapy are simple and are generalizable to routine settings and to all clinicians.

13.4.1.2 The Cognitive Model

The basis for this approach is the set of interactions depicted in Box 13.6. Although intervention can be focused on one or all of the elements in this diagram, notice that the patients' beliefs are central. Therefore, changing the patient's beliefs should be sufficient to interrupt or reverse the vicious circles that maintain the whole set of problems. This is the principle that underlies cognitive therapy. The approach is derived from psychological treatments which aim to reduce *emotional* problems, particularly depression, by changing the way that patients *think* about events and about themselves (Beck et al, 1979). In other words, it tries to change patients' appraisals (Chapter 3).

Essentially there are two stages to cognitive therapy of patients with somatizing symptoms (Sharpe et al, 1992). The first is to help the patient

Box 13.6   A cognitive model of functional symptoms

Symptoms are maintained by a series of vicious circles, in which patients' beliefs about their symptoms are central.

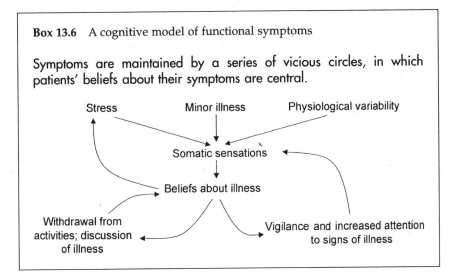

identify the beliefs that maintain the problem. The second is to help the patient change those beliefs.

13.4.2 Identifying Patients' Beliefs

Two types of belief are distinguished in cognitive therapy: the immediate, **automatic thoughts** that symptoms trigger and more **enduring assumptions** about illness and treatment. The thoughts and fears that symptoms trigger are elicited by simply asking about 'the first thought that comes into your head when you notice [symptom]?' Where patients routinely take evasive action quickly (such as lying down in response to feelings of tiredness in chronic fatigue), the first thoughts are often about having to do this. What these patients fear about the symptoms can often be elicited by asking, instead, what they think would have happened had they not taken evasive action.

Being confused about their symptoms is part of many patients' problems, so clinicians receive confused accounts in their turn. Confusion and exaggeration are worst when discussion is in general terms. Therefore the interview should focus on concrete instances: 'Tell me about the worst time you had the symptoms in the past week/month' or 'Tell me about the most recent attack.' This approach is illustrated in Box 13.7.

The patient's enduring assumptions about illness and treatment are not so easily made explicit. Nevertheless, they emerge during conversation.

Box 13.7 Elements of cognitive therapy for functional problems

These extracts from the treatment of a man with irritable bowel syndrome by a counsellor in primary care illustrate the main features of a cognitive therapy approach. The counsellor also scheduled consultations to reduce the doctor's role in maintaining the problem.

Identifying beliefs that maintain the problem

Clinician's question	Patient's answer
'What's your first thought when you notice your symptoms coming on?'	'I've got to get to the toilet.'
'What's the worst that would happen if you couldn't get to one?'	'I'd dirty myself.'
'When did you last dirty yourself?'	'I can't remember; I don't think it's ever happened.'
'How do you know that's what would happen?'	'I just know—I have to go.'
'How long do you think you could hold on for?'	'I don't know. I just get there as quickly as I can.'

Changing beliefs

Clinician's invitation	Patient's response
'OK, you've learned to avoid dirtying yourself by dashing to the toilet as quickly as possible after the symptoms start. We need some more information. Can you find out for me what happens when you wait for a minute before going? Obviously this will be difficult and you won't be able to do it at work or when there's someone else around, so let's think about how you could try this out at home without getting embarrassed by what might happen.'	'Initially he discovered that he could, in some circumstances, delay going to the toilet. He gradually extended the period until he discovered that he could cope with his symptoms without the toilet.'
'You've told me that the symptoms often come on when you're arguing with your wife. You feel that you—and your bowels—get tied up in knots. Let's think about whether dealing with these situations differently has any effect on your symptoms. Can we think about how else you might respond when you think a row is beginning?'	'By seeing his wife's irritability as a sign of her own stress, he became became more tolerant of it. By role-play with the counsellor, he learned to handle disagreements without becoming so upset.'

Scheduling consultation	
Clinician's strategy	Result
'You've been coming to see your doctor whenever you feel you can't cope any longer—about every two weeks. So let's make an appointment now to see him in two weeks' time. I want you to keep the appointment whether or not you are feeling bad. Come and see me in a week's time, and come sooner if you finish these experiments before then.'	In time, consultations became less frequent. After increasing to regular three-monthly intervals, appointments about bowel problems ended altogether.

Typical assumptions are that 'Pain always means that something is seriously wrong' or that 'Doctors should be able to explain or cure every physical problem.' Assumptions about clinicians' attitudes to the patient emerge in comments such as 'Doctors can't be bothered with me' or 'You all think I'm just a pain in the neck.'

13.4.3 Challenging Patients' Beliefs

13.4.3.1 Contradicting the Patient

The most obvious—and common—approach is simply to say that the patient's belief is wrong and to say that a different belief is true. Unfortunately, this is an unsuccessful method of attitude change, even in a public bar or at a political meeting. Inside the clinic it can destroy the clinician–patient relationship. It devalues the patient's own attempts to make sense of the problem and provides further evidence that 'They don't understand.' Where the relationship has deteriorated to include anger and resentment on the patient's side, reactance is a natural response to being told that a belief is wrong (Chapter 9). The anonymous, written information or group-based teaching of the sort that is included in many pain management programmes might have an advantage in this respect. The impersonal nature of information given in this way helps to reduce the risk that a patient feels personally provoked to reactance.

13.4.3.2 Collaborative Empiricism

However, social psychology tells us that people are much more likely to change their beliefs where they feel that they are changing from their own choice. Therefore, cognitive therapy adopts an approach that is called collaborative empiricism. This means that the clinician does not contradict the patient's beliefs. Instead, the clinician collaborates with the patient in testing their validity. Simply asking patients for the **evidence** for what they believe can expose to the patient the *absence* of evidence. **Alternative explanations** can be sought for the symptoms. Although, ideally, the patient will be prompted to supply these, the clinician may need to provide basic information or concepts. Particularly important are the ways that stress can affect the body (Chapter 3) and the processes that can create symptoms without pathology being present (Chapter 5). The third—and most protracted—task is to engage the patient in **hypothesis testing**: i.e., evaluating and comparing these competing explanations. Some testing is done during consultations, for example, by prompting the patient to list and evaluate evidence for and against each explanation. However, ordinary life between consultations provides the ultimate laboratory for such tests (Box 13.7).

13.4.3.3 Inducing Behavioural Change

From the viewpoint of cognitive therapy, changing behaviour is the most powerful way of changing beliefs. That is, once new behaviour is induced in a patient, the patient develops a belief about being able to perform that behaviour! This, of course, is opposite to the view that patients tend to have: that confidence comes first. Behaviour can often be most easily changed as part of gradual hypothesis testing. For instance, the best way for a patient with irritable bowel syndrome to find out if he can delay dashing to the toilet in response to his symptoms is to try delaying! In this way, the clinician can induce change without contradicting the patient's belief that change would be impossible (Box 13.7).

13.4.4 Being Realistic: Limitations of the Cognitive Approach

13.4.4.1 The Functions of Symptoms

Patients' beliefs are central to cognitive therapy. However, clinicians' ability to change patients' beliefs is severely constrained by the reality of patients' lives (Chapter 9). Therefore the success and pace of the approaches described here depend, realistically, on other factors. The consequences of the symptoms for the patient and family are critical. They do not just cause disability and disrupt family relationships. They can come to have important functions. Often, they help to organize family relationships because they establish who should be dependent on whom. They can help to stop other family or personal problems from being addressed. They can even increase family income from disability allowances. For some patients, life might well be worse were they to lose their symptoms.

13.4.4.2 Opportunity for Change

The patient's and family's opportunity for change concerns the extent to which they have the skills and resources to live without the symptoms. A blank response to the simple question: 'How would life be different without your symptoms?' suggests that the opportunity for change feels very limited. Cognitive therapy is therefore not a panacea. In practice it will often be complemented by helping patients to imagine, then practise, a way of life in which familiar symptoms no longer provide the structure for it.

13.4.4.3 Emotional Problems

Some patients have emotional needs that cannot be dealt with in the ways described here. Severe emotional needs would test the plausibility of the cognitive model in Box 13.6. For instance, Chapter 5 showed that a history of intensive physical investigation and treatment without evidence of pathology is a clue that severe psychological problems are present that are associated with childhood abuse. At present, many clinicians assume that specialist psychologically trained personnel are needed to provide psychotherapy for these patients. However, because these kinds of problems are rarely disclosed to clinicians in physical health care, it is simply not known whether they can be addressed satisfactorily by general practitioners, physicians, surgeons, nurses or others. There are reasons to think that they might. Chapter 3 showed that even brief disclosure of traumatic events has health benefits. Moreover, there is no evidence to support the view that disclosures which are not followed through by longer-term counselling are destructive. Indeed, it is likely that these fears largely reflect clinicians' desire to protect themselves from such disclosures. Therefore it is possible that clinicians could do a great deal, at least at primary care level, to help patients with emotional problems.

13.5 WHEN THE CLINICIAN IS PART OF THE PROBLEM

Where symptoms persist and clinical consultations continue, clinicians become important elements of patients' social network. Therefore they must analyse their role in maintaining patients' problems. The obvious risk is that consultation—and the attendant attention, reassurance, prescription and other intervention—becomes contingent on symptom report and dependent behaviour. When this happens, the clinician is drawn into reinforcing symptoms and dependence. Of course, refusal to see a suffering patient is impractical except as an admission that the relationship has broken down. Instead, however, the timing of consultation can be linked to factors other than patients' symptoms and complaints. Most simply, future consultations can be scheduled in advance at a frequency which matches the patient's recent level of consultation. This simple change removes the link between consultation and patient complaint and dependence (Smith et al, 1995). Consultation can even become a reward for achieving therapeutic tasks rather than a reward for failure (Box 13.7).

13.6 CONCLUSION

Two fundamental principles underlie the approaches described in this chapter. One is the importance of identifying the patients' own beliefs and of working with those. The second is the need to acknowledge patients' sense of authority and to *collaborate* with the patient in their need to test and modify their beliefs. These principles are very important in health care. They are the key to meeting the needs of somatizing patients who, for many clinicians, are the largest single 'diagnostic' group that they have to deal with. However, the principles are of much more general importance. They guide psychological approaches to patients in general, including those with cancer and other serious physical pathologies (Chapter 14).

KEY POINTS

- Somatization accounts for a vast proportion of health care.
- Functional diagnoses often deceive patients and clinicians into believing that a syndrome has been explained.
- Somatizing patients have a range of psychological needs that are shared by patients with other physical illnesses.

- These needs include the need to be helped to understand symptoms, to be reassured about them, to adjust to living with them, and to have help with emotional problems.
- Successful engagement with a somatizing patient depends on showing understanding of the patient's perspective and accepting the reality of the symptoms.
- Careful explanation can change the patient's agenda from physical to psychological needs.
- Cognitive therapy has been applied in specialist settings but its principles are generally applicable.
- Patients' beliefs are central in cognitive therapy, but they are often best changed by first changing the patient's behaviour.
- A collaborative relationship and empirical approach is central to treatment.
- Therapeutic approaches in somatization can be applied to other groups of patients where psychological needs coexist with physical pathology.

Chapter 14

PSYCHOLOGICAL TREATMENT OF PHYSICAL DISEASE

KEY CLINICAL ISSUES

- Can psychological methods treat physical disease, or only its psychological effects?
- Should a patient avoid psychological stress after myocardial infarction?
- Can patients overcome cancer by the power of the mind alone?
- Which clinicians should meet patients' psychological needs?
- Should counsellors be available to all patients with serious physical illness?

14.1 PSYCHOLOGICAL TREATMENT FOR PHYSICAL DISEASE

Previous chapters have addressed the psychological needs that surround physical illness and treatment. Implications for the psychological management of patients have flowed from understanding these needs. However, Chapters 3 and 4 showed that psychological factors are connected to physical disease processes and that these connections have been traced in detail for two major sets of diseases: heart disease and cancer. A test of the importance of these factors would be whether they can be recruited in treating disease. That is, can psychological factors reverse the disease process? Specific psychological treatments have been developed for both heart disease and cancer. This chapter will describe them and examine the evidence that they treat the disease processes themselves.

14.2 STRESS MANAGEMENT FOR HEART DISEASE

14.2.1 Can Stress Management Treat the Disease?

Heart disease has been linked to stress in scientific research (Chapter 4) as well as popular beliefs (Chapter 6). Unfortunately, the two views of stress are very different. Therefore many cardiac patients respond in counter-productive ways to their own beliefs about the dangers of stress, or to clinical advice to 'reduce stress' that is well meaning but misleading or ambiguous. Box 14.1 illustrates a 'stress management' approach that is based on the scientific account of stress that was outlined in Chapters 3

Box 14.1   Stress management after myocardial infarction

X returned home eight weeks ago to his wife and 18-year-old son after hospital treatment following a myocardial infarction. He is anxious about returning to work, and the specialist nurse in the cardiology clinic devised the following programme of stress management for him.

Identify challenges. X appeared tense but was not very clear why. The nurse asked him to keep a diary (Box 14.2) and to note any situation where he felt himself becoming more tense or upset. Two weeks later he and the nurse discussed his notes. The main challenges were arguments with his son and fears about work.

Reduce exposure to challenges. Relationships at home are strained by his being at home all day. He is moody and irritable and his son resents his criticism. He would be helped by having a fulfilling activity that took him out of the house for part of the day. Work could achieve this. The main fears about work concern having too much responsibility and managing and disciplining members of his team. He can reduce responsibility by requesting a move to a different role.

Reappraise challenges. He allowed himself to feel pressured at work out of fear of losing his job should he not do whatever was asked as well as he could. The nurse helped him to decide what was a reasonable level of work and to estimate the (low) probability that he would lose his job if he worked at this level. They discussed how he and the family would cope if he did lose his job.

The nurse also helped X to reappraise his son's assertiveness. It reflected his need to feel grown up, and perhaps his own frustration at not having a job. It was not a rejection of his father, whom he had regularly and anxiously visited in hospital.

Problem-focused coping. Instead of reacting automatically to challenges, the nurse rehearsed with him how he could give himself time to think before reacting to his son's provocation (counting to 10, leaving the

Continued

room). He needed to work to replace a relationship of hostility with his son with a relationship of equals, for example by asking him for advice sometimes. He thought of similar ways to delay responding to requests for help at work, so as to give himself time to decide the right response.

Palliative coping: weaken the stress response. X learned relaxation skills, first of all by listening to a relaxation tape at home daily. Then he practised at home without the tape, before learning to relax when challenged at home or work.

Support. X's friends from before his heart attack had been drinking companions. He feared that they would not understand that he could no longer drink like he used to, so he avoided them. The nurse elicited from X that one of his friends had a son of similar age; another had recently been away from work because of 'stress'; and another had been edgy since promotion. X and the nurse discussed how he would explain his changed drinking habits, and they prepared ways of responding to all conceivable reactions from his friends.

and 4. The components of stress management training vary from one programme to another. Nevertheless there are common features. Patients are taught to identify sources of challenge in their lives. Where appropriate, they are helped to reduce their exposure to them. They are taught to appraise them in less threatening ways, and they are taught ways to cope with the challenges more effectively. This kind of approach is widely used, particularly in cardiac rehabilitation and secondary prevention of myocardial infarction. In practice, it is usually combined with other interventions, including exercise training, nutritional advice and information and explanation about heart disease.

Even when it is the main ingredient, stress management does seem to be an effective treatment approach in heart disease. In angina pectoris, it improves exercise capacity and reduces symptoms (Bundy et al, 1994, 1998). After myocardial infarction, several benefits of stress management training have been documented. Physiological responses to challenges have been reduced (Gatchel et al, 1986). A self-help programme that is based on stress management has reduced health care use as well as emotional distress (Lewin et al, 1992). A nursing support follow-up programme that incorporated stress management reduced reinfarction and halved cardiac deaths (Frasure-Smith and Prince, 1989). Reinfarction rate has also been reduced by a similar approach, which focused specifically on reducing patients' hostile and time-pressured ways of appraising and coping with everyday challenges (Friedman et al, 1986).

14.2.2 The Components of Stress Management Training

14.2.2.1 Identifying Challenges

Patients are typically confused about what the main things are that challenge them. Careful interviewing can often identify the challenges. However, general questions are uninformative. Instead, interviewing should be focused on specific instances. The techniques are similar to those described in Chapter 13 for patients without pathology. Questions about the 'time you felt *most* worked up', or the '*last* time you felt yourself getting stressed' will be more informative than questions about 'what upsets you' or 'what makes you feel stressed'. Even interviewing patients in this way is a limited approach, however. Everyday life between clinical consultations provides the best source of direct evidence (Chapter 13). Therefore when patients are asked to keep diary records from day to day the information is more immediate, the patients are themselves encouraged to participate and take responsibility and they begin to learn skills of enquiring into their own behaviour (Box 14.2).

14.2.2.2 Minimizing Challenges

First of all, patients can be protected from those challenges that are avoidable. Unfortunately the simplistic, but common, injunction to 'avoid stress' is often misunderstood by clinicians and patients alike. It can lead to patients giving up pleasurable or exciting activities. These activities are often important in maintaining positive mood or self-esteem. They can connect the patient to social support networks, and even prevent the patient and spouse from irritating each other. In these cases, life without such activities will be more challenging and more stressful than life with them. Therefore patients' and clinicians' misunderstanding of this point has serious effects. Cardiac invalidism is one result of patients' mistakenly giving up rewarding activity (Chapter 7). Clinicians' belief in the need to 'avoid stress' explains the eerie and frightening silence of some coronary care units. The attempt to minimize stress in these units has led to minimizing stimulation of all kinds. The unintended result is a monotonous background of silence against which patients appraise the slightest unexpected sound or the slightest untoward event as signifying a serious crisis. The absence of any external distraction exposes the patients also to challenges generated from their own thoughts and fears.

Understanding the psychological mechanisms that link stress to heart disease helps the clinician to provide sounder advice than the injunction to 'avoid stress'. The most important point is that, rather than being

Box 14.2 Using a diary to identify challenges

Diaries can help patients and clinicians to make sense of confusing feelings. This extract is from a diary that was completed by a patient at the start of a stress management programme delivered by a specialist nurse (Box 14.1).

Instructions: Keep this diary with you. Fill it in every time you feel yourself becoming more worked up, stressed or upset.

Time and date	What was happening	What thoughts went through my head	What did I do?	How did I feel?
Monday 3 p.m.	Nothing. Just reading the paper	Going back to work	Nothing	Tense, panic
Tuesday 11 a.m.	Argument with [son]	What a mess his room is	Told him to clear it up	Angry
Wednesday 5 p.m.	Argument with [son] about going out tonight	He doesn't care about me—only himself	Just argued, shouted	Worked up, heart racing
Thursday 1 a.m.	Lying in bed	He hasn't come home. What's he doing? I told him to be back by midnight	Told him off when he came in at 1 a.m.	Angry

defined *objectively*, challenges must be defined according to whether the patient *perceives* them as challenges; in particular whether the patient appraises them as requiring difficult problem-focused coping (Chapter 4). This means that patients' appraisals (Chapter 3) are central in defining what is challenging and what is not. One patient might appraise returning to work as a major challenge that can only be managed with difficulty. For another, the same job might be a source of support—or of distraction from greater difficulties at home. In hospital care, Chapter 12 shows that many challenges concern events that do *not* happen, such as being left without clear and understandable information, or not having questions anwered. Sadly, such challenges are routine in inpatient and outpatient care. Fortunately, they are normally avoidable.

14.2.2.3 Changing Appraisals

Clinical care entails many challenges that cannot be so easily avoided. Hormonal responses show that admission to hospital itself is a challenge that triggers stress (Tolson et al, 1965). Simply telling patients that they have high blood pressure (Rostrup and Ekeberg, 1992) or, in laboratory conditions at least, urging them to keep it down (Suls et al, 1986), can be sufficiently stressful to increase blood pressure! Other stressors cannot be avoided because they are internally generated, such as fears about what one's symptoms might signify.

For challenges that cannot be avoided, the clinician can use the model of stress outlined in Chapter 3 to help minimize their impact on the patient. The primary need therefore is to ensure that challenges are appraised in such a way as to minimize stress. Often this can be achieved by simply providing patients with appropriate explanation (Box 11.4). For instance, instead of exacerbating hypertension by telling patients that they are hypertensive, they can be told also that this problem can be remedied and that it has been identified in time to stop it from causing health problems.

14.2.2.4 Improving Coping

Problem-focused coping. Reducing exposure to unnecessary challenges is, of course, one product of effective problem-focused coping. Box 14.1 described a patient with additional demands for problem-focused coping. He needed to change his ways of responding to social challenges that were unavoidable. In particular, he needed to replace hostile behaviour towards his son with conciliatory and respectful attempts to improve the relationship. This patient needed also to solve problems presented by relationships with friends and colleagues in such a way as to release emotional support from them.

Palliative coping: inhibiting the stress response. Chapter 3 described the stress response, but also the opposite 'relaxation response'. This is elicited by Western techniques of relaxation training and biofeedback, as well as by Eastern techniques including yoga and meditation (Benson and Klipper, 1975). Using techniques like this to inhibit stress responses makes sense to patients because it links with beliefs about the importance of minimizing stress. It also offers a degree of perceived control (Chapter 11), and learning a skill provides distraction from distressing thoughts and rumination. Focusing on minimizing the stress *response* in this way is more realistic than attempts to minimize exposure to stressful *challenges*.

Arguably, this approach should be regarded as problem-focused coping as much as emotion-focused, palliative coping, because it can influence the disease process. For example, relaxation techniques can alone reduce hypertension (Patel, 1997). However, whether their effects are clinically important depends on whether sufficient attention is given to teaching patients how to generalize the relaxation or meditation skills into everyday life. In practice, therefore, this approach is best used together with stress management that allows patients to identify sources of stress to which relaxation techniques can be applied (Steptoe, 1993; Johnston, 1997).

14.3 PSYCHOLOGICAL TREATMENT FOR CANCER

14.3.1 Can Psychotherapy Treat Cancer?

Just as with heart disease, there is evidence that psychological factors contribute to development of cancer (Chapter 4). This points to the theoretical possibility that patients might be able to use psychological techniques to counter the disease process itself. However, Chapter 4 showed that the role of psychological factors in cancer is much less compelling and less clear than the evidence about heart disease. Correspondingly, evidence about the effects of psychological treatment is also less compelling and much more controversial.

The most persuasive evidence is that programmes of supportive meetings of groups of patients, led by a clinician, have apparently prolonged survival of patients with metastatic breast cancer and malignant melanoma (Fawzy et al, 1993; Spiegel et al, 1989). The findings are not very strong, however, and have not convinced some readers (Box 14.3). An earlier

---

Box 14.3   Does psychological therapy improve survival
from cancer?

Fawzy et al (1993) randomly allocated patients with malignant
melanoma to a six-week programme of group therapy for 1.5 hours
weekly or to a routinely treated control group. The aims of therapy were
to improve patients' control over their lives by:

• information about melanoma and its treatment
• stress management
• help with problem-focused coping
• psychological support by the group.

The figures below indicate that survival, recorded six years later, was
significantly improved by the programme at a 5% significance level. That
means that there was less than a 5% probability that these results arose
by chance, given the variability in outcomes across both groups.

	Therapy group	Control group
Survived	31	24
Died	3	10

However, the sample was quite small for this kind of study. Fox (1995)
pointed out that, had there been one fewer death in the control group,
or one more in the treated group, the difference in survival would no
longer have been statistically significant.

---

report claimed similar effects from a specially devised form of individual
psychotherapy (Grossarth-Maticek et al. 1984). Evaluation of this report
is difficult because aspects of the methodology were not very clearly
reported (Pelosi and Appleby, 1992).

Even if this set of findings is reliable, their interpretation is not straightforward. Survival is a questionable criterion for judging the effects of psychological treatment. First, the quality of the extra life gained is important,
not just its length. Secondly, survival reflects many processes in addition
to tumour growth. Psychological treatment might have improved survival
by, for instance, improving self-care or adherence to medical care.

Some evidence that psychological treatment affects disease processes is
needed to counter these arguments. One of the studies that showed

lengthened survival has gone some way to demonstrating this. Psychological treatment was shown to have improved one index of immune function (Fawzy et al, 1990) as well as reducing disease recurrence (Fawzy et al, 1993). There is other evidence that immune function can be improved by psychological methods. Relaxation techniques (Chapter 3, Box 3.3) can improve aspects of immune function in healthy subjects (VanRood et al, 1993). Immune function which is suppressed by a serious medical diagnosis can be improved by stress management procedures (Antoni et al, 1991). These effects on immune function are theoretically very interesting. However, it is too soon to know whether any of them have any clinical significance.

14.3.2 The Components of Psychotherapy for Cancer

Unfortunately, descriptions of psychological interventions in research literature are often very sketchy (Chapter 1). In particular, they rarely provide information about how patients experience the intervention. This is important because, as previous chapters have shown, what patients experience is often very different from what clinicians think they are providing. It is therefore unfortunate that this perspective is missing from the accounts in which psychotherapy has apparently prolonged survival in patients with cancer. Nevertheless, from the therapists' perspective, it seems that these programmes of group or individual therapy have been designed specifically to improve problem-focused coping, to help patients to express their own feelings, to help them identify and express their own clinical and other needs and to support them in ensuring that their needs are met. These therapeutic procedures counter key aspects of the 'cancer-prone personality' (Chapter 4). Therefore the way that the preliminary effects of psychotherapy on survival fit the emerging theory about psychological factors in cancer (Chapter 4) is encouraging.

14.3.3 Should Psychotherapy be Used to Treat Cancer?

As well as being encouraging, the way that treatment reports fit the theory should also sound a warning. Cancer is a frightening affliction that strikes largely at random and over which patients have, in reality, little or no control. Researchers are people, too, so they probably want to make cancer seem explicable by showing why it affects the people that it does and by showing that patients have the responsibility for overcoming it. It is hard to explain in any other way the fact that various clinical theories have 'blamed' cancer on deficits of patients' personality for decades (Cassileth, 1995). These claims have long pre-dated the evidence that supports them. Rearchers' own human desire to reduce the threat associated with cancer might have compounded the well-known tendency for researchers to discover what they expect—or want—to find!

Psychosocial interventions that have improved survival with cancer were, in fact, originally designed to improve patients' well-being. Changes in survival were incidental to this aim. There are other reports in which, although well-being has been improved, survival was unaffected (e.g., Linn et al, 1982). Until research is much more conclusive than it is now, improving the *psychological* well-being of patients with cancer should be the primary aim of *psychological* treatment (Bottomley, 1998). This is not a difficult aim to achieve. Any reasonable treatment is almost certain to be better than none (Meyer and Mark, 1995). Treatments that have been evaluated and shown to be helpful are legion. They include relaxation, imagery, group support, professional support, individual and couples counselling and various kinds of psychotherapy. The fact that almost any psychological input is helpful reflects the depth of psychological need and the poverty of routine psychological care in most cancer care settings.

14.3.4 Sensitivity to Patients' Preferences

All things considered, therefore, it is inconceivable that any psychological treatment could ethically be presented to patients as a way to influence tumour progression. The disease process is too complex. The critical psychological variables are too fluid and ill defined and their effects are too weak. Therefore, it would be unethical for a clinician to tell a patient that people are able to 'fight cancer', or that fighters will 'win through'. Unfortunately this happens (Box 14.4). More careful messages can allow patients the freedom to fight if they wish, but without incurring the blame if they lose, or guilt if they decline to try.

Because of the uncertainty that surrounds evidence in this area, clinicians have the converse obligation, too. The link that can be traced from psychological and social variables through the endocrine and immune systems to cancer requires the clinician to be open to the *possibility* of psychological influence. Therefore anecdotal reports that link tumour regression to mental activity, such as visualizing the body fighting the cancer, should be taken seriously (Grossarth-Maticek and Eysenck, 1991). For a patient to seize on the possibility of mental influence over cancer can be

---

Box 14.4   The costs of fighting

X had undergone 'lumpectomy' for breast cancer a year previously. She had apparently coped well at first, but then grew depressed and was referred for psychological help. In the course of this she revealed the costs to her of feeling responsible for fighting her disease.

He [surgeon] told me that I should fight the cancer. That made me feel it was somehow my fault. Then I was talking to the nurse and she said that cancer's caused by stress. That made it worse somehow. I felt it sort of meant it [cancer] was because I'd failed, I hadn't coped with my life. It was reading about her [Linda McCartney: a public figure who died of breast cancer] in the papers that made me think. She did all the right things, didn't she—exercise, diet and the rest. And still she got it. It made me think—it's not my fault, is it?

The surgeon and nurse each had something important that they wanted to communicate to X about coping with cancer. Might they have done this without burdening her?

---

a way to maintain hope. However, the clinician should then protect the patient from feeling responsible if and when the 'fight' is lost.

14.3.5 The Cancer-Prone Personality in the Clinic

Chapters 8 and 10 showed the extent to which clinicians and patients conspire to avoid clinicians being upset by patients' suffering. A common scenario in the cancer clinic is when a patient who is very upset suppresses overt signs of distress in the clinician's presence. Patients often describe 'fighting back their tears' so as not to burden the clinician. They apologize if they do cry, as if behaving improperly. Similarly, patients only rarely assert their own needs and avoid being seen as demanding, let alone as complaining. Clinicians typically support this passive patient role (Chapter 10). In these ways, the interactions of patients with clinicians replay and reinforce the main features of the 'cancer-prone' personality! This suggestion is consistent with the evidence that patients who survived for longest with cancer were those whom their clinicians regarded as most poorly adjusted (Derogatis et al, 1979).

Another way of stating this is to point out that many clinicians are routinely providing a kind of psychological management for patients with cancer which research has suggested *worsens* prognosis. The fact that this practice is unwitting does not make it any more defensible. For clinicians to reverse this process will require attention to the factors described in other chapters (Chapter 10) that prevent patients from expressing their emotional feelings and that encourage passivity. Recall that denial is not necessarily a maladaptive response, since it predicts longer survival from breast cancer and protects against emotional disturbance (Chapter 4). Therefore the clinician must identify the fine line between, on the one hand, colluding with patients to avoid them expressing their distress and, on the other, respecting patients' right to deny the illness or its importance should they wish to cope in this way.

14.3.6 Adjuvant Psychological Therapy

One approach to psychotherapy in patients with cancer has been described in particular detail. The aims of 'adjuvant psychological therapy' reflect what is known about the cancer-prone personality (Greer, 1997; Moorey and Greer, 1989; Box 14.5). Therefore it has been devised to reverse the psychological factors that appear to contribute to the disease process. In practice, however, it is aimed (and presented to patients) as a way to improve psychological well-being. It is a form

---

Box 14.5   Adjuvant psychological therapy

This approach to psychological treatment of patients with cancer has several aims that reflect the research literature about coping with cancer. The treatment has several components, each designed to deliver one or more of its aims (Moorey and Greer, 1989).

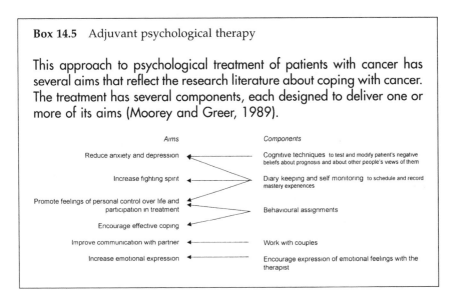

of cognitive therapy. It therefore has much in common with the treatment approach described in detail for somatizing patients (Chapter 13). One of its core principles is that the distress that patients feel is a result of their beliefs and how they appraise events. A second principle is that it is based on 'collaborative empiricism'. That is, the therapist collaborates with the patient to help the patient discover the evidence needed to change the patient's beliefs.

Because adjuvant psychological therapy embodies aims that reflect evidence about the cancer-prone personality (Chapter 4), it is not entirely under the direction of the patient. In particular, there is a strong emphasis on increasing 'fighting spirit' and encouraging patients not to 'give in' to the disease and to return to their previous normal activities. However, fighting is a problematic concept (Chapter 8). Therefore, in clinical practice it is important to identify whether the aims of treatment are those of the patient or the therapist (Box 14.6).

Adjuvant psychological therapy eases emotional distress in patients with breast cancer, and this effect lasts for at least four months (Greer et al, 1992; Moorey et al, 1998). However, it is not clear how well it prepares patients for the longer term where clinical outcome is poor. For a complete picture, we need to know the effects of psychological treatment on coping with recurrence and adjusting to certainty of death (Chapter 8).

14.3.7 Choosing Psychological Treatment in Practice

The problem of responding to psychological needs in patients with cancer does not lie in deciding precisely what is the best thing to do. The main problem is to ensure that effective psychological support of *any* kind is provided. Similarly, it is probably misguided for clinicians to be too concerned with what they need to do to *treat* a patient psychologically. The evidence of Chapter 8 is that patients can generally find their own way of adjusting to disease, but are often prevented from doing so by problems of communication with family and clinicians. Therefore the priority for clinicians in providing support should be to ensure that patients can decide how they wish to use the support, so that they are free to choose the trajectory of adjustment that they wish to follow. At the present state of knowledge, it is best to regard the patients as the experts in emotional adjustment to cancer. A recent study confirms that patients can be trusted to decide about the help that is needed. In a trial of adjuvant psychological therapy with men with testicular cancer, most patients declined it. When the patients were followed up, their emotional

Box 14.6   Trajectories of adjustment: distinguishing patients' from therapists' aims

Two patients with breast cancer illustrate different trajectories that adjustment can follow. A different therapist worked with each. Do the trajectories reflect diverging aims of the patients or of the therapists?

Patient X

X, 60, was depressed following the death of her mother and her own diagnosis of breast cancer. Although told that her prognosis was 'good', her thoughts had turned to death. She felt hopeless about the future and felt that people did not care for her. She had withdrawn socially and stayed at home doing little. She had given up voluntary work that she used to carry out in a local hospital.

The therapist helped her gradually to return to her previous activities. To start with, she was encouraged to carry out small tasks, such as cleaning the house, that she had been neglecting. In time, she resumed social contacts and returned to her voluntary work.

Patient Y

Y, 55 was depressed following her husband's heart attack 12 months ago, and diagnosis of her own breast cancer six months later. She said that she could not 'find the energy' for activities that used to interest and occupy her before she was diagnosed. She said that she tried and failed to do her housework and that she wanted to return to work as a care assistant but did not feel strong enough.

The therapist invited her to question what she found rewarding and fulfilling and helped her to identify goals other than those she was, out of habit, aiming for. She decided not to go back to her work but to concentrate on rebuilding her relationship with her husband (whom she began to realize she 'hardly knew' because they had both been so busy before they were ill). She decided that the house did not need to be as tidy as she used to keep it. She decided that it was no longer necessary to pretend to be 'strong'. By disclosing her own needs to her close family and friends, she found that relationships with them were deepened. She said that cancer had prompted her to 'take a look at her life'.

state improved similarly whether they received the treatment or not (Moynihan et al, 1998).

14.4 CONCLUSION: COUNSELLING AND DUALISM

This chapter has shown that the psychological management of heart disease and cancer should not be considered in isolation from the treatment of the disease itself. Psychological factors can be recruited to help reverse disease processes. Conversely, routine psychological management can even replay psychological factors that *strengthen* the disease process. It follows that psychological management should be integral to clinical care.

The increased recognition of the importance of psychological factors in managing physical illness has led to a growing level of provision of counselling. Patients are able to see counsellors in addition to the clinicians who direct or provide their physical treatment. Ironically, however, the provision of counselling separate from the routine interactions of medical and surgical care perpetuates a dualist approach to health care (Chapter 2) whereby concerns of mind and body are separated (Moynihan et al, 1998). This can be inefficient and counter-productive. It is now routine in some clinics that clinicians in charge of patients' physical treatment continue to be psychologically damaging, but then refer their patients to counsellors or others to pick up the pieces. In general, many patients' psychological needs can and should be addressed in the course of routine clinical care. Too hasty recourse to specialist counselling, psychotherapy or support staff will excuse the deficits in treatment that continue to exacerbate patients' psychological needs.

KEY MESSAGES

- Stress management is an effective psychological component of treatment for heart disease.
- Stress management means reducing stressful appraisals of challenges, improving coping and inhibiting the stress response.
- It is unhelpful just to tell cardiac patients to 'avoid stress'.
- Psychological techniques *might* improve survival from cancer but should not be presented to patients as a way of reversing disease.
- These treatments increase patients' emotional expression and their use of problem-focused coping to achieve their needs.
- Routine clinical care reinforces aspects of the 'cancer-prone personality'.

- Any reasonable psychological help in cancer is better than none. The most important role for clinicians is not to make things worse.
- Good psychological management should be an integral part of clinical care.
- Routine provision of counsellors to address psychological needs might help to perpetuate clinicians' damaging psychological management of their patients.

Chapter 15

USING PATIENTS' PERSPECTIVE TO EVALUATE CARE

KEY CLINICAL ISSUES

- What makes a patient questionnaire valid?
- Which is the best way of measuring quality of life?
- Could patient questionnaires be used to decide a patient's psychological needs?
- How can patients' views be used to evaluate the quality of a clinical service?
- Is it a sign of good-quality care when patients say they are satisfied?

Systematic evaluation has become very important to health care. It is now recognized as intrinsic to quality care because it allows clinicians and managers to monitor their performance and to maintain or improve their skills or service. Evaluation also meets pressure for cost-effectiveness from public and private funders of care. In turn, the patient's perspective is now widely viewed as central to evaluation. However, it is not simple to assess patients' views. There are many different approaches that can be taken. These different approaches reflect different assumptions about what health care is for (Chapter 2). The questions that are asked obviously shape the answers that are obtained. Therefore this chapter will review the various choices that confront the clinician who wishes to measure outcome or to evaluate a clinical intervention or service (Box 15.1).

Assessing patients' perspective often involves measuring subjective phenomena. Unfortunately, the science and technology of subjective measurement are often not understood when such measurements are made in health care. Therefore it is important first to be clear about some of the principles of subjective measurement before going on to review how they can be applied.

Box 15.1   How can patients' perspective be used to evaluate care?

This decision tree shows some of the choices that a clinician or researcher can make about how to use patients' perspective in evaluation. Specific choices are explained in the text.

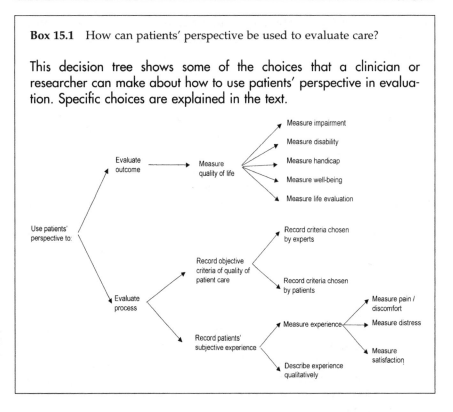

15.1   PRINCIPLES OF SUBJECTIVE MEASUREMENT

Principles of psychological measurement are addressed in detail in several sources (see Oppenheim, 1992). Therefore the aim here is just to clarify some common misapprehensions that arise in evaluating clinical care.

15.1.1   Confidence in What is being Measured

Unfortunately it is common that a measurement does not tell us what we think it does. Often measurements do not tell us anything at all that is useful. This is the problem of 'invalidity' of a measurement. One instance is the mistaken use of analgesic requirement to indicate level of postoperative pain or speed of recovery (Chapter 12). What this actually tells us is not at all clear; it is as likely to measure patients' willingness to complain. A more important example is that patients usually reply positively when asked in questionnaires whether they are satisfied with their care. It is therefore tempting to infer that patients are normally satisfied. This means, however, neglecting the more likely explanation that the question does not measure satisfaction at all. Instead, this kind of question probably measures a concern to please clinicians or not to look ungrateful (Williams, 1994).

15.1.1.1 Statistical Validation

The **validity** of an assessment procedure is therefore the degree to which it can be trusted to measure what is intended. Ensuring validity is rarely simple. If a gold standard is available, we can measure the extent to which the assessment agrees with it, or predicts it (sometimes called **criterion validation**). In practice, such standards are hardly ever available in this field. If they were, a new measurement procedure would not be needed! An alternative approach is to seek relationships, not with a gold standard, but with another similar assessment procedure. This strategy, called **concurrent** validation, has an in-built contradiction. If a new assessment is validated entirely by its relationship with an existing one, then the new one measures something that we can already find out! A further way of validating an assessment procedure is to show that it produces results that can be predicted on clinical or theoretical grounds (**construct validity**). For instance, a new measure of patient satisfaction should be able to confirm that patients seen by clinicians trained in communication skills are more satisfied. In practice, however, new assessments are usually devised to measure aspects of care that are *not* assessed adequately by existing procedures, where there is no gold standard and where theory is not a valuable guide.

Moreover, despite the respect that these approaches to validity receive from clinicians and researchers alike, their value is somewhat illusory. The illusion results from reading too much into statistical significance (Chapter 1). Typically, the degree of relationship that is considered acceptable with the gold standard, the alternative questionnaire or the theoretical prediction is very small. For instance, a correlation of 0.5 between the assessment and a gold standard will be highly statistically significant in a large sample but will mean that only 25% (0.5^2) of the variance (or variability) in the assessment is explained. Therefore, only a tiny proportion of the variance is shown to be valid in this sense (Box 15.2). A clinician normally needs better evidence than this that a measurement can be trusted.

15.1.1.2 Content Validation

For clinicians, the most important source of validity is to ensure that the content of an assessment adequately reflects the domain that is being

Box 15.2   Statistical validation

It is often claimed that a questionnaire 'is valid' because it correlates with a gold standard (such as a clinical outcome or another, well-established and accepted questionnaire). This diagram shows why such a claim should be regarded with caution. The ellipses represent the information provided by two such sets of scores. The information is the variability (or variance) of the scores. Suppose that a new questionnaire correlates at 0.50 with a gold standard (quite a high correlation in this kind of work). This means that 25% (0.5^2) of the information overlaps. The remaining 75% of the information is telling us something different from the gold standard. Strictly, therefore, only 25% of the information given by the new questionnaire is validated in this way.

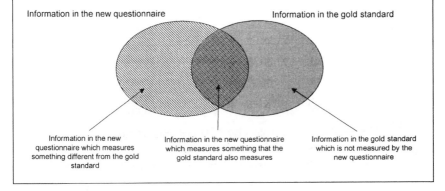

Information in the new questionnaire   Information in the gold standard

Information in the new questionnaire which measures something different from the gold standard

Information in the new questionnaire which measures something that the gold standard also measures

Information in the gold standard which is not measured by the new questionnaire

assessed (**content validity**; Box 15.3). Suppose that a clinician wanted to measure patients' experience of a disease or treatment. One way to start would be first to listen to patients talking freely about their experience and to note the words and phrases that they used. A questionnaire can then be formed from these terms. This procedure was used to produce the questionnaire items in Box 8.2, whereby patients described their experience of cancer. This procedure protects against the danger that the content of an assessment reflects clinicians' or researchers' *assumptions* about what matters to patients, rather than what actually *does* matter to them.

Content validity is not just a matter of choosing the right observations to make or questions to ask. It also concerns the way that the individual results are combined. For instance, it is common to calculate an overall questionnaire score by summing scores across several items. This requires two assumptions. The first is that the items do have something in

---

Box 15.3 Achieving content validity: evaluating patients' experience of colonoscopy

Patients' experience is important in evaluating the delivery of routine procedures. In this example, a procedure was devised to measure patients' experience of colonoscopy. For the procedure to be content-valid, it was essential that it measured aspects of experience that mattered to patients (Salmon et al, 1994).

Step 1. 20 patients were asked about their recent experience of colonoscopy. The words and phrases that they used to describe it were noted. Removing synonyms and esoteric terms left 31 different words or phrases. Each was written in opposite forms and given a scale, as illustrated below.

I was worried	7	6	5	4	3	2	1	I was not worried
I understood what was happening	7	6	5	4	3	2	1	I did not understand what was happening
It was painful	7	6	5	4	3	2	1	It was not painful
I was sore	7	6	5	4	3	2	1	I was not sore
Staff were interested in me	7	6	5	4	3	2	1	Staff were not interested in me

Step 2. These items were rated by 110 patients. A statistical technique (principal components analysis) was used to identify clusters of items which patients tended to answer in the same way. These clusters indicated three separate components of the patients' experience: 'worry', 'physical discomfort' and 'satisfaction'. Patients were given scores for their experiences on each component (by summing the scores on the items belonging to the relevant cluster).

Step 3. These scores for consecutive patients were used to evaluate aspects of the service. Different endoscopists achieved similar levels of satisfaction and physical discomfort, but the most experienced endoscopist achieved the lowest level of worry in his patients. It appeared that he was the best able to anticipate and detect patients' fears and to provide effective reassurance.

---

common, and specialized statistical techniques can help in this respect (Box 15.3). The second is that each item is equally important. Although this is almost always incorrect, making this assumption simplifies measurement considerably.

15.1.1.3 Limits of Validity

It should be clear that validity of measurement is a more complex and less cut-and-dried issue than is often appreciated. To claim that an assessment 'has validity' or 'is valid' is simplistic and misleading because it implies that validity is a property that is either present or absent. Instead, the clinician or researcher has to be aware of the different ways in which an assessment procedure can be justified as revealing what it is claimed to reveal.

15.1.2 Problems of Variability

A separate set of measurement problems arises from the variability that is intrinsic to most subjective phenomena. Responses to a single intervention vary from patient to patient and, within an individual patient, from day to day or year to year. Therefore assessments must be sufficiently numerous and widely dispersed (across time, patients, clinicians or clinics) to be **representative** of the patient, clinic, hospital, practice or clinician which is at issue.

A second source of variability arises between assessments that are made in different ways, by different people or at slightly different times. This kind of variability is known as the unreliability (or error) of measurement. Therefore **reliability** can be quantified by the degree to which different ways of measuring the same thing—the different items in a questionnaire, for example—interrelate.

15.2 EVALUATING SUBJECTIVE OUTCOMES

15.2.1 Objective Outcomes and Subjective Quality of Life

Traditionally, outcome is evaluated according to major clinical criteria. Mortality is unambiguous. Many indices of morbidity can also be ascertained objectively by the clinician or manager in the course of a routine clinical service. For many procedures, such indicators remain critical. It is natural to measure the improvement in outcome of heart transplantation or treatment of cancer by increases in survival. However, a large amount of health care cannot be so simply evaluated. This includes areas of treatment where outcomes are not so clear-cut, and care that is symptomatic or palliative rather than curative. Therefore the outcomes that are becoming increasingly important concern patients' subjective experience.

Patients' judgements of the quality of their lives are now widely viewed as the main way of evaluating health and treatment outcomes. Quality of life has also been seen as a way of comparing effects of different treatments—even in different illnesses. Resources can then be directed where the best improvements in quality of life are obtained. References to quality of life in clinical and research literature have proliferated in recent years and the clinician wishing to measure quality of life faces a bewildering array of choices of instrument. The present account will not substitute for the detailed reviews and reference works that are available (Bowling, 1995a; Fallowfield, 1990). Instead, it will introduce some *psychological* issues that arise for the clinician who wants to decide either how to measure quality of life or the importance to attach to measurements of quality of life that have been made by others. These issues are often glossed over by clinicians and researchers alike.

15.2.2 What is Quality of Life?

15.2.2.1 The Multiple Meanings of Quality of Life

It is important to appreciate that quality of life does *not* refer to a clearly defined entity, with an accepted measurement procedure. There are so many different ways of defining and measuring it that an apparently simple statement, for instance that 'treatment X improves quality of life', is virtually meaningless without much more information. The multiplicity of meanings of the term arises from two developments in thinking about illness that have gathered pace over the last half-century. Each has had a major influence on ideas about quality of life.

15.2.2.2 Origins of the Quality of Life Concept

Levels of impact of illness. One development has been the appreciation that the impact of a disease or disorder extends beyond the traditional concerns of medical care to include the individual's psychological and social functioning (Chapter 7). It is useful to have different terms to reflect the different levels at which a disease affects people's lives, and Box 15.4 shows currently accepted definitions of these. The extent of **disability**, **handicap** or **dependence** does not just depend on the level of physical **impairment** that the condition or its treatment causes. Among other influences, effects at those levels depend on social and psychological factors, including the expectations and support of other people, and how the patients cope with the condition. Therefore, because the impact of a disease at these different levels cannot be predicted from the physical characteristics of the disease, it must be assessed directly.

Box 15.4 Levels of impact of illness

In general, the impact of an illness can be assessed at different levels. Impairment and disability most closely reflect the disease process, whereas handicap and dependency are influenced by society also. Well-being and life evaluation are sensitive to the individual's own reflection on life.

Life evaluation	*The individual's view of life.*
↑	
Psychological wellbeing	*Feelings of health and happiness*
↑	
Dependency	*Reliance on others to meet normal needs*
↑	
Handicap	*The disadvantage that occurs because disability restricts normal social roles*
↑	
Disability	*Restriction of ability to perform an activity*
↑	
Impairment	*Abnormality or loss of anatomical structure or of physiological or psychological function.*
↑	
Disease or disorder	

Positive and negative definitions of health. The second development has been a more theoretical one: a change from a negative to a positive definition of health. Clinicians tend to define health negatively—as the absence of disease. The first attempts at a positive definition of health defined it as a 'state of complete physical, mental and social well-being' (World Health Organization, 1958). This idealistic definition is of little practical help to clinicians. However, the change in orientation that it signalled has stimulated a great deal of research into feelings of well-being and happiness. It has become clear that these are independent of disease and unhappiness (Warburton and Sherwood, 1996). That is, just being free from disease or misery does not mean that an individual feels happy. It follows from this that well-being should be assessed in its own right.

15.2.3 Measuring Quality of Life

The diversity of quality of life assessments reflects the two influences described above. Assessments ask about different levels of psychosocial function (Box 15.4) and they vary in whether they take a positive or negative focus. They also ask in different ways. The

---

Box 15.5 Measuring quality of life

Quality of life is not a single concept. These items from commonly used questionnaires reflect very different definitions of quality of life. In particular they differ in the level at which they assess the impact of illness (Box 15.4) and whether they have a negative or positive focus.

Impairment

Tick the reply which is closest to how you are feeling.[a]

Lack of appetite	Not at all ☐	A little ☐	Quite a bit ☐	Very much ☐
Tension	Not at all ☐	A little ☐	Quite a bit ☐	Very much ☐

Disability

What degree of difficulty do you have with bending to the floor?[b]
  None ☐   Mild ☐   Moderate ☐   Severe ☐   Extreme ☐

Handicap

Here are some problems that people can have in their daily life. For each one, tick Yes or No to show whether it is true for you.[c]

	Yes	No
I'm finding it hard to make contact with people	☐	☐

Illness-related handicap

As a result of your physical health have you accomplished less than you would like during the past four weeks?[d]
  Yes ☐   No ☐

Life evaluation

How often do you feel that your life has been worthwhile?[e]
  Not at all ☐ A little ☐   Some of the time ☐   Quite a lot ☐
  Most of the time ☐

---

[a] Rotterdam Symptom Checklist: deHaes et al (1990); [b] Western Ontario and McMaster Universities Arthritis Index (WOMAC): Bellamy et al (1988); [c] Nottingham Health Profile: Hunt et al (1985); [d] The Short-Form 36: Stewart et al (1988); [e] Life Closure Scale: Dobratz (1990).

---

diversity of assessment procedures that results is illustrated in Box 15.5.

15.2.3.1 Impairment and Disability

The simplest, but most limited, assessments focus on impairment. Hip or knee replacement would be evaluated at this level by finding the angle to which the patient could flex the joint. Both physical and emotional problems are included at this level. Therefore reactions to cancer could be assessed by noting emotional or physical symptoms that have arisen. Other measurement procedures focus on disability: i.e., the restrictions to normal activity that are caused by the impairment. These limitations include, for example, being unable to bend to the floor because of arthritis.

15.2.3.2 Handicap and Dependency

To assess limitations at the level of handicap, activities must be assessed that are important to patients' ordinary life. Choosing these activities is, however, not always easy. For instance, the traditional concern with return to employment reflected an economically oriented view of what life is for. It is not appropriate for those who, for reasons other than health, do not work. Functionally oriented quality of life questionnaires therefore typically include many separate domains such as social activities, emotional state and sexual function. The problem then is whether and how to aggregate these different domains to produce a single score. The simplest response is to accept that quality of life is multidimensional and to use separate scores for each domain. If a single score is desired, then the component scores can simply be added together to provide one, but this assumes that each is equally important. Instead, scores can be weighted according to their importance to an 'average' individual (e.g., Sickness Impact Profile; Bergner, 1988). In practice, few individuals' priorities in life exactly match those of the 'average' individual.

Unfortunately, many of the domains that *are* important to people's quality of life, such as money and religion, rarely feature on standard quality of life scales (Bowling, 1995b). Yet another problem was seen in Chapter 8: the importance of different domains of life tends to change in response to major health problems (Kreitler et al, 1993). To get round these complications, procedures have been devised whereby domains of life are weighted by each individual according to the importance that he/she attaches to them (Ruta and Garratt, 1994). Eliciting domains from individuals is not perfectly straightforward and different domains can emerge depending on how it is done (Bowling, 1995b). Therefore, although these techniques are clearly more sensitive to patients' individuality than are others, it is important to appreciate that no amount of methodological and statistical sophistication can provide a perfect index of quality of life.

15.2.3.3 Illness-Related Handicap

Because patterns of impairment and disability reflect the specific disease or disorder, many scales have been developed for specific medical conditions (Bowling, 1995a). The term 'health-related quality of life' is sometimes used, although 'illness-related handicap' would be more accurate. This approach can be appropriate where a specific disease or disorder is concerned. In practice, questions often ask for patients' judgements of how illness has affected their lives (Box 15.5). This assumes that patients know the extent to which constraints on their lives are because of illness. In many instances this will not be the case. For instance, a tendency to blame illness for life's problems obviously invalidates this approach.

15.2.3.4 Beyond Handicap and Dependency

Well-being. At first sight, assessing happiness or well-being offers a way around the difficulties entailed in measuring different domains of quality of life. Well-being can be measured on the assumption that the individual will provide a single score that aggregates the domains that matter according to the degree to which they matter. This way, the clinician or researcher need not be concerned with how the domains are weighted. This is one justification for the 'short cut' of using psychiatric questionnaires, such as the Hospital Anxiety and Depression Scales (Zigmond and Snaith, 1983), as indicators of quality of life. A simpler approach—with a focus on well-being rather than unhappiness—is to ask the individual for a single global rating of subjective health or quality of life.

The limitation of this approach for a clinician is that patients often report their health or well-being as 'good', despite having major or chronic diseases or disabilities (Jenkinson, 1994). That is, a feeling of being healthy can coexist with disease. Assessments like this tell us how patients feel about their lives, but underestimate patients' suffering and needs.

Acceptance of illness. One of the psychological tasks that confronts patients with chronic illness is acceptance of the reality of the disease and of the need to adjust their lives to it (Chapter 8). Despite its importance, ways of measuring this are not yet available. Although one questionnaire has been called the 'Acceptance of Illness Scale', its content suggests that it measures something different: negative attitudes to illness (Felton et al, 1984).

Life evaluation. Chapter 8 showed that illness also has effects on the ways that people evaluate their lives. Existential and spiritual concerns become important. Measuring life satisfaction or life evaluation is a step in this direction because these terms imply the patient's *evaluation*, rather than *description*, of life. For instance, a scale to measure life satisfaction, on which respondents reflect on past and present life, has been developed for elderly people (Neugarten et al, 1961). A measure of the quality of dying, which also includes reflection on life, is available (Dobratz, 1990; Box 15.5).

Existential and spiritual domains have normally been excluded from measurements of quality of life, but they *can* be measured. For instance, questionnaires have been devised to measure the 'meaning' of illness (Fife, 1995) or feelings of spiritual well-being (Ellison, 1983) or purpose in life (Crumbaugh and Maholick, 1964; Reker and Peacock, 1981). Although there is little experience of their use clinically, it is clear that these dimensions of quality of life are not closely related to impairment, disability and handicap (Cohen et al, 1995; Salmon et al, 1996). Moreover, these dimensions matter particularly to people who are seriously ill (Cohen et al, 1996).

15.2.4 Using Measurements of Quality of Life

15.2.4.1 Individual Patients

Despite the absence of consensus about how to measure quality of life, neglecting it means neglecting the patient's perspective. Without this perspective, conclusions and decisions about illness and treatment are liable to reflect clinicians' assessments, which are unreliable guides to what patients think (Slevin et al, 1988). However, because of the unreliability that surrounds any measurement of this kind, it is implausible that an individual patient's management could ethically be decided by the score on a quality of life questionnaire. A score might, though, help to inform a clinician's judgement.

15.2.4.2 Health Care Evaluation and Planning

Unreliability matters less when quality of life assessments are used to inform decisions that affect large numbers of patients, such as in evaluating health care with a view to resource allocation. The unreliability is simply lost in the average. For this purpose, measurement of quality of life has been extended to more complex indices which reflect both the improved *quality* of life and increased (or decreased) *duration* of life that might result from treatment (Spiegelhalter et al, 1992).

Calculation of these so-called QALYs (quality-adjusted life years) is beyond the scope of this book. However, it is important to appreciate that they entail further assumptions, particularly about the ways that people evaluate periods of time at different levels of suffering (Rosser, 1998). This approach is hard to reconcile with the intensity with which most patients value life (and the chance of prolonging it), even to the extent of apparently disregarding unpleasant side effects of treatment that severely compromise quality of life (Schneiderman et al, 1993; Slevin, 1992). For instance, even a very slight chance of delaying death will often be felt sufficient to justify noxious chemotherapy (Slevin et al, 1990). Calculation of QALYs also entails complex statistical procedures. We have seen already in this chapter that statistical methods do not protect against the need to make assumptions. They merely put the assumptions into effect—and often entail new ones. Therefore, although sophisticated measurement techniques can assist decision making, they should not be allowed to hide the reality that all such decisions are based on value judgements.

15.2.4.3 Reporting Quality of Life

This chapter has shown that different ways of measuring quality of life reflect very different assumptions as to what it is. It follows that any decision to use a specific measurement procedure should be carefully justified. Furthermore, any statement about quality of life should be qualified by describing the way it was measured. Unfortunately this is rarely done (Gill and Feinstein, 1994).

15.3 EVALUATING THE PROCESS OF CARE

To this point, the chapter has focused on assessing the *outcome* of care. An alternative focus is on the *process* of care (Box 15.1). For some clinical interventions, this is the only approach that can be taken. These include exploratory procedures and care that occurs in the absence of clinical problems such as screening. In evaluating the process of care there are also difficult decisions as to what to measure. As we have seen in quality of life assessment, value judgements about what should be measured cannot be avoided.

15.3.1 Using Objective Criteria

15.3.1.1 Expert-Identified Criteria

Objective criteria can often be identified that are generally agreed to be important. These include brevity of waiting times, cleanliness of the clinic and readability of written information provided. Because these are objectively identifiable, they can be assessed without any reference to patients at all. Even clinicians' communication skills can be assessed in this way (Box 15.6).

15.3.1.2 Patient-Identified Criteria

There are, however, limitations of relying on experts to choose the criteria. Clinicians are not, in general, very accurate at detecting their patients' concerns (Chapter 10). Therefore the criteria that clinicians choose often differ from what patients think are most important (Drew et al, 1989). The

---

Box 15.6   Using objective criteria to assess quality of communication

The quality of care can be assessed by first deciding on objective criteria of quality and then recording whether they are met in any specific instance. For instance, the criteria below were chosen by experts to represent properties of communication that matter to patients. They are used to assess the quality of communication by clinicians in training. Patients' own subjective experience of the quality of consultation correlates with the extent to which these criteria are met (Humphris and Kaney, 1999).

Did the clinician:
  Greet the patient?
  Confirm the patient's name?
  Provide own name?
  Explain own position and role?
  Use open questions to explore the problem?
  Use reflection (repeating and rephrasing the patient's statements) to show empathy?
  Use non-verbal behaviour to show interest?
  Summarize and confirm understanding of information that the patient provided?
  Explain the action plan?
  Confirm patient's understanding of, and agreement with, the plan?

'average' patient's view can be found by surveying a representative sample of patients. A list of objective quality criteria that has been obtained in this way would be grounded in patients' views of what is important. That is, it would be content-valid (see above). It could then be used to compare different settings, or to check on maintenance of quality of care over time in a single setting.

15.3.1.3 Patients as the Observers

Objective observations. Once they have been identified, the objective criteria of quality care could be observed by clinicians, managers or external personnel. However, there are obvious advantages to recruiting patients as the observers. For instance, primary care patients can be asked whether the health centre answers the telephone quickly when they call or whether appointments are available when they need them (Baker, 1993).

Subjective observations. Patients' views of care do not, of course, depend only on its objective characteristics. They are influenced also by the patients' expectations and their history of related treatment and experiences. Therefore patients can be asked for their *subjective evaluation*, rather than objective observation, of discrete elements of care. In one example of this kind of recording scheme for hospital inpatients, they are asked for their view of the adequacy of cleaning of the ward, visiting arrangements, level of noise, food, pain control and the nurses' and doctors' behaviour (Gritzner, 1993).

15.3.2 Patients' Experience of Care

15.3.2.1 Identifying the Components of Experience

The focus, above, on discrete, objective elements of care is useful for some purposes. In particular, it can help to identify specific problematic— or positive—aspects of the way that care is delivered. However, for other purposes we need to know about patients' experience of care as a whole.

This itself is complex, because patients' experience is multifaceted and it resists being captured in a single question. Indeed, the words or expressions that patients use to describe an experience of health care are vast in number. Nevertheless, this diversity of terms normally reflects a limited number of underlying components of experience. A familiar analogy is the experience of colour. Most of us think that we see a limitless number of hues around us. In reality, we see only three colours. Every hue that can be seen results from a different combination of the primary colours: red, green and blue. In the same way, apparently different subjective experiences of care can reflect variations in a small number of underlying components. Fortunately, statistical procedures are available that can identify these components. A complete example, from identifying the words that patients use to describe their experience, through to obtaining a score which can be used to quantify the experience, is illustrated in Box 15.3 for one routine invasive investigation.

That study identified three components that underlay patients' experience. These were: pain and physical discomfort; emotional distress; and satisfaction. These dimensions probably apply quite generally to challenging medical and surgical procedures, since similar ones have emerged in childbirth (Salmon and Drew, 1992) and surgery (Johnston, 1984). Nevertheless, different groups of patients use very different language for different procedures. Therefore, it is important to carry out the complete cycle for any procedure which is to be evaluated. The results in one procedure cannot simply be generalized to another.

15.3.2.2 The Independence of the Components

The components that result from this kind of statistical procedure are independent. This is not just a statistical point. It means, for instance, that whether or not patients are in pain does not affect whether they are satisfied and emotionally calm; conversely, a patient could be dissatisfied but in no pain at all. The colonoscopy patients described in Box 15.3 were equally *satisfied* whether or not their endoscopist was experienced or inexperienced, but patients of the inexperienced endoscopists were the more *worried*. Because the components are independent, procedures which are intended to improve one component can have unpredicted effects on others. For example, childbirth by Caesarean section is less painful for the mother than is vaginal delivery, but it is also more distressing and less satisfying (Salmon and Drew, 1992).

Because patients have different experiences on each component, it will often be impossible to classify an intervention as improving or worsening patients' experience overall or to classify a particular patient as having a good or bad experience: different dimensions would point to different answers. To produce a single index, scores on each dimension could simply be added together, but this would mean assuming that each dimension matters equally to the patient. In practice, one or other dimension has normally been regarded as most important.

Traditionally, care surrounding medical and surgical procedures has been geared to minimizing pain and discomfort, and sometimes emotional distress. Increasingly, however, patient satisfaction is seen as the key dimension. Despite being only one component of patients' experience, its popularity in evaluating health care merits a separate section in this chapter.

15.3.2.3 The Concept of Satisfaction

The growing importance of patient satisfaction reflects the increasing consumerism of health care (Chapter 2). Some writers even go as far as to claim that 'customer satisfaction' should be regarded as an element of health status (see Williams, 1994). There are, however, important problems with the concept of satisfaction.

The main problem is that most patients probably do not have a consumerist concept of satisfaction in relation to health care. Satisfaction or dissatisfaction is simply not an issue for them. They do not approach medical care with the kinds of consumerist expectations with which they approach the consumption of other goods and services. Another way of explaining this is to point out that the passive role that many patients adopt (Chapters 11 and 12) is incompatible with feeling dissatisfied (Williams, 1994). Without the potential for dissatisfaction, there can be no concept of satisfaction.

Patients accept as 'normal' a very wide range of behaviour by clinicians. In practice, feelings of dissatisfaction—or satisfaction—with clinical care probably only arise when there have been gross departures from what they regard as normal (Nelson and Larson, 1993). This does not mean that a patient cannot answer when asked about satisfaction. Hearing the question immediately triggers the patient to think in terms of satisfaction. However, the patient does not necessarily then think in the way that the clinician might assume. Typically, patients' responses to simple satisfaction questions indicate extremely high levels of satisfaction. Very few patients identify themselves as dissatisfied (Fitzpatrick, 1993; Williams, 1994). The main thing that this tells us is that in formal surveys, just as in individual consultations, patients are reluctant to criticize their clinicians.

Where answers do vary, they depend more on interpersonal than technical aspects of care (Fitzpatrick, 1993). For instance, for the colonoscopy patients in Box 15.3, feeling satisfied meant feeling that staff were warm, interested in the patient and informative. Therefore, it would not be difficult for a scurrilous or technically poor clinician to satisfy a patient.

Box 15.7   The different meanings of 'being satisfied'

There are many reasons why patients might respond positively to simple questions about satisfaction with care (Williams, 1994).

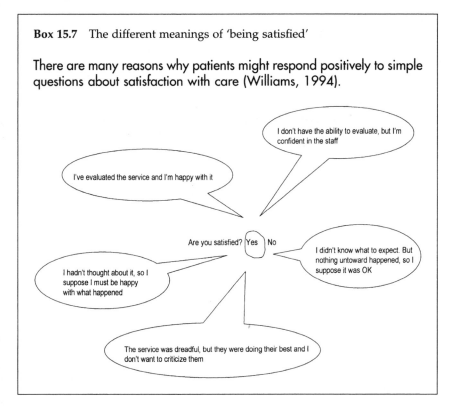

There are other influences on how satisfied patients say they are which further weaken the value of these ratings as indicators of quality of care (Fitzpatrick, 1993). The satisfied patients tend to be older or less well educated (Hall and Dornan, 1990), healthier, at least in terms of mental health (Cleary et al, 1991; Marshall et al, 1996), and happier with the world in general (Fitzpatrick and Hopkins, 1993). Therefore, when patients respond positively to simple questions about satisfaction, there can be a variety of different meanings (Box 15.7). That is, simple measures of satisfaction are unlikely to be valid.

15.3.2.4 Measuring Satisfaction

Nevertheless, when they are carefully constructed, questions about satisfaction do measure a property of the patient–clinician relationship that is clinically important. Patients who say they are satisfied are the most likely to comply with treatment advice (Chapter 9). There is also some evidence that they have a better clinical outcome (Fitzpatrick and Hopkins, 1981, 1993). Therefore Box 15.8 illustrates how questions can be constructed so

---

Box 15.8 Measuring satisfaction

The question about satisfaction in Box 15.7 was uninformative. These examples are likely to be more informative. Note the specific design principles described in the text that they incorporate.

No service can get everything right. We need *your* views so that we can improve our service in future. Please answer these questions as honestly as possible. Do not write your name. *Your answers will not be seen by any of the people who have looked after you.*

	Strongly agree	On balance, agree	Neither agree nor disagree	On balance, disagree	Strongly disagree
The doctor used words that I could not understand	☐	☐	☐	☐	☐
Everything I wanted to know was explained to me	☐	☐	☐	☐	☐
The staff treated me with respect	☐	☐	☐	☐	☐
There are ways in which this clinic could improve its care	☐	☐	☐	☐	☐

---

that they produce useful answers. The main principles that need to be applied are described below.

How to ask questions. Although patients tend to answer positively when presented with simple and transparent questions about satisfaction, there are several ways of designing questionnaires to yield more variable responses (Fitzpatrick, 1991; Robinson et al, 1998). Obviously, patients must be convinced that their responses are **confidential** and that the assessor is **neutral**. The use of **specific questions** is more revealing than global evaluations (Thompson, 1993). Where **factual questions** precede satisfaction questions, patients might be more prepared to give honest answers. Similarly, **instructions** for the questionnaire are important. A questionnaire that states that 'no service can get everything right' will probably be better at eliciting negative feelings than one that says 'we want to know how satisfied our customers are'. Questions and response choices can be framed so as to **avoid explicit statements of dissatisfaction** (Ware and Hays, 1988). For instance, questions can ask, not about the deficiencies of care, but about scope for improving it.

How to structure answers. The requirements for response options are those that are relevant to questionnaires generally. **'Yes/no'** answers are appropriate when the occurrence or absence of an objective feature of care is at issue, but this choice does not do justice to the subtleties of subjective experience. **'Agree/disagree'**, perhaps with intermediate points, is an alternative but questions should be worded so that 'agreement' does not always indicate satisfaction (so as to exclude the possibility that a general tendency to agree appears, incorrectly, as satisfaction). Defining satisfied and dissatisfied responses, alike, by **positive statements** can avoid this kind of bias (e.g., I was happy with the information I was given/I would have liked more information). Intermediate responses can be denoted by **numbered points** or a **visual analogue scale**, with the disadvantages that different patients mean different things by the same response and that it is impossible to conclude that a given score reflects either satisfaction or dissatisfaction. Instead, statements can be used for intermediate points in forming a Likert scale.

15.3.2.5 Qualitative Evaluation of Experience

Any questionnaire only finds out what the questions ask. Therefore clinicians or researchers who use questionnaires can only find out about things that the designers of the questionnaire have already thought of. This means that questionnaires 'censor' what patients tell clinicians (Williams, 1994). Clinicians who use questionnaires in their clinical work with individual patients have to be aware that patients will often have things to communicate that are not included in any questionnaire (Box 15.9). In research and evaluation, the uncritical use of questionnaires can therefore diminish, rather than enhance, the patient's perspective on care (Editorial, 1995).

Qualitative methods (Chapter 1) therefore have an important place in evaluation. Taking this approach, aspects of patients' experience can be identified that had not previously been appreciated. Box 15.10 illustrates how this approach can give rise to answers that are quite different from those that questionnaires provide. The essential feature of qualitative evaluation is that patients are helped to talk about their experience in their own way. This should happen routinely in clinical practice. In practice,

---

Box 15.9   When formal evaluation censors patients

Used sensitively, formal questionnaires and rating scales can help patients to express views and feelings that would otherwise go unnoticed. However, they can also get in the way of good patient–clinician communication. In this example, a nurse and researcher are asking for a child's assessment of pain after surgery. She is using a pain rating scale (one end of which is marked as 'unbearable pain'), but the child wants to tell her something about the pain that does not fit into the rating scale (Byrne et al, 1999).

Nurse	'What is your pain like?'
Child	'It's bad.'
Nurse	'How bad?'
Child	'It's bad. It's—'
Researcher	'If no pain is number 1 and the worst pain is number 10 what number are you?'
Child	'10, 10'
Nurse	'But is it bearable?'
Child	'I don't know what that means.'
Nurse	'Can you stand it?'
Child	'Oh mum tell her to go away. It's bad. It's bad. I've told you.'

---

few clinicians achieve this. Their directive questions, distancing techniques (Chapter 10) and evident authority get in the way.

15.4   CONCLUSION

This chapter is too brief and incomplete to teach the reader how to use patients' perspective to evaluate clinical care. However, it provides a framework for the choices that clinicians face when deciding how care should be evaluated, or when deciding how seriously to take others' evaluations of care. It should, at least, be clear that statements such as 'treatment Y improves quality of life', 'X% of patients are satisfied' or that 'questionnaire Z is valid' are no more than a covenient shorthand and can be downright misleading.

It is easy to be distracted by the apparent attractions of formal approaches to evaluation. However, other chapters in this book have shown that, in routine clinical practice, clinicians often prevent patients from disclosing

Box 15.10   Contrasting qualitative and quantitative evaluation: different perspectives on patient-controlled analgesia (PCA)

Questionnaire surveys of patients' views often give answers that clinicians expect. Therefore they perpetuate assumptions about how patients view their care. These two studies of PCA were carried out on similar patients at a single hospital (Chumbley et al, 1998; Taylor et al, 1996a, 1996b).

Questionnaire survey

200 patients gave these answers to two questions:

How did you feel about PCA?			How much control did you have?		
	Extremely positive	83		Complete	51
	Fairly positive	79		Quite a lot	86
	Neutral	28		Some	47
	Fairly negative	6		A little	11
	Extremely negative	4		None	3

These findings support the assumption that patients are very satisfied with PCA because it gives them control over their pain relief.

Qualitative study

26 patients were prompted to talk about their experience of PCA in their own way. Closed questions were avoided. Their comments about evaluation and control are summarized and illustrated below.

Evaluation. Two-thirds of patients described PCA enthusiastically ('Can't recommend it highly enough') or positively ('Very good, did the trick when you used it'). One third described it negatively ('About as effective as pissing into the wind').

Control. Only one patient spontaneously said anything about feeling in control. Most volunteered that they liked PCA because it saved them from bothering the nurses. When prompted to talk about control, no patient was very positive about it ('When you're in pain you don't care whether you're in control'). Other comments showed problems with PCA that *restricted* patients' control over pain relief. A third of patients described side effects or fears about addiction that stopped them using PCA as much as they wished. Others feared addiction or overdose if they used it 'too much'.

Does asking about PCA in these different ways lead to different conclusions?

important concerns and feelings to them. Formal assessment procedures can even contribute to this process (Box 15.9). Used critically, formal evaluation clearly has the potential to improve patients' care. However, care is even more likely to improve where clinicians who deliver it find out directly about their patients' experience—by asking patients and helping patients to answer.

KEY POINTS

- Patients' perspective is central in evaluating most health care.
- Patients' perspective can be used to evaluate the *outcome* or *process* of care.
- Quantifying patients' perspective requires careful attention to principles of subjective measurement.
- Validating a questionnaire means justifying that it measures what it is claimed to measure.
- In general, 'content validation' is critical for patient questionnaires.
- There is no single measurement of quality of life. Different methods assess impairment, disability, handicap, well-being and life evaluation.
- The process of care can be evaluated by objective indicators of quality or by patients' experience.
- Patients' experience of care is multidimensional. Satisfaction is only one dimension.
- Simple questions about satisfaction are misleading because patients are reluctant to criticize clinicians.
- Satisfaction questionnaires can be designed so as to produce useful responses.
- Satisfaction reflects clinicians' interpersonal style more than quality of technical care.
- Questionnaires can 'censor' what patients have to say. The best way of finding out patients' experience is to ask.

REFERENCES

Aarons H, Forester A, Hall G, Salmon P (1996) Fatigue after major joint arthroplasty: relationship to preoperative fatigue and postoperative emotional state. *Journal of Psychosomatic Research* 41, 225–233

Abbott J, Abbott P (1995) Psychological and cardiovascular predictors of anaesthesia induction, operative and post-operative complications in minor gynaecological surgery. *British Journal of Clinical Psychology* 34, 613–625

Affleck G, Tennen H, Pfeiffer C, Fifield J (1987) Appraisals of control and predictability in adapting to a chronic disease. *Journal of Personality and Social Psychology* 53, 273–279

Anderson EA (1987) Preoperative preparation for cardiac surgery facilitates recovery, reduces psychological distress and reduces the incidence of acute postoperative hypertension. *Journal of Consulting and Clinical Psychology* 55, 514–520

Andrew JM (1970) Recovery from surgery, with and without preparatory instruction, for three coping styles. *Journal of Personality and Social Psychology* 15, 223–226

Antoni MH, Baggett L, Ironson G, LaPerriere A (1991) Cognitive behavioral stress management intervention buffers distress response and immunological changes following notification of HIV1 seropositivity. *Journal of Consulting and Clinical Psychology* 59, 906–915

Armstrong D, Fry J, Armstrong P (1991) Doctors' perceptions of pressure from patients for referral. *British Medical Journal* 302, 1186–1188

Arnold RP, Rogers D, Cook DAG (1990) Medical problems of adults who were sexually abused in childhood. *British Medical Journal* 300, 705–708

Auerbach SM, Martelli MF, Mercuri LG (1983) Anxiety, information, interpersonal impacts, and adjustment to a stressful health care situation. *Journal of Personality and Social Psychology* 44, 1284–1296

Auerbach SM, Meredith J, Alexander JM, Mercuri LG, Brophy C (1984) Psychological factors in adjustment to orthognathic surgery. *Journal of Oral Maxillofacial Surgery* 42, 435–440

Ayton P, Wright G, Rowe G (1997) Medical decision making. In A Baum, S Newman, J Weinman, R West, C McManus (eds) *Cambridge Handbook of Psychology, Health and Medicine.* Cambridge: Cambridge University Press, pp 294–297

Bachen E, Cohen S, Marsland AL (1997) Psycho-immunology. In A Baum, S Newman, J Weinman, R West, C McManus (eds) *Cambridge Handbook of Psychology, Health and Medicine.* Cambridge: Cambridge University Press, pp 35–39

Baez K, Aiarzaguena JM, Grandes G, Pedrero E, Aranguren J, Retolaza A (1998) Understanding patient-initiated frequent attendance in primary care: a case–control study. *British Journal of General Practice* 48, 1824–1827

Baider L, Peretz T, Kaplan DeNour A (1997) The effect of behavioral intervention on the psychological distress of Holocaust survivors with cancer. *Psychotherapy and Psychosomatics* 66, 44–49

Bailey R, Clarke M (1989) *Stress and Coping in Nursing.* London: Chapman & Hall

Baker R (1993) Use of psychometrics to develop a measure of patient satisfaction for general practice. In R Fitzpatrick, A Hopkins (eds) *Measurement of Patients' Satisfaction with their Care.* London: Royal College of Physicians, pp 57–75

Balint M (1957) *The Doctor, his Patient and the Illness.* Tunbridge Wells: Pitman

Ballantyne JC, Carr DB, Chalmers TC, Dear KBG, Angellilo IF, Mosteller F (1993) Postoperative patient controlled analgesia: meta analyses of initial randomized control trials. *Journal of Clinical Anesthesiology* 5, 182–193

Bardram L, Funchjensen P, Jensen P, Crawford ME, Kehlet H (1995) Recovery after laparoscopic colonic surgery with epidural analgesia and early oral nutrition and mobilization. *Lancet* 345, 763–764

Barker A, Mayou R (1992) Psychological factors in patients with nonspecific abdominal pain acutely admitted to a general surgical ward. *Journal of Psychosomatic Research* 36, 715–722

Bar-On D (1986) Professional models vs patient models in rehabilitation after heart attack. *Human Relations* 39, 917–932

Bar-On D (1987) Causal attributions and the rehabilitation of myocardial infarction victims. *Journal of Social and Clinical Psychology* 5, 114–122

Baron RS, Logan H (1993) Desired control, felt control and dental pain. *Motivation and Emotion* 17, 181–204

Bass CM (1990) (ed) *Somatization: Physical Symptoms and Psychological Illness.* Oxford: Blackwell

Bass MJ and the Headache Study Group of the University of Western Ontario (1986) Predictors of outcome in headache patients presenting to family physicians: a one year prospective study. *Headache* 26, 285–294

Beaver K, Luker KA, Owens RG, Leinster SJ, Degner L, Sloan JA (1996) Treatment decision making in women newly diagnosed with breast cancer. *Cancer Nursing* 19, 8–19

Beck AT, Rush AJ, Shaw BJ, Emery G (1979) *Cognitive Therapy of Depression: A Treatment Manual.* New York: Guilford

Beecher HK (1956) Relationship of significance of wound to pain experienced. *Journal of the American Medical Association* 161, 1609–1613

Bellamy N, Buchanan WW, Goldsmith CH, Campbell J, Stitt L (1988) Validation study of WOMAC: a health status instrument for measuring clinically important patient relevant outcomes following total hip or knee arthroplasty in osteoarthritis. *Journal of Orthopaedic Rheumatology* 1, 95–108

Bennett P, Carroll D (1997) Coronary heart disease: impact. In A Baum, S Newman, J Weinman, R West, C McManus (eds) *Cambridge Handbook of Psychology, Health and Medicine.* Cambridge: Cambridge University Press, pp 419–421

Benotsch EG, Christensen AJ, McKelvey L (1997) Hostility, social support, and ambulatory cardiovascular activity. *Journal of Behavioral Medicine* 20, 163–176

Benson H, Klipper MZ (1975) *The Relaxation Response.* New York: William Morrow

Benyamini Y, Leventhal E, Leventhal H (1997) Attributions and health. In A Baum, S Newman, J Weinman, R West, C McManus (eds) *Cambridge Handbook of Psychology, Health and Medicine.* Cambridge: Cambridge University Press, pp 72–77

Bergner M (1988) Development, testing and use of the Sickness Impact Profile. In SR Walker, RM Rosser (eds) *Quality of Life: Assessment and Application.* Lancaster: MTP Press, pp 79–93

Berkman LF (1985) The relationship of social networks and social support to morbidity and mortality. In S Cohen SL, Syme (eds) *Social Support and Health*. Orlando, FL: Academic Press, pp 241–262

Berkman L, Syme SL (1979) Social networks, host resistance and mortality: a nine-year follow-up study of Alameda County residents. *American Journal of Epidemiology* 109, 186–204

Bibace R, Walsh ME (1980) Development of children's concept of illness. *Pediatrics* 66, 912–917

Bibace R, Schmidt LR, Walsh ME (1994) Children's perceptions of illness. In GN Penny, P Bennett, M Herbert (eds) *Health Psychology: A Lifespan Perspective*. Amsterdam: Harwood, pp 13–30

Bishop GD (1991) Understanding the understanding of illness: lay distress representations. In JA Skelton, RT Croyle (eds) *Mental Representation in Health and Illness*. New York: Springer, pp 32–59

Blackburn S, Piper K, Wooldridge T, Hoag JD, Hannan L (1978) Diabetic patients on hemodialysis. *Health and Social Work* 3, 90–104

Blaxter M (1989) The causes of disease: women talking. *Social Science and Medicine* 17, 59–69

Bloom JR, Kang SH, Romano P (1991) Cancer and stress: the effect of social support as a resource. In CL Cooper, M Watson (eds) *Cancer and Stress: Psychological, Biological and Coping Studies*. Chichester: Wiley

Bloor M, McIntosh J (1990) Surveillance and concealment: a comparison of techniques of client resistance in therapeutic communities and health visiting. In S Cunningham-Burley, NP McKeganey (eds) *Readings in Medical Sociology*. London: Routledge, pp 159–181

Bohus B, Koolhaas JM (1993) Stress and the cardiovascular system: central and peripheral physiological mechanisms. In SC Stanford, P Salmon (eds) *Stress: From Synapse to Syndrome*. London: Academic Press, pp 75–117

Boore JRP (1978) *Prescription for Recovery: The Effects of Preoperative Preparation of Surgical Patients on Postoperative Stress, Recovery and Infection*. London: Royal College of Nursing

Bottomley A (1998) Psychotherapy groups and cancer patient survival: chasing fool's gold? *European Journal of Cancer Care* 7, 192–196

Bowlby J (1973) *Attachment and Loss. Vol 2: Separation*. New York: Basic Books

Bowling A (1995a) *Measuring Disease*. Buckingham: Open University Press

Bowling A (1995b) What things are important in people's lives? A survey of the public's judgements to inform scales of health related quality of life. *Social Science and Medicine* 41, 1447–1462

Boyle CM (1970) Differences between patients' and doctors' interpretations of some common medical terms. *British Medical Journal* 2, 286–289

Bradley C (1988) Stress and diabetes. In S Fisher, J Reason (eds) *Handbook of Life Stress, Cognition and Health*. Chichester: Wiley

Bradley C (1994) Contributions of psychology to diabetes management. *British Journal of Clinical Psychology* 33, 11–21

Branstetter E (1969) The young child's response to hospitalization: separation anxiety or lack of mothering care? *American Journal of Public Health* 59, 92–97

Brehm SS, Brehm JW (1981) *Psychological Reactance: A Theory of Freedom and Control*. New York: Academic Press

Brosschot JF, Godaert GLR, Benschop RJ, Olff M, Ballieux RE, Heijnen CJ (1998) Experimental stress and immunological reactivity: a closer look at perceived uncontrollability. *Psychosomatic Medicine* 60, 359–361

Brownell KD (1991) Personal responsibility and control over our bodies: when expectation exceeds reality. *Health Psychology* 10, 303–310

Bulman JR, Wortman CB (1977) Attributions of blame and coping in the 'real world': severe accident victims react to their lot. *Journal of Personality and Social Psychology* 35, 351–363

Bundy C, Carroll D, Wallace L, Nagle R (1994) Psychological treatment of chronic stable angina pectoris. *Psychology and Health* 10, 69–77

Bundy C, Carroll D, Wallace L, Nagle R (1998) Stress management and exercise training in chronic stable angina pectoris. *Psychology and Health* 13, 147–155

Burish TG, Jenkins RA (1992) Effectiveness of biofeedback and relaxation training in reducing the side effects of cancer chemotherapy. *Health Psychologist* 11, 17–23

Burish TC, Carey MP, Wallston KA, Stein MJ, Jamison RN, Lyles JN (1984) Health locus of control and chronic disease: an external orientation may be advantageous. *Journal of Social and Clinical Psychology* 2, 326–332

Bush JP, Melamed BG, Sheras PL, Greenbaum PE (1986) Mother child patterns of coping with anticipatory medical stress. *Health Psychology* 5, 137–157

Butler CC, Evans M (1999) The 'heartsink' patient revisited. *British Journal of General Practice* 49, 230–233

Butler GS, Hurley CA, Buchanan KL, Smith-vanHorne J (1996) Prehospital education: effectiveness with total hip replacement surgery patients. *Patient Education and Counselling* 29, 189–197

Byrne A, Holcombe C, Ellershaw J, Salmon P (1999a) Psychological adjustment to cancer: fighting spirit re-evaluated University of Liverpool (unpublished manuscript)

Byrne A, Morton J, Salmon P (1999b) Clinicians' responses to patients' suffering: pediatric nurses' defences against children's postoperative pain. University of Liverpool (unpublished manuscript)

Cacioppo JT, Anderson BL, Turnquist DC, Petty RE (1986) Psychophysiological comparison processes: interpreting cancer symptoms. In B Anderson (ed) *Women with Cancer: Psychological Perspectives*. New York: Springer, pp 141–171

Cameron L, Leventhal EA, Leventhal H (1995) Seeking medical care in response to symptoms and life stress. *Psychosomatic Medicine* 57, 37–47

Campion PD, Butler NM, Cox AD (1992) Principle agendas of doctors and patients in general practice consultations. *Family Practice* 9, 181–190

Cannon WB (1929) *Bodily Changes in Pain, Hunger, Fear and Rage*, 2nd edition. New York: Appleton

Cannon WB (1942) Voodoo death. *American Anthropologist* 44, 169–181

Carney RM, Freedland KE, Rich MW, Jaffe AS (1995) Depression as a risk factor for cardiac events in established coronary heart disease: a review of possible mechanisms. *Annals of Behavioral Medicine* 17, 142–149

Carroll D, Bennett P, Davey Smith G (1993) Socioeconomic health inequalities: their origins and implications. *Psychology and Health* 8, 295–316

Case RB, Moss AJ, Case N, McDermott M, Eberly S (1992) Living alone after myocardial infarction: impact on prognosis. *Journal of the American Medical Association* 267, 515–519

Cassell EJ (1976) Disease as an 'it': concepts of disease revealed by patients' presentation of symptoms. *Social Science and Medicine* 10, 143–146

Cassileth BR (1995) History of psychotherapeutic intervention in cancer patients. *Supportive Care in Cancer* 3, 264–266

Charmaz K (1995) The body, identity and self: adapting to impairment. *Sociological Quarterly* 36, 656–680

Chesney M, Folkman S, Chambers D (1996) Coping effectiveness training for men living with HIV: preliminary findings. *International Journal of STD & AIDS* 7, 75–82

Christensen AJ, Moran PJ (1998) Psychosomatic research in endstage renal disease: a framework for matching patient to treatment. *Journal of Psychosomatic Research* 44, 523–528

Christensen AJ, Edwards DL, Wiebe JS, Benotsch EG, McKelvey L, Andrews M, Lubaroff DM (1996) Effect of verbal selfdisclosure on natural killer cell activity: moderating influence of cynical hostility. *Psychosomatic Medicine* 58, 150–155

Christensen T, Kehlet H (1993) Postoperative fatigue. *World Journal of Surgery* 17, 220–225

Christensen T, Hjortso NC, Mortensen E, RiisHansen M, Kehlet H (1986) Fatigue and anxiety in surgical patients. *Acta Psychiatrica Scandinavica* 73, 76–79

Chumbley GM, Hall GM, Salmon P (1998) Patient-controlled analgesia: an assessment by 200 patients. *Anaesthesia* 53, 216–221

Chumbley GM, Hall GM, Salmon P (1999) Why do patients feel positive about patient-controlled analgesia? *Anaesthesia* 54, 386–389

Cleary P, Edgman-Levitan S, Roberts M, Moloney T, McMullen W, Walter J, Delbanco T (1991) Patients evaluate their hospital care: a national survey. *Health Affairs* 10, 254–267

Cohen FL (1980) Postsurgical pain relief: patients' status and nurses' medication choices. *Pain* 9, 265–274

Cohen S, Doyle WJ, Skoner DP, Rabin BS, Gwaltney JM (1997) Social ties and susceptibility to the common cold. *Journal of the American Medical Association* 277, 1940–1944

Cohen SR, Mount BM (1992) Quality of life in terminal illness: defining and measuring subjective wellbeing in the dying. *Journal of Palliative Care* 8, 40–45

Cohen SR, Mount BM, Strobel MG, Bui F (1995) The McGill Quality of Life Questionnaire: a measure of quality of life appropriate for people with advanced disease. A preliminary study of validity and acceptability. *Palliative Medicine* 9, 207–219

Cohen SR, Mount BM, Thomas JJN, Mount LF (1996) Existential wellbeing is an important determinant of quality of life: evidence from the McGill Quality of Life Questionnaire. *Cancer* 77, 576–586

Collins NL, Dunkel-Schetter C, Lobel M, Scrimshaw SCM (1993) Social support in pregnancy: psychosocial correlates of birth outcomes and postpartum depression. *Journal of Personality and Social Psychology* 5, 1243–1258

Collins RL, Taylor SE, Skokan LA (1990) A better world or a shattered vision? Changes in perspectives following victimization. *Social Cognition* 8, 263–285

Compas BE, Haaga DAF, Keefe FJ, Leitenberg H, Williams DA (1998) Sampling of empirically supported psychological treatments from health psychology: smoking, chronic pain, cancer, and bulimia nervosa. *Journal of Consulting and Clinical Psychology* 66, 89–112

Conroy RM, Smyth O, Siriwardena R, Fernandes P (1999) *Journal of Psychosomatic Research* 46, 45–50

Cook WW, Medley DM (1954) Proposed hostility and pharasaic virtue scales for the MMPI. *Journal of Applied Psychology* 38, 414–418

Cooper B (1993) Single spies and battalions: the clinical epidemiology of mental disorders. *Psychological Medicine* 23, 891–907

Coulter A (1997) Partnerships with patients: the pros and cons of shared clinical decision-making. *Journal of Health Services Research and Policy* 2, 112–121

Coulter A, McPherson K (1987) Waiting times and duration of hospital stay for common surgical operations: trends over time. *Community Medicine* 9, 247–253

Cox DJ, Gonder-Frederick L, Antoun B, Cryer PE, Clarke WL (1993) Perceived symptoms in the recognition of hypoglycemia. *Diabetes Care* 16, 519–527

Craig TKJ, Boardman AP (1990) Somatization in primary care settings. In CM Bass (ed) *Somatization: Physical Symptoms and Psychological Illness*. Oxford: Blackwell, pp 73–103

Crook P, Stott R, Rose M, Peters S, Salmon P, Stanley I (1998) Adherence to group exercise training: lessons from physiotherapist-led experimental programmes. *Physiotherapy* 84, 366–372

Croyle RT (1990) Biased appraisal of high blood pressure. *Preventive Medicine* 19, 40–44

Croyle RT, Sun YC, Louie DH (1993) Psychological minimization of cholesterol test results: moderators of appraisal in college students and community residents. *Health Psychology* 12, 503–507

Croyle RT, Sun YC, Hart M (1997) Processing risk factor information: defensive biases in health-related judgements and memory. In KJ Petrie, JA Weinman (eds) *Perceptions of Health and Illness*. Amsterdam: Harwood, pp 267–290

Crumbaugh JC, Maholick LT (1964) An experimental study in existentialism: the psychometric approach to Frankl's concept of noogenic neurosis. *Journal of Clinical Psychology* 20, 200–207

Dantzer R (1993) Coping with stress. In SC Stanford, P Salmon (eds) *Stress: From Synapse to Syndrome*. London: Academic Press, pp 167–189

David AS, Wessely SC (1995) The legend of Camelford: medical consequences of a water pollution accident. *Journal of Psychosomatic Research* 39, 1–9

Davies ADM, Peters MP (1989) Stresses of hospitalization in the elderly: nurses' and patients' perceptions. *Journal of Advanced Nursing* 8, 99–105

Davis H, Fallowfield L (1991) Counselling and communication in health care: the current situation. In H Davis, L Fallowfield (eds) *Counselling and Communication in Health Care*. Chichester: Wiley

Davison KP, Pennebaker JW (1997) Virtual narratives: illness representations in online support groups. In KJ Petrie, JA Weinman (eds) *Perceptions of Health and Illness*. Amsterdam: Harwood, pp 463–486

Dean C, Surtees PG (1989) Do psychological factors predict survival in breast cancer? *Journal of Psychosomatic Research* 33, 561–569

Deaton AV (1985) Adaptive noncompliance in pediatric asthma: the parent as expert. *Journal of Pediatric Psychology* 10, 1–14

Debatz DL (1996) Meaning in life: clinical relevance and predictive power. *British Journal of Clinical Psychology* 35, 503–516

Degner LF, Sloan JA (1992) Decision making during serious illness: what role do patients really want to play? *Journal of Clinical Epidemiology* 45, 941–950

deHaes JCJM, VanKnippenberg RCE, Neijt JP (1990) Measuring psychological and physical distress in cancer patients: structure and application of the Rotterdam Symptom Checklist. *British Journal of Cancer* 62, 1034–1038

Derogatis L, Abeloff M, Melisaratos N (1979) Psychological coping mechanisms and survival time in metastatic cancer. *Journal of the American Medical Association* 242, 1504–1508

DeWolfe AS, Barrel RP, Cummings JW (1966) Patient variables in emotional response to hospitalization for physical illness. *Journal of Consulting and Clinical Psychology* 30, 68–72

DiMatteo MR, Hays RD, Prince LM (1986) Relationship of physicians' nonverbal communication skill to patient satisfaction, appointment noncompliance and physician workload. *Health Psychology* 5, 581–594

DiMatteo MR, Sherbourne CD, Hays RD, Ordway L, Kravitz RL, McGlynn EA, Kaplan S, Rogers WH (1993) Physicians' characteristics influence patients' adherence to medical treatment: results from the Medical Outcomes Study. *Health Psychology* 12, 93–102

Ditto PH, Jemmott JB III, Darley JM (1988) Appraising the threat of illness: a mental representational approach. *Health Psychology* 7, 183–200

Dobratz MC (1990) The Life Closure Scale: a measure of psychological adaptation in death and dying. *Hospice Journal* 6, 1–15

Dowrick C (1992) Why do the O'Sheas consult so often? An exploration of complex family illness behaviour. *Social Science and Medicine* 34, 491–497

Dracup K, Moser D (1991) Treatment-seeking behavior among those with signs and symptoms of acute myocardial infarction. *Heart and Lung* 20, 570–575

Drew NC, Salmon P, Webb L (1989) Mothers', midwives' and obstetricians' views on the features of obstetric care which influence satisfaction with childbirth. *British Journal of Obstetrics and Gynaecology* 96, 1084–1088

Drife JO (1993) Errors and accidents in obstetrics. In CA Vincent, M Ennis, RJ Audley (eds) *Medical Accidents*. Oxford: Oxford University Press, pp 34–51

Drossman DA, McKee DC, Sandler RS, Mitchell CM, Cramer EM, Lowman BC, Burger AL (1988) Psychosocial factors in the irritable bowel syndrome. *Gastroenterology* 95, 701–708

Dumas RG, Leonard RC (1963) The effect of nursing on the incidence of postoperative vomiting. *Nursing Research* 12, 12–15

Easterling DV, Leventhal H (1989) Contribution of concrete cognition to emotion: neutral symptoms as elicitors of worry about cancer. *Journal of Applied Psychology* 74, 787–796

Eddy DM (1982) Probabilistic reasoning in clinical medicine: problems and opportunities. In D Kahneman, P Slovic, A Tversky (eds) *Judgement under Uncertainty: Heuristics and Biases*. Cambridge, Cambridge University Press, pp 249–267

Eddy DM, Clanton CH (1982) The art of clinical diagnosis: solving the clinico-pathological exercise. *New England Journal of Medicine* 306, 1263–1268

Editorial (1995) Quality of life and clinical trials. *Lancet* 346, 1–2

Egbert LD, Battit GE, Welch CE, Bartlett MK (1964) Reduction of postoperative pain by encouragement and instruction of patients. *New England Journal of Medicine* 270, 825–827

Eitel P, Hatchett L, Friend R, Griffin KW, Wadhwa N (1995) Burden of self care in seriously ill patients: impact on adjustment. *Health Psychology* 14, 457–463

Ekblom A, Hansson P, Thomsson M, Thomas M (1991) Increased postoperative pain and consumption of analgesics following acupuncture. *Pain* 44, 241–247

Ell K, Nishimoto R, Mediansky L, Mantell J, Hamovitch M (1992) Social relations, social support and survival among patients with cancer. *Journal of Psychosomatic Research* 36, 531–541

Elliott-Binns CP (1973) An analysis of lay medicine. *Journal of the Royal College of General Practitioners* 23, 255–264

Elliott-Binns CP (1986) An analysis of lay medicine: fifteen years later. *Journal of the Royal College of General Practitioners* 36, 542–544

Ellison CW (1983) Spiritual well-being: conceptualization and measurement. *Journal of Psychology and Theology* 11, 330–340

Elstein AS, Holzman GB, Ravitch MM, Metheny WA, Holmes MM, Hoppe RB, Rothert ML, Rovner DR (1986) Comparisons of physicians' decisions regarding oestrogen replacement therapy for menopausal women and decisions derived from a decision analytic model. *American Journal of Medicine* 80, 246–258

Epstein AM, Taylor WC, Seage GR (1985) Effects of patients' socio-economic status and physicians' training and practice on patient–doctor communication. *American Journal of Medicine* 78, 101–106

Erikson EH, Erikson JM, Kivnick HQ (1986) *Vital Involvement in Old Age*. New York: Norton

Esterling BA, Antoni MH, Fletcher MA, Margules S, Scheiderman N (1994) Emotional disclosure through writing or speaking modulates latent Epstein–Barr virus antibody titers. *Journal of Consulting and Clinical Psychology* 62, 130–140

Fahrenberg J (1986) Psychophysiological individuality: a pattern analytic approach to personality research and psychosomatic medicine. *Advances in Behaviour Research and Therapy* 8, 43–100

Fallowfield L (1990) *The Quality of Life: The Missing Measurement in Health Care*. London: Souvenir Press

Fallowfield LJ, Hall A, Maguire GP, Baum M (1990) Psychosocial outcomes of different treatment policies in women with early breast cancer outside a clinical trial. *British Medical Journal* 301, 575–580

Fawzy FI, Kemeny ME, Fawzy NW, Elashoff R, Morton D, Cousins N, Fahey JL (1990) A structured psychiatric intervention for cancer patients. *Archives of General Psychiatry* 47, 729–735

Fawzy FI, Fawzy NW, Hyun CS, Elashoff R, Guthrie D, Fahey JL, Morton DL (1993) Malignant melanoma: effects of an early structured psychiatric intervention, coping, and affective state on recurrence and survival 6 years later. *Archives of General Psychiatry* 50, 681–689

Felton BJ, Revenson TA, Henrichsen GA (1984) Stress and coping in the explanation of psychological adjustment among chronically ill adults. *Social Science and Medicine* 18, 889–898

Feyerabend P (1975) *Against Method: Outline of an Anarchistic Theory of Knowledge*. London: Verso

Fife B (1995) The measurement of meaning in illness. *Social Science and Medicine* 40, 1021–1028

Fink P (1992) Surgery and medical treatment in persistent somatizing patients. *Journal of Psychosomatic Research* 36, 439–447

Fishbein M, Ajzen I (1975) *Belief, Attitude, Intention and Behavior: An Introduction to Theory and Research*. Reading, MA: Addison-Wesley

Fitzgibbon EJ, Murphy D, O'Shea K, Kelleher C (1997) Chronic debilitating fatigue in Irish general practice: a survey of general practitioners' experience. *British Journal of Gneral Practice* 47, 618–622

Fitzpatrick R (1991) Surveys of patient satisfaction II: designing a questionnaire and conducting a survey. *British Medical Journal* 302, 1129–1132

Fitzpatrick R (1993) Scope and measurement of patient satisfaction. In R Fitzpatrick, A Hopkins (eds) *Measurement of Patients' Satisfaction with their Care*. London: Royal College of Physicians, pp 1–17

Fitzpatrick R, Hopkins A (1981) Referrals to neurologists for headaches not due to structural disease. *Journal of Neurology, Neurosurgery and Psychiatry* 12, 1061–1067

Fitzpatrick R, Hopkins A (1993) Patient satisfaction in relation to clinical care: a neglected contribution. In R Fitzpatrick, A Hopkins (eds) *Measurement of*

Patients' Satisfaction with their Care. London: Royal College of Physicians, pp 77–86

Fox BH (1995) Supportive care in cancer. *Cancer* 3, 257–263

Frasure-Smith N, Prince R (1989) Long-term follow up of the Ischaemic Heart Disease Life Stress Monitoring Program. *Psychosomatic Medicine* 51, 485–513

Frasure-Smith N, Lesperance F, Juneau M, Talajic M, Bourassa MG (1999) Gender, depression, and one-year prognosis after myocardial infarction. *Psychosomatic Medicine* 61, 26–37

Frenzel MP, McCaul KD, Glasgow RE, Schafer LC (1988) The relationship of stress and coping to regimen adherence and glycemic control of diabetes. *Journal of Social and Clinical Psychology* 6, 77–87

Friedman M, Thoresen CD, Gill JJ, Ulmer D, Powell LH, Price VA, Brown B, Thompson L, Arbin DD, Breall WS, Bourg E, Levy R, Dixon T (1986) Alteration of Type A behavior and its effect on cardiac recurrences in post myocardial infarction patients: summary results of the recurrent coronary prevention project. *American Heart Journal* 112, 653–665

Fry R (1993) Adult physical illness and childhood sexual abuse. *Journal of Psychosomatic Research* 37, 89–103

Gatchel RJ, Gaffney FA, Smith JE (1986) Comparative efficacy of behavioral stress management versus propranolol in reducing psychophysiological reactivity in post-myocardial infarction patients. *Journal of Behavioral Medicine* 9, 503–513

Gill TM, Feinstein AR (1994) A critical appraisal of the quality of quality-of-life measurements. *Journal of the American Medical Association* 272, 619–626

Glazebrook CP, Lim E, Sheard CE, Standen PJ (1994) Child temperament and reaction to induction of anaesthesia: implications for maternal presence in the anaesthetic room. *Psychology and Health* 10, 55–67

Goldberg D, Gask L, O'Dowd T (1989) The treatment of somatization: teaching techniques of reattribution. *Journal of Psychosomatic Research* 33, 689–695

Goodwin JS, Hunt WC, Key CR, Samet JM (1987) The effect of marital status on stage, treatment and survival of cancer patients. *Journal of the American Medical Association* 258, 3125–3130

Gould TH, Crosby DL, Harmer M, Lloyd SM, Lunn JN, Rees GAD, Roberts DE, Webster JA (1992) Policy for controlling pain after surgery: effect of sequential changes in management. *British Medical Journal* 305, 1187–1193

Greenfield S, Kaplan S, Ware JE (1985) Expanding patient involvement in care: effects on patient outcomes. *Annals of Internal Medicine* 102, 520–528

Greer S (1997) Adjuvant psychological therapy for cancer patients. *Palliative Medicine* 11, 240–244

Greer S, Moorey S, Baruch JDR, Watson M, Robertson BM, Mason A, Rowden L, Law MG, Bliss JM (1992) Adjuvant psychological therapy for patients with cancer: a prospective randomised trial. *British Medical Journal* 304, 675–680

Gritzner C (1993) The CASPE patient satisfaction system. In R Fitzpatrick, A Hopkins (eds) *Measurement of Patients' Satisfaction with their Care*. London: Royal College of Physicians, pp 33–41

Grootenhuis MA, Last BF, van der Wel M, de Graaf-Nijkerk JH (1998) Parents' attribution of positive characteristics to their children with cancer. *Psychology and Health* 13, 67–81

Grossarth-Maticek R, Eysenck HJ (1991) Creative novation behaviour therapy as a prophylactic treatment for cancer and coronary heart disease: part I. Description of treatment. *Behaviour Research and Therapy* 29, 1–16

Grossarth-Maticek R, Schmidt P, Vetter H, Arndt S (1984) Psychotherapy research in oncology. In A Steptoe, A Mathews (eds) *Health Care and Human Behaviour*. London: Academic Press, pp 325–342

Guthrie E (1992) The management of medical outpatients with nonorganic disorders: the irritable bowel syndrome. In F Creed, R Mayou, A Hopkins (eds) *Medical Symptoms not Explained by Organic Disease*. London: Royal College of Psychiatrists and Royal College of Physicians, pp 60–69

Hackett TP, Cassem NH (1973) Psychological adaptation to convalescence in myocardial infarction patients. In JP Naughton, HK Hellerstein, IC Mohler (eds) *Exercise Testing and Exercise Training in Coronary Heart Disease*. New York: Academic Press, pp 253–262

Hampson SE (1997) Illness representations and the self-management of diabetes. In KJ Petrie, JA Weinman (eds) *Perceptions of Health and Illness*. Amsterdam: Harwood, pp 323–347

Hall GM, Salmon P (1997) Patient-controlled analgesia: who benefits? *Anaesthesia* 52, 401–402

Hall J, Dornan M (1990) Patient sociodemographic characteristics as predictors of satisfaction with medical care: a meta-analysis. *Social Science and Medicine* 30, 811–818

Hall JA, Epstein AM, DeCiantis ML, McNeil BJ (1993) Physicians' liking for their patients: more evidence for the role of affect in medical care. *Health Psychology* 12, 140–146

Hampson SE (1997) Illness representations and the self-management of diabetes. In KJ Petrie, JA Weinman (eds) *Perceptions of Health and Illness*. Amsterdam: Harwood, pp 323–347

Hatchett L, Friend R, Symister P, Wadwha N (1997) Interpersonal expectations, social support and adjustment to chronic illness. *Journal of Personality and Social Psychology* 73, 560–573

Haug MR, Ory MG (1987) Issues in elderly patient–provider interactions. *Research on Aging* 9, 3–44

Haynes RB, McKibbon KA, Kanani R (1996) Systematic review of randomised trials of interventions to assist patients to follow prescriptions for medications. *Lancet* 48, 383–386

Haynes SG, Feinleib M (1980) Women, work and coronary disease: prospective findings from the Framingham Heart Study. *American Journal of Public Health* 70, 133–141

Heaven CM, Maguire P (1996) Training hospice nurses to elicit patient concerns. *Journal of Advanced Nursing* 23, 280–286

Heaven CM, Maguire P (1997) Disclosure of concerns by hospice patients and their identification by nurses. *Palliative Medicine* 11, 283–290

Hegel MT, Ayllon T, Thiel G, Oulton B (1992) Improving adherence to fluid restrictions in male hemodialysis patients: a comparison of cognitive and behavioral approaches. *Health Psychology* 11, 324–330

Helgeson VS (1993) Implications of agency and communion for patient and spouse adjustment to a 1st coronary event. *Journal of Personality and Social Psychology* 64, 807–816

Helgeson VS, Taylor SE (1993) Social comparisons and adjustment among cardiac patients. *Journal of Applied Psychology* 23, 1171–1195

Helman CG (1978) 'Feed a cold, starve a fever': folk models of infection in an English suburban community, and their relation to medical treatment. *Culture, Medicine and Psychiatry* 2, 107–137

Helman CG (1985) Psyche, soma, and society: the social construction of psychosomatic disorders. *Culture, Medicine and Psychiatry* 9, 1–26

Helman CG (1994) *Culture, Health and Illness*, 3rd edition. Oxford: Butterworth-Heinemann

Henningsen P, Priebe S (1999) Modern disorders of vitality: the struggle for legitimate incapacity. *Journal of Psychosomatic Research* 46, 209–214

Herbert C, Salmon P (1994) The inaccuracy of nurses' perception of elderly patients' wellbeing. *Psychology and Health* 9, 485–492

Hergenrather JR, Rabinowitz MR (1991) Age-related differences in the organization of children's knowledge of illness. *Developmental Psychology* 27, 952–959

Hirano PC, Laurent DD, Lorig K (1994) Arthritis education studies, 1987–1991: a review of the literature. *Patient Education and Counselling* 24, 9–54

Hogbin B, Fallowfield LJ (1989) Getting it taped: the bad news consultation with cancer patients. *British Journal of Hospital Medicine* 41, 330–333

Hopkins A (1990) Stress, the quality of work, and repetition strain injury in Australia. *Work and Stress* 4, 129–138

Hopkins A (1992) The management of patients with chronic headache not due to obvious structural disease. In F Creed, R Mayou, A Hopkins (eds) *Medical Symptoms not Explained by Organic Disease*. London: Royal College of Psychiatrists and Royal College of Physicians of London, pp 34–46

Horne R (1997) Representations of medication and treatment: advances in theory and measurement. In KJ Petrie, JA Weinman (eds) *Perceptions of Health and Illness*. Amsterdam: Harwood, pp 155–188

House JS, Robbins C, Metzner HL (1982) The association of social relationships and activities with mortality. *American Journal of Epidemiology* 116, 123–140

Howitt A, Armstrong D (1999) Implementing evidence based medicine in general practice: audit and qualitative study of antithrombotic treatment for atrial fibrillation. *British Medical Journal* 318, 1324–1327

Humphris G, Kaney S (1999) Evaluating communications skills training. University of Liverpool (unpublished manuscript)

Hunt LM, Jordan B, Irwin S (1989) Views of what's wrong: diagnosis and patients' concepts of illness. *Social Science and Medicine* 28, 945–956

Hunt SM, McEwen J, McKenna SP (1985) Measuring health status: a new tool for clinicians and epidemiologists. *Journal of the Royal College of General Practitioners* 35, 185–188

Ingham JG, Miller PM (1986) Self-referral to primary care: symptoms and social factors. *Journal of Psychosomatic Research* 30, 49–56

Innui TS, Yourtee EL, Williamson JW (1976) Improved outcomes in hypertension after physician tutorials. *Annals of Internal Medicine* 84, 646–651

Isen AM, Rosenzweig AS, Young MJ (1991) The influence of positive affect on clinical problem solving. *Medical Decision Making* 11, 221–227

Jacobsen PB, Manne SL, Gorfinkle K, Schorr O, Rapkin B, Redd WH (1990) Analysis of child and parent behavior during painful medical procedures. *Health Psychology* 9, 559–576

Janis IL (1958) *Psychological Stress*. New York: Wiley

Janoff-Bulman R (1992) *Shattered Assumptions: Towards a New Psychology of Trauma*. New York: Free Press

Janz NK, Becker MH (1984) The health belief model a decade later. *Health Education Quarterly* 11, 1–47

Jenkinson C (1994) Measuring health and medical outcomes: an overview. In C Jenkinson (ed) *Measuring Health and Medical Outcomes*. London: UCL Press, pp 1–6

Johnson JE, Leventhal H (1974) Effects of accurate expectations and behavioral instructions on reactions during a noxious medical examination. *Journal of Personality and Social Psychology* 29, 710–718

Johnson MH, Breakwell G, Douglas W, Humphries S (1998) The effects of imagery and sensory detection distractors on different measures of pain: how does distraction work? *British Journal of Clinical Psychology* 37, 141–154

Johnston DW (1997) Hypertension. In A Baum, S Newman, J Weinman, R West, C McManus (eds) *Cambridge Handbook of Psychology, Health and Medicine*. Cambridge: Cambridge University Press, pp 500–501

Johnston M (1982) Recognition of patients' worries by nurses and by other patients. *British Journal of Clinical Psychology* 21, 255–261

Johnston M (1984) Dimensions of recovery from surgery. *International Review of Applied Psychology* 33, 505–520

Johnston M (1998) Hospitalization in adults. In A Baum, S Newman, J Weinman, R West, C McManus (eds) *Cambridge Handbook of Psychology, Health and Medicine*. Cambridge: Cambridge University Press, pp 121–123

Johnston M, Vogele C (1993) Benefits of psychological preparation for surgery: a meta-analysis. *Annals of Behavioral Medicine* 15, 245–256

Jones K, Fowles AJ (1984) *Ideas on Insitutions*. London: Routledge

Kane RL, Wales J, Bernstein L, Liebowitz A, Kaplan S (1984) A randomized controlled trial of hospice care. *Lancet* 1, 890–894

Karasek RA, Theorell TG (1990) *Healthy Work*. New York: Basic Books

Keefe FJ, Caldwell DS, Baucom D, Salley A, Robinson E, Timmons K, Beaupre P, Weisberg J, Helms M (1996) Spouse-assisted coping skills training in the management of osteoarthritic knee pain. *Arthritis Care and Research* 9, 279–291

Kelly MP, May D (1982) Good and bad patients: a review of the literature and a theoretical critique. *Journal of Advanced Nursing* 7, 147–156

Kendall PC, Williams L, Pechacek TF, Graham LE, Shisslak C, Herzoff N (1979) Cognitive behavioral and patient education interventions in cardiac catheterization procedures: the Palo Alto Medical Psychology Project. *Journal of Consulting and Clinical Psychology* 47, 49–58

Kiecolt-Glaser JK, Glaser R (1995) Psychoneuroimmunology and health consequences: data and shared mechanisms. *Psychosomatic Medicine* 57, 269–274

Kiecolt-Glaser JK, Williams DA (1987) Self-blame, compliance and distress among burn patients. *Journal of Personality and Social Psychology* 53, 187–193

Kiecolt-Glaser JK, Page GC, Marucha PT, MacCullum RC, Glaser R (1998) Psychological influences on surgical recovery. *American Psychologist* 53, 1209–1218

Klein RF, Kliner VA, Zipes DP, Troyer WG, Wallace AG (1968) Transfer from a coronary care unit. *Archives of Internal Medicine* 122, 104–108

Kleinman A (1980) *Patients and Healers in the Context of Culture: An Explanation of the Borderland between Anthropology, Medicine and Psychology*. Berkeley CA: University of California Press

Krantz DS, Baum A, Wideman MH (1980) Assessment of preferences for self-treatment and information in health care. *Journal of Personality and Social Psychology* 39, 977–990

Kreitler S, Chaitchik S, Rapoport Y, Kreitler H, Algor R (1993) Life satisfaction and health in cancer patients, orthopedic patients and healthy individuals. *Social Science and Medicine* 36, 547–556

Krespi MR, Ahmad R, Bone M, Worthington B, Salmon P (1999a) *Haemodialysis patients' beliefs about renal failure and its treatment.* University of Liverpool (unpublished manuscript)

Krespi MR, Ahmad R, Bone M, Worthington B, Salmon P (1999b) *Haemodialysis patients' evaluation of their lives.* University of Liverpool (unpublished manuscript)

Kubler-Ross E (1970) *On Death and Dying.* London: Tavistock

Kulik JA, Mahler HIM (1987) Effects of preoperative roommate assignment on preoperative anxiety and recovery from coronary bypass surgery. *Health Psychology* 6, 525–543

Kulik JA, Mahler HIM (1989) Social support and recovery from surgery. *Health Psychology* 8, 221–238

Kulik JA, Mahler HIM (1993) Emotional support as a moderator of adjustment and compliance after coronary artery bypass surgery: a longitudinal study. *Journal of Behavioral Medicine* 16, 45–64

Kulik JA, Moore PJ, Mahler HIM (1993) Stress and affiliation: hospital room-mate effects on preoperative anxiety and social interaction. *Health Pychology* 12, 118–124

Laerum E, Johnsen N, Smith P, Larsen S (1987) Can myocardial infarction induce positive changes in family relationships? *Family Practice* 4, 302–305

Lalljee M, Lamb R, Carnibella G (1993) Lay prototypes of illness: their content and use. *Psychology and Health* 8, 33–49

Lander J (1990) Fallacies and phobias about addiction and pain. *British Journal of Addiction* 85, 803–809

Langer EJ, Abelson RP (1972) The semantics of asking a favor: how to succeed in getting help without really dying. *Journal of Personality and Social Psychology* 24, 26–32

Langer EJ, Janis IL, Wolfer JA (1975) Reduction of psychological distress in surgical patients. *Journal of Experimental Social Psychology* 11, 155–165

Langer EJ, Blanl A, Chanowitz B (1978) The mindlessness of ostensibly thoughtful action: the role of 'placebic' information in interpersonal interaction. *Journal of Personality and Social Psychology* 36, 635–642

Lavies N, Hart L, Rounsefell B, Runciman W (1992) Identification of patient, medical and nursing staff attitudes to postoperative opioid analgesia: stage 1 of a longitudinal study of postoperative analgesia. *Pain* 48, 313–319

Lazarus RS (1999) *Stress and Emotion.* London: Free Association Books

Lazarus RS, Folkman S (1984) *Stress, Appraisal and Coping.* New York: Springer

Lee-Jones C, Humphris G, Dixon R, Hatcher MB (1997) Fear of recurrence: a literature review and proposed cognitive formulation to explain exacerbation of recurrence fears. *Psychooncology* 6, 95–105

Leigh JM, Walker J, Janaganathan P (1977) Effect of preoperative anaesthetic visit on anxiety. *British Medical Journal* 2, 987–989

Leserman J, Li Z, Hu YJB, Drossman, DA (1998) How multiple types of stressors impact on health. *Psychosomatic Medicine* 60, 175–181

Leventhal EA, Leventhal H, Schacham S, Easterling DV (1989) Active coping reduces reports of pain from childbirth. *Journal of Consulting and Clinical Psychology* 57, 365–371

Leventhal H, Benyami Y (1997) Lay beliefs about health and illness. In A Baum, S Newman, J Weinman, R West, C McManus (eds) *Cambridge Handbook of Psychology, Health and Medicine.* Cambridge: Cambridge University Press, pp 131–135

Levine J, Warrenburg S, Kerns R, Schwartz G, Delaney R, Fontana A, Gradman A, Smith S, Allen S, Cascione R (1987) The role of denial in recovery from coronary heart disease. *Psychosomatic Medicine* 49, 109–117

Levinson DJ (1990) A theory of life-structure development in adulthood. In CN Alexander, EG Langer (eds) *Higher Stages of Human Development: Perspectives on Adult Growth*. New York: Oxford University Press, pp 35–53

Levis DJ (1991) A clinician's plea for a return to the development of nonhuman models of psychopathology: new clinical observations in need of laboratory study. In MR Denny (ed) *Fear, Avoidance and Phobias: A fundamental Analysis*. Hillsdale, NJ: Erlbaum, pp 395–427

Levy SM, Herberman RB, Whiteside T, Sanzo K, Lee J, Kirkwood J (1990) Perceived social support and tumor estrogen/progesterone receptor status as predictors of natural killer cell activity in breast cancer patients. *Psychosomatic Medicine* 52, 73–85

Lewin B, Robertson IH, Cay EL, Irving JB, Campbell M (1992) Effects of self-help post-myocardial-infarction rehabilitation on psychological adjustment and use of health services. *Lancet* 339, 1036–1040

Ley P (1979) Memory for medical information. *British Journal of Social and Clinical Psychology* 18, 245–255

Ley P (1988) *Communicating with Patients*. London: Chapman & Hall

Ley P (1997) Compliance among patients. In A Baum, S Newman, J Weinman, R West, C McManus (eds) *Cambridge Handbook of Psychology, Health and Medicine*. Cambridge: Cambridge University Press, pp 281–284

Lindeman CA, Stetzer SL (1973) Effects of preoperative visits by operating room nurses. *Nursing Research* 22, 4–15

Linn BS, Linn MW, Klimas NG (1988) Effects of psychophysical stress on surgical outcome. *Psychosomatic Medicine* 50, 230–244

Linn MW, Linn BS, Harris R (1982) Effects of counseling for late stage cancer patients. *Cancer* 49, 1048–1055

Little P, Williamson I, Warner G, Gould C, Gantley M, Kinmouth AL (1997a) Open randomised trial of prescribing strategies in managing sore throat. *British Medical Journal* 314, 722–727

Little P, Gould C, Williamson I, Warner G, Gantley M, Kinmouth AL (1997b) Reattendance and complications in a randomised trial of prescribing strategies for sore throat: the medicalising effect of prescribing antibiotics. *British Medical Journal* 315, 350–352

Lorber J (1975) Good patients and problem patients: conformity and deviance in a general hospital. *Journal of Health and Social Behavior* 16, 213–225

Lowe CJ, Raynor DK, Courtney EA, Purvis J, Teale C (1995) Effects of self medication programme on knowledge of drugs and compliance with treatment in elderly patients. *British Medical Journal* 310, 1229–1230

Luker KA, Beaver K, Leinster SJ, Owens RG (1996) Meaning of illness for women with breast cancer. *Journal of Advanced Nursing* 23, 1194–1201

Lupton D (1994) *Medicine as Culture: Illness, Disease and the Body in Western Societies*. London: Sage

Lydeard S, Jones R (1989) Factors affecting the decision to consult with dyspepsia. *Journal of the Royal College of General Practitioners* 39, 495–498

Lyth IM (1988) *Containing Anxiety in Institutions: Selected Essays*, Volume 1. London: Free Association Books

Mabeck CE, Olesen F (1997) Metaphorically transmitted diseases: how do patients embody medical explanations? *Family Practice* 14, 271–278

Maguire P (1985) Barriers to psychological care of the dying. *British Medical Journal* 291, 1711–1713

Maguire P (1990) Can communication skills be taught? *British Journal of Hospital Medicine* 43, 21–56

Maguire P (1998) Breaking bad news. *European Journal of Surgical Oncology* 24, 188–199

Maguire P, Faulkner A (1988) How to do it. *British Medical Journal* 297, 972–974

Maguire P, Booth K, Elliott C, Jones B (1996a) Helping health professionals involved in cancer care acquire key interviewing skills: the impact of workshops. *European Journal of Cancer* 32A, 1486–1489

Maguire P, Faulkner A, Booth K, Elliott C, Hillier V (1996b) Helping cancer patients disclose their concerns. *European Journal of Cancer* 32, 78–81

Mahler HIM, Kulik JA (1991) Health care involvement preferences andsocial-emotional recovery of male coronary-artery-bypass patients. *Health Psychology* 10, 399–408

Malmo RB, Shagass C (1949) Physiologic study of symptom mechanisms in psychiatric patients under stress. *Psychosomatic Medicine* 11, 25–29

Manyande A, Salmon P (1998) Effects of preoperative relaxation training on postoperative analgesia: immediate increase and delayed reduction. *British Journal of Health Psychology* 3, 215–224

Manyande A, Chayen S, Priyakumar P, Smith CCT, Hayes M, Higgins D, Kee S, Phillips S, Salmon P (1992) Anxiety and endocrine responses to surgery: paradoxical effects of preoperative relaxation training. *Psychosomatic Medicine* 54, 275–287

Manyande A, Berg S, Gettins D, Stanford SC, Mazhero S, Marks DF, Salmon P (1995) Preoperative rehearsal of active coping imagery influences subjective and hormonal responses to abdominal surgery. *Psychosomatic Medicine* 57, 177–182

Marchant-Haycox S, Salmon P (1997) Patients' and doctors' strategies in consultations with unexplained symptoms: interactions of gynecologists with women presenting menstrual problems. *Psychosomatics* 38, 440–450

Marchant-Haycox S, Liu D, Nicholas N, Salmon P (1998) Patients' expectations of outcome of hysterectomy and alternative treatments for menstrual problems. *Journal of Behavioral Medicine* 21, 283–297

Markland D, Hardy L (1993) Anxiety, relaxation and anaesthesia for day-case surgery. *British Journal of Clinical Psychology* 32, 493–504

Marshall GN, Hays RD, Mazel R (1996) Health status and satisfaction with health care: results from the medical outcomes study. *Journal of Consulting and Clinical Psychology* 64, 380–390

Marteau TM, Kidd J, Cuddeford L, Walker P (1996) Reducing anxiety in women referred for colposcopy using an information booklet. *British Journal of Health Psychology* 1, 181–189

Martelli MF, Auerbach M, Alexander J, Mercury LG (1987) Stress management in the health care setting: matching interventions with patient coping styles. *Journal of Consulting and Clinical Psychology* 55, 201–207

Marucha PT, KiecoltGlaser JK, Faveghi M (1998) Mucosal wound healing is impaired by examination stress. *Psychosomatic Medicine* 60, 362–365

Maslach C (1982) *Burnout: The Cost of Caring*. Englewood Cliffs, NJ: Prentice Hall

Maslach C, Jackson SE, Leiter MP (1996) *Maslach Burnout Inventory Manual*, 3rd edition. Palo Alto, CA: Consulting Psychologists' Press

Mason JW, Maher JT, Hartley LH, Mougey E, Perlow MJ, Jones LG (1976) Selectivity of corticosteroid and catecholamine response to various natural stimuli. In G Serban (ed) *Psychopathology of Human Adaptation*. New York: Plenum

McArdle JMC, George WD, McArdle CS, Snith DC, Moodie AR, Hughson AVM, Murray GD (1996) Psychological support for patients undergoing breast cancer: a randomised study. *British Medical Journal* 312, 813–817

McFarland C, Ross M, DeCourville N (1989) Women's theories of menstruation and biases in recall of menstrual symptoms. *Journal of Personality and Social Psychology* 57, 522–531

McNeil BJ, Pauker SG, Sox HE, Tversky A (1982) On the elicitation of preferences for alternative therapies. *New England Journal of Medicine* 306, 1259–1262

Meehl PE (1986) Causes and effects of my disturbing little book. *Journal of Personality Assessment* 50, 370–375

Melamed BG, Siegel LJ (1975) Reduction of anxiety in children facing hospitalization and surgery by use of filmed modeling. *Journal of Consulting and Clinical Psychology* 43, 511–521

Meyer D, Leventhal H, Gutman M (1985) Commonsense models of illness: the example of hypertension. *Health Psychology* 4, 115–135

Meyer TJ, Mark MM (1995) Effects of psychosocial interventions with adult cancer patients: a meta-analysis of randomised experiments. *Health Psychology* 14, 101–108

Miller SM, Mangan CE (1983) Interacting effects of information and coping style in adapting to gynecologic stress: should the doctor tell all? *Journal of Personality and Social Psychology* 45, 223–236

Miller SM, Brody DS, Summerton J (1988) Styles of coping with threat: implications for health. *Journal of Personality and Social Psychology* 54, 142–148

Miranda J, Perez-Stable EJ, Munoz RF, Hargreaves W, Henke CJ (1991) Somatization, psychiatric disorder, and stress in utilization of ambulatory medical services. *Health Psychology* 10, 46–51

Moorey S, Greer S (1989) *Psychological Therapy for Patients with Cancer: A New Approach*. Oxford: Heinemann

Moorey S, Greer S, Bliss J, Law M (1998) A comparison of adjuvant psychological therapy and supportive counselling in patients with cancer. *Psychooncology* 7, 218–228

Moos RH, Schaefer JA (1984) The crisis of physical illness: an overview and conceptual approach. In R Moos (ed) *Coping with Physical Illness 2: New Perspectives*. New York: Plenum

Morley S (1997) Pain management. In A Baum, S Newman, J Weinman, R West, C McManus (eds) *Cambridge Handbook of Psychology, Health and Medicine*. Cambridge: Cambridge University Press, pp 234–237

Morris J, Royle GT (1988) Offering patients a choice of surgery for early breast cancer: a reduction in anxiety and depression in patients and their husbands. *Social Science and Medicine* 26, 583–585

Morriss R, Gask L, Ronalds C, Downes-Grainger E, Thompson H, Leese B, Goldberg D (1998) Cost effectiveness of a new treatment for somatised mental disorder taught to general practitioners. *Family Practice* 15, 119–125

Morriss RK, Gask L, Downes-Grainger E, Thompson H, Goldberg D (1999) Clinical and patient satisfaction outcomes of a new treatment of somatized disorder taught to general practitioners. *British Journal of General Practice* 49, 263–267

Moynihan C, Bliss JM, Davidson J, Burchell L, Horwich A (1998) Evaluation of adjuvant psychological therapy in patients with testicular cancer: randomised controlled trial. *British Medical Journal* 316, 429–435

Nagy M (1948) The child's theories concerning death. *Journal of Genetic Psychology* 73, 3–27

Nelson EC, Larson C (1993) Patients' good and bad surprises: how do they relate to overall patient satisfaction? *Quality Review Bulletin* 19, 89–94

Neu S, Kjellstrand CM (1986) Stopping long-term dialysis: an empirical study of withdrawal of life-supporting treatment. *New England Journal of Medicine* 314, 14–20

Neugarten BL, Havighurst RJ, Tobin SS (1961) The measurement of life satisfaction. *Journal of Gerontology* 16, 134–143

Oates JDL, Snowdon SL, Jayson DWH (1994) Failure of pain relief after surgery. *Anaesthesia* 49, 755–758

O'Boyle CA, McGee H, Hickey A, O'Malley K, Joyce CRB (1992) Individual quality of life in patients undergoing hip replacement. *Lancet* 339, 1088–1091

Obrist PA (1981) *Cardiovascular Psychophysiology.* New York: Academic Press

O'Connor AP, Whicker CA, Germino BB (1990) Understanding the cancer patient's search for meaning. *Cancer Nursing* 13, 167–175

Oppenheim AN (1992) *Questionnaire Design, Interviewing and Attitude Measurement.* London: Pinter

Orme CM, Binik YM (1989) Consistency of adherence across regimen demands. *Health Psychology* 8, 27–43

Parker JC, Singsen BH, Hewett JE, Walker SE, Hazelwood SE, Hall PJ, Holsten DJ, Rodon CM (1984) Educating patients with rheumatoid arthritis: a prospective analysis. *Archives of Physical Medicine and Rehabilitation* 65, 771–774

Parkes CM (1972) *Bereavement: Studies of Grief in Adult Life.* London: Tavistock

Parkes CM (1998) Coping with death and dying. In A Baum, S Newman, J Weinman, R West, C McManus (eds) *Cambridge Handbook of Psychology, Health and Medicine.* Cambridge: Cambridge University Press, pp 91–94

Parkes CM, Relf M, Couldrick A (1997) *Counselling in Terminal Care and Bereavement.* Leicester: BPS Books

Patel C (1997) Stress management and hypertension. *Acta Psychiatrica Scandinavica* 640, 155–157

Patel C, Marmot M (1988) Can general practitioners use training in relaxation and management of stress to reduce mild hypertension? *British Medical Journal* 296, 21–24

Paterson J, Moss-Morris R, Butler SJ (1999) The effect of illness experience and demographic factors on children's illness representations. *Psychology and Health* 14, 117–129

Peerbhoy D, Hall GM, Parker C, Shenkin A, Salmon P (1998) Patients' reactions to attempts to increase passive or active coping with surgery. *Social Science and Medicine* 47, 595–601

Pelosi AJ, Appleby L (1992) Psychological influences on cancer and ischaemic heart disease. *British Medical Journal* 304, 1295–1298

Pennebaker JW (1982) *The Psychology of Physical Symptoms.* New York: Springer

Pennebaker JW (1993) Putting stress into words: health, linguistic and therapeutic implications. *Behaviour Research and Therapy* 31, 539–548

Pennebaker JW, Susman JR (1988) Disclosure of traumas and psychosomatic processes. *Social Science and Medicine* 26, 327–332

Pennebaker JW, Mayne TJ, Francis ME (1997) Linguistic predictors of adaptive bereavement. *Journal of Personality and Social Psychology* 72, 863–871

Persky VW, Kempthornerawson J, Shekelle RB (1987) Personality and risk of cancer: 20-year followup of the Western Electric study. *Psychosomatic Medicine* 49, 435–449

Peters S, Stanley I, Rose M, Salmon P (1998) Patients with medically unexplained symptoms: sources of patients' authority and implications for demands on medical care. *Social Science and Medicine* 46, 559–565

Petrie KJ, Weinman JA (1997) Illness representations and recovery from myocardial infarction. In KJ Petrie, JA Weinman (eds) *Perceptions of Health and Illness.* Amsterdam: Harwood, pp 441–461

Petrie KJ, Weinman J, Sharpe N, Buckley J (1996) Role of patients' view of their illness in predicting return to work and functioning after myocardial infarction: longitudinal study. *British Medical Journal* 312, 1191–1194

Pettingale KW, Morris T, Greer S, Haybittle JL (1985) Mental attitudes to cancer: an additional prognostic factor. *Lancet* 1, 7–50

Peveler R, Kilkenny L, Kinmouth AL (1997) Medically unexplained physical symptoms in primary care: a comparison of self-report screening questionnaires and clinical opinion. *Journal of Psychosomatc Research* 42, 245–252

Philip AE (1988) Psychological predictors of outcome after myocardial infarction. In T Elbert, W Langosch, A Steptoe, D Vaitl (eds) *Behavioural Medicine in Cardiovascular Disorders.* Chichester: Wiley, pp 193–204

Pick B, Molloy A, Dinds C, Pearce S, Salmon P (1994) Postoperative fatigue following coronary bypass surgery: relationship to emotional state and to the catecholamine response to surgery. *Journal of Psychosomatic Research* 38, 599–607

Poulter NR, Khaw KT, Hopwood BEC, Mugambi M, Peart WS, Rose G, Sever PS (1990) The Kenyan Luo migration study: observations on the initiation of a rise in blood pressure. *British Medical Journal* 300, 967–972

Prigerson HG (1992) Socialization to dying: social determinants of death acknowledgment and treatment among terminally ill geriatric patients. *Journal of Health and Social Behavior* 33, 378–395

Radley A (1988) *Prospects of Heart Surgery: Psychological Adjustment to Coronary Bypass Grafting.* New York: Springer

Radley A (1994) *Making Sense of Illness.* London: Sage

Ramsey NL (1982) Effects of hospitalization on the child and family. In MJ Smith, JA Goodman, NL Ramsey, SB Pasternack (eds) *Child and Family: Concepts of Nursing Practice.* New York: McGraw-Hill

Raps CS, Peterson C, Jonas M, Seligman MEP (1982) Patient behavior in hospitals: helplessness, reactance or both? *Journal of Personality and Social Psychology* 42, 1036–1041

Reed PG (1987) Spirituality and wellbeing in terminally ill hospitalized adults. *Research in Nursing and Health* 10, 335–344

Reichsman F, Levy NB (1972) Problems in adaptation to maintenance hemodialysis: a four-year study of 25 patients. *Archives of Internal Medicine* 130, 859–865

Reilly J, Baker G, Rhodes J, Salmon P (1999) The association of sexual and physical abuse with somatization: characteristics of patients presenting with irritable bowel syndrome and non-epileptic attack disorder. *Psychological Medicine* 29, 399–406

Reker GT, Peacock EJ (1981) The Life Attitude Profile (LAP): a multidimensional instrument for assessing attitudes toward life. *Canadian Journal of Behavioral Science* 13, 264–273

Richards MA, Ramirez AJ, Degner LF, Fallowfield LJ, Maher EJ, Neuberger J (1995) Offering choice of treatment to patients with cancers. A review based on a symposium held at the 10th Annual Conference of the British Psychosocial Oncology Group, December 1993. *European Journal of Cancer* 31A, 112–116

Ridgway V, Mathews A (1982) Psychological preparation for surgery: a comparison of methods. *British Journal of Clinical Psychology* 21, 271–280

Riley V (1981) Psycho-neuroendocrine influences on immuno-competence and neoplasia. *Science* 212, 1100–1109

Robinson EJ, Whitfield M (1985) Improving the efficiency of patients' comprehension monitoring: a way of increasing patients' participation in general practice consultation. *Social Science and Medicine* 21, 915–919

Robinson PN, Salmon P, Yentis SM (1998) Maternal satisfaction. *International Journal of Obstetric Anesthesia* 7, 32–37

Rosenberg SJ, Peterson RA, Hayes JR, Hatcher J, Headen S (1988) Depression in medical inpatients. *British Journal of Medical Psychology* 61, 245–254

Rosengren A, OrthGomer K, Wedel H, Wilhelmsen L (1993) Stressful life events, social support and mortality in men born in 1933. *British Medical Journal* 307, 1102–1105

Rosser R (1998) Quality of life assessment. In A Baum, S Newman, J Weinman, R West, C McManus (eds) *Cambridge Handbook of Psychology, Health and Medicine*. Cambridge: Cambridge University Press, pp 310–314

Rostrup M, Ekeberg O (1992) Awareness of high blood pressure influences on psychological and sympathetic responses. *Journal of Psychosomatic Research* 36, 117–123

Roter DL, Hall JA (1992) *Doctors Talking with Patients/Patients Talking with Doctors: Improving Outcomes in Medical Visits*. Wesport, CT: Auburn House

Rowe G, Wright G, Ayton P (1998) Judgement and decision-making. In A Baum, SE Taylor, J Singer (eds) *Handbook of Psychology and Health*, Volume 4. Hillsdale, NJ: Erlbaum, pp 21–25

Ruble DN (1977) Premenstrual symptoms: a reinterpretation. *Science* 197, 291–292

Ruta D, Garratt AM (1994) Health status to quality of life measurement. In C Jenkinson (ed) *Measuring Health and Medical Outcomes*. London: UCL Press, pp 138–159

Safer MA, Tharps QJ, Jackson TC, Leventhal H (1979) Determinants of three stages of delay in seeking care at a medical care clinic. *Medical Care* 17, 11–29

Salkovskis PM, Clark DM (1990) Affective responses to hyperventilation: a test of the cognitive model of panic. *Behaviour Research and Therapy* 28, 51–61

Salmon P (1994) Psychological factors in surgical recovery. In HB Gibson (ed) *Psychology, Pain and Anaesthesia*. London: Chapman & Hall, pp 229–258

Salmon P, Drew NC (1992) Multi-dimensional assessment of women's experience of childbirth: relationship to obstetric procedure, antenatal preparation and obstetric history. *Journal of Psychosomatic Research* 36, 317–327

Salmon P, Hall GM (1997) A theory of postoperative fatigue: an interaction of biological, psychological and social processes. *Pharmacology, Biochemistry and Behavior* 56, 623–628

Salmon P, Manyande A (1996) Good patients cope with their pain: postoperative analgesia and nurses' perceptions of their patients' pain. *Pain* 68, 63–68

Salmon P, May C (1995) Patients' influence on doctors' behavior: a case study of patient strategies in somatization. *International Journal of Psychiatry in Medicine* 25, 319–329

Salmon P, Quine J (1989) Patients' intentions in primary care: measurement and preliminary investigation. *Psychology and Health* 3, 103–110

Salmon P, Evans R, Humphrey D (1986) Anxiety and endocrine changes in surgical patients. *British Journal of Clinical Psychology* 25, 135–141

Salmon P, Pearce S, Smith CCT, Heys A, Manyande A, Peters N, Rashid J (1988) The relationship of preoperative distress to endocrine and subjective responses to surgery: support for Janis' theory. *Journal of Behavioral Medicine* 11, 599–613

Salmon P, Sharma N, Valori R, Bellenger N (1994) Patients' intentions in primary care: relationship to physical and psychological symptoms, and their perception by general practitioners. *Social Science and Medicine* 38, 585–592

Salmon P, Manzi F, Valori RM (1996a) Measuring the meaning of life for patients with incurable cancer: the life evaluation questionnaire (LEQ). *European Journal of Cancer* 32A, 755–760

Salmon P, Woloshynowych M, Valori R (1996b) The measurement of beliefs about physical symptoms in English general practice patients. *Social Science and Medicine* 42, 1561–1567

Salmon P, Peters S, Stanley I (1999) Patients' perceptions of medical explanations for somatisation disorders: qualitative analysis. *British Medical Journal* 318, 372–376

Savage R, Armstrong D (1990) Effect of a general practitioner's consulting style on patients' satisfaction: a controlled study. *British Medical Journal* 301, 968–970

Scambler A, Scambler G, Craig D (1981) Kinship and friendship networks and women's demand for primary care. *Journal of the Royal College of General Practitioners* 31, 746–750

Schachter S, Singer J (1962) Cognitive, social and physiological determinants of emotion. *Psychological Review* 69, 379–399

Scharloo M, Kaptein A (1997) Measurement of illness perceptions in patients with chronic somatic illness: a review. In KJ Petrie, JA Weinman (eds) *Perceptions of Health and Illness*. Amsterdam: Harwood, pp 103–154

Scheier MF, Matthews KA, Owens JF, Magovern GJ, Lefebvre RC, Abbott RA, Carver CS (1989) Dispositional optimism and recovery from coronary artery bypass surgery. *Journal of Personality and Social Psychology* 57, 1024–1040

Schmidt LR (1998) Hospitalization in children. In A Baum, S Newman, J Weinman, R West, C McManus (eds) *Cambridge Handbook of Psychology, Health and Medicine*. Cambridge: Cambridge University Press, pp 124–127

Schmitt FE, Wooldridge PJ (1973) Psychological preparation of surgical patients. *Nursing Research* 22, 108–116

Schneiderman LJ, Kaplan RM, Pearlman RA, Teetzel H (1993) Do physicians' own preferences for life-sustaining treatment influence their perceptions of patients' preferences? *Journal of Clinical Ethics* 4, 28–33

Schwartz S, Griffin T (1986) *Medical Thinking: The Psychology of Medical Judgement and Decision Making*. New York: Springer

Seligman MEP (1975) *Helplessness: On Depression, Development, and Death*. San Francisco: Freeman

Selye H (1956) *The Stress of Life*. New York: McGraw-Hill

Sharpe M, Peveller R, Mayou R (1992) The psychological treatment of patients with functional somatic symptoms: a practical guide. *Journal of Psychosomatic Research* 36, 515–529

Sharpe M, Mayou R, Seagroatt V, Surawy C, Warwick H, Bulstrode C, Dawber R, Lane D (1994) Why do doctors find some patients difficult to help? *Quarterly Journal of Medicine* 87, 187–193

Sharpe M, Hawton K, Simkin S, Surawy C, Hackmann A, Klimes I, Peto T, Seagroatt V (1996) Cognitive therapy of the chronic fatigue syndrome: a randomized controlled trial. *British Medical Journal* 312, 22–26

Shaw RE, Cohen F, Doyle B, Palesky J (1985) The impact of denial and repressive style on information gain and rehabilitation outcomes in myocardial infarction patients. *Psychosomatic Medicine* 47, 262–273

Shontz FC (1975) *The Psychological Aspects of Physical Disease and Disability*. New York: Macmillan

Shorter E (1992) *From Paralysis to Fatigue: A History of Psychosomatic Illness in the Modern Era*. New York: Free Press

Siegman AW, Dembroski TM, Crump D (1992) Speech rate, loudness and cardiovascular reactivity. *Journal of Behavioral Medicine* 15, 519–532

Sigelman C, Maddock A, Epstein J, Carpenter W (1993) Age differences in understanding of disease causality: AIDS, colds and cancer. *Child Development* 64, 272–284

Sime AM (1976) Relationship of preoperative fear, type of coping, and information received about surgery to recovery from surgery. *Journal of Personality and Social Psychology* 34, 716–724

Skevington SM (1995) *The Psychology of Pain*. Chichester: Wiley

Slevin ML (1992) Quality of life: philosophical question or clinical reality? *British Medical Journal* 305, 466–469

Slevin ML, Plant H, Lynch D, Drinkwater J, Gregory WM (1988) Who should measure quality of life, the doctor or the patients? *British Journal of Cancer* 57, 109–112

Slevin ML, Stubbs L, Plant HJ, Wilson P, Gregory WM, Armes PJ, Downer SM (1990) Attitudes to chemotherapy: comparing views of patients with cancer with those of doctors, nurses and the general public. *British Medical Journal* 300, 1458–1460

Slugoski BR (1995) Mindless processing of requests? Don't ask twice. *British Journal of Social Psychology* 34, 335–350

Smith G (1991) Pain after surgery. *British Journal of Anaesthesia* 67, 233–234

Smith GR, Rost K, Kashner TM (1995) A trial of the effect of a standardized psychiatric consultation on health outcomes and costs in somatizing patients. *Archives of General Psychiatry* 52, 238–243

Smith RC, Greenbaum DS, Vancouver JB, Henry RC, Reinhart MA, Greenbaum RB, Dean HA, Mayle JE (1990) Psychosocial factors are associated with health care seeking rather than diagnosis in irritable bowel syndrome. *Gastroenterology* 98, 293–301

Smyth JM, Soefer MH, Hurewitz A, Stone AA (1999) The effect of tape-recorded relaxation training on wellbeing, symptoms, and peak expiratory flow rate in adult asthmatics: a pilot study. *Psychology and Health* 14, 487–501

Sontag S (1978) *Illness as Metaphor*. New York: Vintage

Speckens AEM, van Hemert AM, Spinhoven P, Hawton KE, Bolk JH, Rooijmans GM (1995) Cognitive behavioural therapy for medically unexplained physical symptoms: a randomised controlled trial. *British Medical Journal* 311, 1328–1332

Spiegel D, Bloom JR, Kraemer HC, Gottheil E (1989) Effect of psychosocial treatment on survival of patients with metastatic breast cancer. *Lancet* 2, 888–891

Spiegelhalter DJ, Gore SM, Fitzpatrick R, Fletcher AE, Jones DR, Cox DR (1992) Quality of life measures in health care. III: resource allocation. *British Medical Journal* 305, 1205–1209

Stanley I, Peters S, Rose M, Salmon P (1999) Persistent unexplained physical symptoms: challenging the explanatory validity of somatization in primary care. University of Liverpool (unpublished)

Steptoe A (1983) Stress, helplessness and control: the implications of laboratory studies. *Journal of Psychosomatic Research* 27, 361–367

Steptoe A (1993) Stress and the cardiovascular system: psychosocial perspective. In SC Stanford, P Salmon (eds) *Stress: From Synapse to Syndrome*. London: Academic Press, pp 119–141

Stewart AL, Hays RD, Ware JE (1988) The MOS short form general health survey: reliability and validity in a patient population. *Medical Care* 26, 724–735

Stimson GV (1974) Obeying doctor's orders: a view from the other side. *Social Science and Medicine* 8, 97–104

Stroebe MS, Stroebe W (1991) Does 'grief work' work? *Journal of Consulting and Clinical Psychology* 59, 479–482

Stuart S, Noyes R (1999) Attachment and interpersonal communication in somatization. *Psychosomatics* 40, 34–43

Suls J, Fletcher B (1985) The relative efficacy of avoidant and nonavoidant coping strategies: a metaanalysis. *Health Psychology* 4, 249–288

Suls J, Wan CK (1989) Effects of sensory and procedural information on coping with stressful medical procedures and pain: a meta-analysis. *Journal of Consulting and Clinical Psychology* 57, 372–379

Suls J, Wan CK (1993) The relationship between trait hostility and cardiovascular reactivity: a quantitative review and analysis. *Psychophysiology* 30, 1–12

Suls J, Sanders GS, Lebrecque MS (1986) Attempting to control blood pressure without systematic instruction: when advice is counterproductive. *Journal of Behavioral Medicine* 9, 567–578

Tagliacozzo DL, Mauksch HO (1972) The patient's view of the patient's role. In EG Jaco (ed) *Patients, Physicians and Illness*, 2nd edition. New York: Free Press, pp 172–185

Taylor CB, Bandura A, Ewart CK, Miller NH, DeBusk RF (1985) Exercise testing to enhance wives' confidence in their husbands' cardiac capability soon after clinically uncomplicated acute myocardial infarction. *American Journal of Cardiology* 55, 635–638

Taylor NM, Hall GM, Salmon P (1996a) Patients' experiences of patient-controlled analgesia. *Anaesthesia* 51, 525–528

Taylor NM, Hall GM, Salmon P (1996b) Is patient-controlled analgesia controlled by the patient? *Social Science and Medicine* 43, 1137–1143

Taylor SE (1979) Hospital patient behavior: reactance, helplessness or control? *Journal of Social Issues* 35, 156–184

Taylor SE, Lichtman RR, Wood JV (1984) Attributions, beliefs about control and adjustment to breast cancer. *Journal of Personality and Social Psychology* 46, 489–502

Temoshok L (1990) On attempting to articulate the biopsychosocial model: psychological-psychophysiological homeostasis. In HS Friedman (ed) *Personality and Disease*. New York: Wiley

Tennen H, Affleck G (1990) Blaming others for threatening events. *Psychological Bulletin* 108, 209–232

Tessler R, Mechanic D, Dimond M (1976) The effect of psychological distress on physician utilization: a prospective study. *Journal of Health and Social Behavior* 17, 353–364

Thompson A (1993) Inpatients' opinions of the quality of acute hospital care: discrimination as the key to measurement validity. In R Fitzpatrick, A Hopkins (eds) *Measurement of Patients' Satisfaction with their Care*. London: Royal College of Physicians, pp 19–32

Thompson SC, Cheek PR, Graham MA (1988) The other side of perceived control: disadvantages and negative effects. In S Spacapan, S Oskamp (eds) *The Social Psychology of Health: The Claremont Applied Social Psychology Conference*, Volume 2. Beverly Hills, CA: Sage, pp 69–94

Tolson WW, Mason JW, Sachar EJ, Hamburg DA, Handlon JH, Fishman JR (1965) Urinary catecholamine responses associated with hospital admission in normal human subjects. *Journal of Psychosomatic Research* 8, 365–372

Totman R (1976) Cognitive dissonance in the placebo treatment of insomnia: a pilot experiment. *British Journal of Medical Psychology* 49, 393–400

Tuckett D, Boulton M, Olson C, Williams A (1985) *Meetings between Experts: An Approach to Sharing Ideas in Medical Consultations*. London: Tavistock

Turk DC, Meichenbaum D, Genest M (1983) *Pain and Behavioral Medicine: A Cognitive Behavioral Perspective*. New York: Guilford

Turnquist DC, Harvey JH, Anderson BL (1988) Attributions and adjustment to life-threatening illness. *British Journal of Clinical Psychology* 27, 55–65

Tversky A, Kahneman D (1981) The framing of decisions and the psychology of choice. *Science* 211, 453–458

Valori R (1993) Lines written on reading another review article about the irritable bowel syndrome. *Lancet* 341, 36–37

Valori R, Woloshynowych M, Bellenger N, Aluvihare V, Salmon P (1996) The Patients Requests Form: a way of measuring what patients want from their general practitioner. *Journal of Psychosomatic Research* 40, 87–94

van de Kar A, Knottnerus A, Meertens R, Dubois V, Kok G (1992) Why do patients consult their general practitioner? Determinants of their decision. *British Journal of General Practice* 42, 313–316

vanDulmen AM, Fennis JFM, Bleijenberg G (1996) Cognitive behavioural group therapy for irritable bowel syndrome: effects and long-term follow-up. *Psychosomatic Medicine* 58, 508–514

van Rood YR, Bogaards M, Goulmy E, VanHouwelingen HC (1993) The effects of stress and relaxation on the in vitro immune response in man: a metaanalytic study. *Journal of Behavioral Medicine* 16, 163–181

Volicer BJ, Isenberg MA, Burns MW (1977) Medical surgical differences in hospital stress factors. *Journal of Human Stress* 3, 3–13

Walsh ME, Bibace R (1991) Children's conceptions of AIDS: a developmental analysis. *Journal of Pediatric Psychology* 16, 273–285

Warburton DM, Sherwood N (eds) (1996) *Pleasure and Quality of Life*. Chichester: Wiley

Ware J, Hays R (1988) Methods for measuring patient satisfaction with specific medical encounters. *Medical Care* 26, 393–402

Warwick HMC, Salkovskis PM (1985) Reassurance. *British Medical Journal* 290, 10–28

Wason PC, Johnson-Laird PN (1972) *Psychology of Reasoning: Structure and Content*. London: Batsford

Waterworth S, Luker K (1990) Reluctant collaborators: do patients want to be involved in decisions concerning care? *Journal of Advanced Nursing* 15, 971–976

Watson D, Pennebaker JW (1989) Health complaints, stress, and distress: exploring the central role of negative affectivity. *Psychological Review* 96, 234–254

Watson M, Haviland JS, Greer S, Davidson J, Bliss JM (1999) Influence of psychological response on survival in breast cancer: a population-based cohort study. *Lancet* 354, 1331–1336

Waxler-Morrison N, Hislop TG, Mears B, Kan L (1991) Effects of social relationships on survival for women with breast cancer: a prospective study. *Social Science and Medicine* 33, 177–183

Webb S, Lloyd M (1994) Prescribing and referral in general practice: a study of patients' expectations and doctors' actions. *British Journal of General Practice* 44, 165–169

Weinman J, Petrie KJ, Moss-Morris R, Horne R (1996) The Illness Perception Questionnaire: a new method for assessing cognitive representations of illness. *Psychology and Health* 11, 431–445

Weisman AD, Worden JW (1976) The existential plight in cancer: significance of the first 100 days. *International Journal of Psychiatry in Medicine* 7, 1–15

Weiss D, Sriwatanakul K, Alloza J, Weintraub M, Lasagna L (1983) Attitudes of patients, house staff and nurses towards postoperative analgesic care. *Anesthesia and Analgesia* 62, 70–74

White GL, Knight TD (1984) Misattribution of arousal and attraction: effects of salience of explanations for arousal. *Journal of Experimental Social Psychology* 20, 55–64.

Whitehead JE, Crowell MD, Heller BR, Robinson JC, Schuster MM, Horn S (1994) Modeling and reinforcement of the sick role during childhood predicts adult illness behavior. *Psychosomatic Medicine* 56, 541–550

Whiteman MC, Fowkes FGR, Deary IJ (1997) Hostility and the heart. *British Medical Journal* 315, 379–380

Wilder-Smith CH, Schuler L (1992) Postoperative analgesia: pain by choice? The influence of patient attitudes and patient education. *Pain* 50, 257–262

Wilkinson RG (1992) Income distribution and life expectancy. *British Medical Journal* 304, 165–168

Wilkinson S (1991) Factors which influence how nurses communicate with cancer patients. *Journal of Advanced Nursing* 16, 677–688

Williams B (1994) Patient satisfaction: a valid concept? *Social Science and Medicine* 38, 509–516

Williams JGL, Jones JR, Workhoven MN, Williams B (1975) The psychological control of preoperative anxiety. *Psychophysiology* 12, 50–54

Williams JMG, Watts FN, MacLeod C, Mathews A (1997) *Cognitive Psychology and Emotional Disorders*, 2nd edition. Chichester: Wiley

Williams RB, Barefoot JC, Califf RM, Haney TL, Saunders WB, Pryor DB, Hlatky MA, Siegler IC, Mark DB (1992) Prognostic importance of social resources among patients with CAD. *Journal of the American Medical Association* 267, 520–524

Wilson HF (1981) Behavioral preparation for surgery: benefit or harm? *Journal of Behavioral Medicine* 4, 79–102

Wilson-Barnett J (1978) Patients' emotional responses to barium X-rays. *Journal of Advanced Nursing* 3, 37–46

Woloshynowych M, Valori R, Salmon P (1998) General practice patients' beliefs about their symptoms. *British Journal of General Practice* 48, 885–889

World Health Organization (1958) *The First Ten Years: The Health Organization.* Geneva: World Health Organization

Wortman CB, Silver RC (1989) The myths of coping with loss. *Journal of Consulting and Clinical Psychology* 57, 349–357

Wright B (1991) *Sudden Death: Intervention Skills for the Caring Professions.* Edinburgh: Churchill Livingstone

Zigmond AS, Snaith RP (1983) The hospital anxiety and depression scale. *Acta Psychiatrica Scandinavica* 67, 361–370

Zola IK (1973) Pathways to the doctor from person to patient. *Social Science and Medicine* 7, 677–689

INDEX

The Wiley Series in

CLINICAL PSYCHOLOGY

Ian H. Gotlib and Constance L. Hammen	Psychological Aspects of Depression: Toward a Cognitive-Interpersonal Integration
Max Birchwood and Nicholas Tarrier (Editors)	Innovations in the Psychological Management of Schizophrenia: Assessment, Treatment and Services
Robert J. Edelmann	Anxiety: Theory, Research and Intervention in Clinical and Health Psychology
Alastair Agar (Editor)	Microcomputers and Clinical Psychology: Issues, Applications and Future Developments
Bob Remington (Editor)	The Challenge of Severe Mental Handicap: A Behaviour Analytic Approach
Colin A. Espie	The Psychological Treatment of Insomnia
David Peck and C.M. Shapiro (Editors)	Measuring Human Problems: A Practical Guide
Roger Baker (Editor)	Panic Disorder: Theory, Research and Therapy
Friedrich Fösterling	Attribution Theory in Clinical Psychology
Anthony Lavender and Frank Holloway (Editors)	Community Care in Practice: Services for the Continuing Care Client
John Clements	Severe Learning Disability and Psychological Handicap